Lebanon's Second Republic

Florida A&M University, Tallahassee
Florida Atlantic University, Boca Raton
Florida Gulf Coast University, Ft. Myers
Florida International University, Miami
Florida State University, Tallahassee
University of Central Florida, Orlando
University of Florida, Gainesville
University of North Florida, Jacksonville
University of South Florida, Tampa
University of West Florida, Pensacola

Lebanon's Second Republic

Prospects for the Twenty-first Century

Edited by Kail C. Ellis

University Press of Florida

Gainesville · Tallahassee · Tampa · Boca Raton
Pensacola · Orlando · Miami · Jacksonville · Ft. Myers

07 06 05 04 03 02   6 5 4 3 2 1

Library of Congress Cataloging-in-Publication Data
Lebanon's second republic: prospects for the twenty-first century /
edited by Kail C. Ellis.
p. cm.
Based on a seminar held at Villanova University, Villanova, Pa., 1998, jointly
sponsored by the Center for Arab and Islamic Studies of Villanova University
and the Lebanese American University.
Includes bibliographical references and index.

ISBN: 978-1-61610-114-5

1. Lebanon—Politics and government—1990—Congresses. I. Ellis, Kail C. II. Villanova
University. Center for Arab and Islamic studies. III. Jami'ah al Lubnaniyah al-Amirikiyah.
DS87.54 .L418 2002
956.9204'4—dc21 2002018077

The University Press of Florida is the scholarly publishing agency for the State
University System of Florida, comprising Florida A&M University, Florida Atlantic
University, Florida Gulf Coast University, Florida International University, Florida State
University, University of Central Florida, University of Florida, University of North
Florida, University of South Florida, and University of West Florida.

University Press of Florida
15 Northwest 15th Street
Gainesville, FL 32611–2079
http://www.upf.com

Contents

Tables

Preface

On 2–3 October 1998, a seminar was held at Villanova University, Villanova, Pennsylvania, titled "Lebanon in the Twenty-first Century." Jointly sponsored by the Center for Arab and Islamic Studies of Villanova University and the Lebanese American University, the seminar featured presentations and discussions by noted national and international scholars, diplomats, and others interested in Lebanon.

Works on contemporary Lebanon are hardly an anomaly. Since the beginning of Lebanon's civil war in 1975, Lebanon's sectarian politics and its relationships with the Palestinians and its neighbors, Israel and Syria, have been the subject of many outstanding studies. With the arrival of peace in the 1990s, numerous excellent books have analyzed Lebanon's prospects for reconciliation and reconstruction. Lebanon's contemporary history has been so thoroughly explored that recent scholarship has returned to probing the important lessons offered by Great Power rivalry and the turbulent history of sectarian nationalism in nineteenth-century Mount Lebanon under the Ottomans.

This volume includes discussion of contemporary politics and international relations, recognizing Lebanon's central role in regional conflicts. It then looks at other forces that will determine Lebanon's future. The book features chapters that argue that Lebanon's future is very much dependent on the progress of Muslim-Christian relations, on the viability of its educational system (that will enable its citizens to contribute to its economic development), and on the way that the concerns of women, urban planning, and the ecological crises are being addressed. The analysis of these topics will be of interest to scholars of women's issues, urban studies, and the environmental movement, as well as to specialists of the region.

Many people helped to make this volume possible and I am grateful for their support. In particular I wish to acknowledge Interstate Resources, which generously provided financial assistance toward the expenses of the seminar. I am also grateful to Father Edmund J. Dobbin, O.S.A., president of Villanova University, for his long-time support for the Center for Arab and Islamic Studies; he graciously attended the banquet and welcomed the participants and guests. The participation of Mr. Mohamad Chatah, Lebanon's ambassador to the United States at the time, and Mr. John Kelly, former U.S. ambassador to Lebanon, is also gratefully acknowledged. Both of these individuals gave addresses and contributed greatly to the discussions.

I am also indebted to Nabeel Haidar of the Lebanese American University in Lebanon, who arranged for his university's cosponsorship and who collaborated with me in planning the seminar, Antoine Frem, who provided generous financial assistance, and Michael Hudson, James Bill, Edmund Ghareeb, and Barbara Stowasser, all of whom have provided invaluable advice and assistance. I am also grateful for the assistance of my colleagues at Villanova. In particular, I would like to thank Hafeez Malik, who has provided support and encouragement in difficult situations, and Helen Lafferty and Louise Fitzpatrick, who were always ready to lend a helping hand and give moral support. In addition, Kathryn Johnson, my secretary, handled the logistics for the seminar with her usual efficiency and skill, Maureen Cavanaugh helped with the travel arrangements, and Angèle M. Ellis and Carolyn Lea provided excellent technical support in editing and proofreading the manuscript. I am very grateful for their assistance. I would also like to acknowledge Jouhaina Hobeiche, who has given me a home from which to observe events in Lebanon, and Toufic Traad Kmeid and Angèle Hobeiche Kmeid, whose wisdom and love for Lebanon provided the inspiration for this work and much more.

Lebanon's Challenge

Reclaiming Memory and Independence

Kail C. Ellis

In the fall of 1990, Lebanon's fifteen-year nightmare of civil conflict and foreign invasions seemed to be coming to an end. Most of the surviving members of the 1972 Lebanese Parliament had been summoned to Ta'if in October 1989 to craft a new constitutional arrangement, the Document of National Reconciliation. Included in the Ta'if Agreement was a recommitment to political confessionalism, with certain adjustments. When the agreement was approved by the Lebanese Parliament with amendments on 21 August 1990,[1] many Lebanese hoped it would signify Lebanon's renewal, its "second republic." Others, however, viewed the document as a more conservative version of the National Pact of 1943, for despite its emphasis on national unity, it enshrined Lebanon's traditional confessional political system, which divides power among the country's religious communities. Moreover, in the view of many Lebanese, the agreement codified Syrian hegemony over Lebanon. The constitutional authority that was established by the Ta'if Agreement could not be fully implemented until October 1990, when Syrian forces were finally able to depose the rival government of General Michel Aoun, who had tried to build unity among Lebanese by blaming outside forces for Lebanon's misery.

From this unsettled beginning, political and economic life resumed in Lebanon, but much unfinished business remained. Lebanon needed to address the ongoing political, social, economic, and religious problems that led to the war, the instability of its southern border with Israel after the withdrawal of Israeli troops in May 2000, and the onerous presence of 35,000–40,000 Syrian peacekeepers. Above all, Lebanon had to come to terms with its history.

For the Lebanese beginning a new century, confronting the past was not only painful but also overwhelming. Denial and historical amnesia became coping mechanisms in the face of thousands of lives lost, unspeakable crimes committed against the innocent, unresolved political, economic, and social issues, and, especially, the complicity of the Lebanese in their own destruction. Guilt for the war was placed on outside forces—the United States, Israel, the Palestinians, and Syria, among others. Even the redevelopment of central Beirut became a symbol of the attempt to bypass the historical experience of the war. As one observer noted, "There has been a concerted effort to wipe clean the surface of central Beirut, to purify it of all historical associations in the forms of its buildings; to render it pure space, pure commodity, pure real estate. The most obvious and striking potential war memorial—in a country that seems to have forgotten its long war—the shrapnel-scarred statue in Martyrs' Square, apparently will be completely repaired."[2]

In Lebanon's postwar culture of forgetting, affluence, social position, and religious sect count more than social justice, and daily cruelties and neglect remain unspoken national secrets. But memory, according to St. Augustine, also has the power "to evoke future actions, occurrences or hopes."[3] Its images can be creatively combined to conjure new possibilities. Lebanon needs its memory if it is to create a viable future.

Lebanon must also find its voice in the cacophony of regional politics and redefine its role in the world economy. The two are intertwined. The outcome of the Middle East peace process, which will define Lebanon's relationships with both Syria and Israel, will also determine whether Lebanon will regain its sovereignty. Lebanon's survival depends on regional peace.

During the civil war, Lebanon lost the competitive economic edge that in the 1950s and 1960s made it "the Switzerland of the Middle East." Its decline was spurred not only by its internal problems but also by changes in the rest of the Arab world. Technical and educational advances in the Gulf countries lessened the need for Lebanon's service-oriented workforce; New York and London became centers of Arab banking. Lebanon's own professional class was decimated by emigration as economic activity dropped, debt and inflation rose, and the national currency was devalued.

Compounding these problems today is Lebanon's inability to resettle thousands of internal war refugees or to find a solution to the presence of an estimated 400,000 Palestinian refugees. The conflict between Hizballah and Israel in the south, the increasing public and foreign debt, and the lack of investment by Lebanese expatriates awaiting the outcome of the peace process have exacerbated Lebanon's economic decline.

It is against this complex background that this volume explores Lebanon's past and the possibilities for its future. An overview of Lebanon as an experiment in multicultural interdependence provides the framework for understanding the Lebanese context. This is followed by chapters under three general headings: Lebanon and the Middle East Peace Process; Religion, Culture, and Gender; and Problems of Urbanization, Ecology, and the Economy.

Overview

"Overview: Lebanon as an Experiment in Multicultural Interdependence," by Hafeez Malik, traces Lebanon's unique history as a multicultural and multireligious entity from 1590 to the present. According to Malik, the reason Muslim-Christian coexistence lasted for centuries is that it existed within a tradition of "no conqueror and no vanquished." Malik outlines four periods in the development of modern Lebanon: intersectarianism and "modernism," 1590–1635; Maronite-Druze equilibrium, 1697–1842; the *mutasarrifiyyah* (governorate) of Mount Lebanon, 1861–1914; and the emergence of the Republic of Lebanon, 1920–present. The present is dominated by ongoing regional conflict and the policies of the United States, which has replaced Great Britain and France as a regional and global power. Malik observes that the United States has always placed Lebanon within the context of a Middle Eastern policy in which Lebanon was not a priority. Central to U.S. interests have been its relationship with Israel, the protection of oil companies in the Gulf states, and, during the cold war, its balance of power with the Soviet Union. Malik concludes with certain questions about Lebanon's uniqueness as a multicultural state and its future relationship with the countries in the region. He cautions that any attempts to destroy Lebanon's ethnic-religious balance will imperil its continued existence.

Part I. Lebanon and the Middle East Peace Process

This section comprises four chapters: "The Regional Struggle for Lebanon"; "Israeli-Lebanese Relations: A Future Imperfect?"; "The Dilemma of the Palestinians in Lebanon"; and "U.S. Policy toward Lebanon." The first and fourth chapters are authored by this volume's editor, the second is by Kirsten Schulze, a scholar with expertise on Lebanese-Israeli relations, and the third is by Julie Peteet, an anthropologist who has written extensively on the Palestinians.

"The Regional Struggle for Lebanon" argues that the weakness of Lebanon's inter-sect political system has allowed outside forces to influence its domestic affairs. At the same time, Lebanon's strategic location has made entanglements in the region's conflicts impossible to avoid. The chapter examines the roles of Syria, Israel, and the Palestinians in Lebanon, although Lebanon's future relations with each of these actors is unclear. Many have hoped that the successful conclusion of the peace negotiations between Israel and Syria would result in a shift of the regional balance of power, reducing Syria's suzerainty over Lebanon. This does not seem likely. If and when peace does come to the region, Syria will continue to exercise political dominance over Lebanon. Lebanon's importance to Syria's economy and regional security permits no other outcome.

Lebanese-Israeli relations, therefore, are inextricably linked to Israel's future relations with Syria. Despite Israel's unilateral withdrawal from south Lebanon in May 2000, there can be no formal peace between Lebanon and Israel until Israel also withdraws from the Golan Heights. The future of the Palestinians in Lebanon is less hopeful. Opposition to their continued presence is one issue that unites Lebanese of all factions, with few exceptions. The new Lebanese constitution explicitly states that there shall not be any colonization of Lebanese territory and that Lebanese territory is for the Lebanese.[4] Implicit in this statement is the Lebanese stance that the Palestinians should not be resettled permanently in Lebanon.

Palestinians living in Lebanon face physical danger and suffer the afflictions of poverty, unemployment, and political disenfranchisement. They are marginalized by a peace process that holds out no hope of repatriation to Palestine. Given the opposition to granting them Lebanese citizenship and allowing their permanent settlement in Lebanon, the Palestinians have sought protection from further displacement by redefining their place in Lebanon as a legal minority.

Kirsten Schulze examines Israeli-Lebanese relations from the perspective of each country. Historically, Israeli leaders believed that a natural alliance could be developed with the Maronite Christian community and, by extension, with Lebanon. Both Israel and Lebanon have looked to the West, had a Western orientation, and been minority states in a predominantly Arab-Muslim environment. Lebanon's ethno-religious political system, however, has prevented a unified stance toward Israel from emerging. Lebanese Muslims generally have regarded Israel as a foreign implant, while Christian attitudes have been split. The Greek Orthodox, attuned to Arab nationalism, have aligned themselves with the Muslims; the Maronites, whose strong independent national identity placed them at odds with Arab nationalism, have favored Israel.

After reviewing the unresolved issues in the peace process for Israel and Lebanon, Schulze concludes that there are no intrinsic obstacles to normal relations between the two countries. Both Israel and Lebanon would benefit from cooperation in the areas of tourism, infrastructure, transport, and water, once the important issues of military security, Palestinian refugees, water rights, and economic development have been addressed. More important, Israel will need to change its traditional policy of favoring the Maronite community to one of sensitivity to all of Lebanon's religious and ethnic communities if relations between the two countries are to improve.

Julie Peteet explores the worldview of the Palestinian refugees in Lebanon from an anthropological perspective. The Palestinian refugees not only face physical danger and human rights abuses but also suffer the afflictions of poverty, unemployment, and political disenfranchisement. The Declaration of Principles on Palestinian self-rule in Jericho and the Gaza Strip, signed by the Palestine Liberation Organization (PLO) and Israel at Oslo on 13 September 1993, did not address the situation of the Palestinians in Lebanon. This omission renewed fears that Lebanon would have to accept the Palestinians permanently after any Israeli-Palestinian peace settlement. In the discourse of recrimination and historical amnesia, most Lebanese have come to blame the Palestinians for the civil war and vehemently oppose giving them permanent status. According to Peteet, "If one looks at the meaning of the Lebanese civil war for the Palestinians in an anthropological framework, it was about spatiality. The war redefined space and its meaning." In one sense, "the Palestinian refugee camps serve as Lebanon's war memorials. Their continued existence is testimony to the reputed cause of the war, and their recontainment represents a tangible victory for the Lebanese."

The Palestinian refugees are now entering their fourth generation in Lebanon. For more than fifty years, their experience has been one of perpetual crisis. Years of violence and terror have been punctuated by brief periods of quiet and safety, with resulting despair. The younger generation of Palestinians does not envision a future in which the situation in Lebanon will improve. Peteet concludes that unless Palestinian efforts to form effective social organizations and negotiate with the Lebanese government succeed, the current Palestinian-Lebanese relationship will only breed more violence.

"U.S. Policy toward Lebanon" traces U.S.-Lebanese relations in the context of U.S. objectives in the region. These include the now-familiar goals of the security and well-being of Israel, the need to maintain influence in Arab countries in order to access and control Middle Eastern oil, and, during the cold war, preventing the Soviet Union from achieving power in the Middle East. These goals have been paramount for the United States. The long history of U.S. intervention in Lebanon has included the sending of troops during Lebanon's civil war in 1958 and securing the evacuation of the PLO from Beirut in 1982. It was, however, U.S. involvement in the disastrous Multinational Force and the negotiations between Israel and Lebanon and the ill-fated 17 May 1983 Lebanese-Israeli agreement that led to the final withdrawal of U.S. forces from Lebanon in March 1984. With that withdrawal, the United States acknowledged Syria's primacy in Lebanon and its role as the policeman of the region, creating a new focus for U.S. policy in Lebanon. The chapter concludes that Lebanon will continue to remain hostage to the Middle East peace process and that the United States will continue to pursue a pragmatic policy in Lebanon, acknowledging Syria's dominance.

Part II. Religion, Culture, and Gender

The chapters in this section deal with cultural issues that have shaped Lebanon, including Muslim-Christian relations, the status of higher education, and the status of women in postwar Lebanon.

Muslim-Christian relations are examined by Paul Sayah and Mohammad Sammak. In "Muslim-Christian Relations in Lebanon: A Christian Perspective," Sayah discusses from a Christian perspective the historical relationship between the main Muslim and Christian communities in Lebanon. Of seminal importance in the relationship between the two communities are the pastoral letters issued by the Catholic Patriarchs of the Orient in 1991, 1992, and 1994; the *Post Synodal Apostolic Exhortation* of 1995, written by Pope John Paul II, which sought to give Lebanese Catholics (principally Maronites) a guide for future action; and a memorandum given to the Lebanese prime minister by the Maronite patriarch in 1998, outlining Christian concerns. Sayah quotes a passage from the *Apostolic Exhortation* that sums up the Christian position on the relationship with

Muslims: "Arab Christians are an integral part of the cultural identity of Muslims, just as Muslims are an integral part of the cultural identity of Christians. We are responsible for each other before God and humanity."[5]

The *Apostolic Exhortation* called for change in Catholic attitudes toward Muslims, which ultimately could have a strong political and social impact on the Arab world. During his visit to Lebanon in May 1997, Pope John Paul II called upon Catholics to accept integration in the Arab world if they wanted to ensure their long-term presence in Lebanon and the region.

The obstacles to peaceful Christian-Muslim relations in Lebanon include the presence of foreign troops, the resettlement of Lebanese citizens displaced by the civil war, and the reintegration of Christians into the political life of the country. Sayah concludes with the hope that both communities will work together to build a Lebanon that can ensure justice, equality, and freedom for all its citizens.

A Muslim perspective on Muslim-Christian relations is given by Mohammad Sammak in "Religion and Politics: The Case of Lebanon." According to Sammak, history demonstrates that the region's ethnic and religious diversity turned from strength to liability when European powers tried to use religious minorities as a wedge to dominate the Middle East. This policy continued in Israel's attempts to foster the creation of a Christian ministate in Lebanon both in the 1950s and during the 1975–90 civil war. Despite these efforts, Sammak observes that Lebanese religious leaders never approved the military actions of any side in the civil war, nor did they give their blessing to any of the warlords. They did, however, support the Ta'if Agreement and its goal of balancing religious and confessional interests, rather than eradicating them.

For Sammak, the theological basis for Muslim-Christian understanding is the Quranic verse "Nearest among them in love to the believers wilt thou find those who say 'we are Christians.'" This verse, he states, is at the core of Arab-Christian-Muslim nationality and Lebanese national identity. It also provides the motif for an Arab-Islamic heritage to which all Lebanon's citizens can relate.

Sammak's discussion of the Islamic-Christian Committee for National Dialogue, established in 1993, indicates that tangible efforts have been made to promote Muslim-Christian relations. Minimally, the committee tries to preempt threats (both internal and from abroad) to the coexistence of Muslims and Christians by organizing seminars and conferences and issuing policy statements to the media on issues of concern to Muslims and

Christians. Sammak concludes that Muslim-Christian dialogue has many dimensions, but its effectiveness is rooted primarily in the search for truth in the other's point of view in an atmosphere where goodwill and a willingness for reconciliation prevail.

The role of education in repositioning Lebanon as an educational and cultural center in the Middle East is discussed by Nabeel Haidar in "Lebanon as a Regional Educational and Cultural Center." Prior to the 1975–90 civil war, Lebanese universities and colleges attracted students from all over the world and produced many leaders. Lebanon's uniquely vibrant secular society made its educational system especially attractive to the Arab countries. Haidar outlines the types of governmental and private schools in Lebanon and reviews their strengths and weaknesses. He notes that one of the advantages of the private schools over those administered by the government is the quality of their language instruction. Fluency in several foreign languages, Haidar observes, gives Lebanese students a definite economic edge in a global marketplace.

The weakness shared by both educational systems is their failure to forge the identity of the Lebanese citizen. Haidar recommends the establishment of educational programs geared toward progressively bringing new generations of young Lebanese to a healthy respect for the norms of civil life. Only when students are so educated will the rights of all citizens be guaranteed.

Haidar contends that the rich history of Lebanese universities will be a major factor in the revival of Lebanon as a cultural and educational center. He concludes by affirming that Lebanon's strength lies in its atmosphere of academic and social freedom, where new ideas are nurtured and the creative spirit can flourish.

Mona Khalaf discusses the impact of Lebanon's civil war on women in "Women in Postwar Lebanon." Tracing the significant milestones in women's rights in the twentieth century, Khalaf notes that much remains to be accomplished, not only in Lebanon but in the rest of the world as well. The Lebanese civil war merely accentuated the disadvantages that Lebanese women were already experiencing, including discrimination in employment and wages that are only 50 to 75 percent of those earned by men.

Khalaf assesses the impact of the war on family life, the participation of women in the labor force, the feminization of poverty, and equal access to education. She argues that the legal status of women in Lebanon is problematic since the Lebanese Constitution does not spell out clearly the equality between the sexes. Legislation, although giving lip service to the social and economic rights of all citizens, differentiates between men and women in the workplace. The absence of a unified personal-status law also discriminates against women and violates the principle of equality of all citizens before the law, since each of Lebanon's religious sects has its own tribunals to deal with marriage, divorce, custody, inheritance, guardianship, and adoption.

Khalaf notes a major setback for women's rights in Lebanon: the opposition of religious leaders to former president Elias Hrawi's proposal for an optional civil marriage law that would have guaranteed equality between men and women and allowed intercommunitarian marriages. She concludes by offering recommendations for the ongoing fight of Lebanese women for civil rights but cautions that the problems women face will not be solved if they are formulated in terms of women versus men.

Khalaf's arguments mirror those of other women's rights organizations such as Tayyar al-Almani (Movement for Secularism), founded in 1980 by Gregoire Haddad, the Greek Catholic bishop of Beirut. The Tayyar is an interdenominational organization whose goal is a civil marriage law that will guarantee equality between men and women and apply human rights legislation to personal status laws, since secular personal status codes will promote civil society. According to Marie Rose Zalzal, Tayyar's secretary-general, "When rights are protected by civil law, no one will be able to pretend to be the 'porte parole' of God and then realize his own plans in the name of God. Unfortunately, very few organizations are working on a unified civil code. It is mostly the *Tayyar*. Even secularists in parliament fear raising the issue of personal status codes."[6]

The reform of Lebanon's marriage and family laws faces serious obstacles. Although leaders of both the Muslim and Christian confessions opposed the legislation, acceptance of secular jurisdiction in personal status laws will be especially difficult for the Muslim community. In Lebanon, as in most Arab and Islamic countries, the structure and regulation of family matters has always been acknowledged as the purview of Islamic law. Removing the family from this jurisdiction, or even granting the option to do so, is seen as impermissible.[7]

Part III. Problems of Urbanization, Ecology, and the Economy

The chapters in this section examine the ways in which problems of urbanization, ecology, and the economy will determine the quality of life in twenty-first-century Lebanon. In "The Emerging Urban Landscape of Lebanon," Michael Davie presents a history of the development of Lebanon's cities and towns from the Ottoman period to the present. He argues that Lebanon's urban landscape is the product of the economy in a political context. According to Davie, Lebanon's sprawling, chaotic urban landscape physically expresses the failure of its liberal economy to come to grips with its structural and political weaknesses.

The end of the 1975–90 civil war brought to power a new elite whose goal was to make Beirut a locus of national and regional prosperity. The elite developed a plan to modernize the city and provide amenities unavailable elsewhere in the Middle East. At first glance, the activity generated by the rebuilding of Beirut's center city gave observers grounds for optimism. Davie points out, however, that the Lebanese political system, which was largely responsible for the lack of urban planning before the war, has not been reformed. Most important, there is little room for the development of new political parties or of a new political consciousness among urban citizens, who are still required to vote in their ancestors' rural place of origin.

Davie concludes that the Third World pattern of Lebanese cities—business and upper-class residential areas giving way to increasingly crowded middle-class and lower-class areas, which are ringed by slums and refugee camps—will continue. Palestinian camps and nomad settlements at the periphery of cities will exist as long as a low-wage workforce is required to build urban infrastructure and there is no permanent settlement for refugees. Upper-class residential areas will maintain their exclusive character, but few new ones will be created because of lack of space. Davie bases his analysis on the prediction that Lebanon's liberal economic system and confessional political system will be maintained. As a result, Lebanon's vaunted reconstruction is simply a replication of previous urban failures and will foster social unrest and urban violence.

Fouad Hamdan, in "The Ecological Crisis in Lebanon," details the role of the environmental organization Greenpeace in Lebanon. Founded in 1971 in the Quaker tradition of "bearing witness," Greenpeace emulates the nonviolent disobedience of the American civil rights movement and the example of Mahatma Gandhi. It has cooperated with local Lebanese activists in calling attention to numerous environmental disasters. Decades of uncontrolled urban and industrial development and over fifteen years of war have produced an ecological crisis in Lebanon. Deforestation, polluted drinking water, uncontrolled dumping of toxic waste from industrial and urban areas, lack of waste management programs, and the overpopulation of the narrow coastal zone and cities are rampant. Even more insidious was the use of Lebanon during the war as a dumping ground for toxic waste imported from Italy, Belgium, and Germany.

Greenpeace coordinates its work in Lebanon with its regional campaign to pressure governments to ratify the protocols and amendments of the 1976 Barcelona Convention, which banned direct and indirect pollution of the Mediterranean basin. Hamdan offers the broad outlines of a solution to Lebanon's ecological problems and urges the Lebanese government to rebuild the country on an environmentally sound basis.

Wassim Shahin, in "The Lebanese Economy in the Twenty-first Century," begins with an analysis of the Hariri government's 1994 Horizon 2000 plan. Although never formally adopted, the plan provided a blueprint for governmental action and anticipated projections for major macroeconomic variables in the Lebanese economy from 1995 to 2007. After investigating the causes of Lebanon's current economic situation, Shahin recommends a plan that could promote growth, equity, and stability. These changes include reforming the tax system, improving tax collection, abolishing waste, and setting priorities for expenditures. Administrative reform and reducing the deficit and debt service are particularly important, as Lebanon needs to achieve a stable currency and low inflation.

According to Shahin, the state of the Lebanese economy in the twenty-first century will depend on political as well as economic variables. He urges Lebanon to automate its banking facilities to become more competitive in attracting regional and international funds. Shahin also advocates industrial quality control and tax-funded expenditures on research and development as ways to improve the Lebanese economy. He believes that unless Lebanon adopts fiscal and monetary policy reforms, it will not achieve economic stability in the twenty-first century.

Shahin develops a model for an Arab Economic and Monetary Union, based on that of the European Community, but he uncovers many flaws in the hypothetical organization. In his view, Lebanon should not become involved in such an organization even if it were to be established. Given current political and economic realities, it is more advantageous for Lebanon to establish independent objectives and policies. This path does not, however, preclude Lebanon from cooperating with other Arab countries or from sharing information with them on global issues.

Conclusion

Shortly before the end of the Lebanese civil war in 1990, the Lebanese historian Kamal Salibi wrote:

> Lebanon today is a political society condemned to know and understand the real facts of its history if it seeks to survive. How the thorny complexities of the present conflict in Lebanon will be resolved is not a matter for historians to determine. Certainly, however, no political settlement in the country can be lasting unless it takes questions of history into account. Before the people of Lebanon can hope to develop the degree of social solidarity that can enable them to stand together as a coherent and viable political community, they have to know precisely what they are, and how they relate to the world around them. This means that they have to learn exactly why and how they came to be Lebanese, given the original historical and other differences between them. Otherwise, regardless of how the present quarrel in Lebanon is patched up, they will continue to be so many tribes (the current euphemism is "spiritual families"); each tribe forever suspicious and distrustful of the others; each tribe always alert, extending feelers to the outside world in different directions, probing for possible sources of external support in preparation for yet another round of open conflict.[8]

Lebanon's future in the twenty-first century is uncertain. As the authors of this volume demonstrate, Lebanon must deal not only with a painful past but also with a present in which it is held hostage to regional politics. Despite understandable pessimism, there are signs that Lebanon will not only survive but thrive in the new century. Whatever its flaws, Lebanon's confessional democracy is remarkably durable. Lebanon has existed within internationally recognized borders since 1920, and years of civil war and involvement in regional conflicts have not managed to destroy it. Its religious communities, however contentious and divided, are part of a framework that forces compromise, as one faction can never completely dominate another. Most Lebanese, Muslim and Christian alike, affirm that Lebanon must continue to exist and that Christians and Muslims share a common heritage. Lebanon is accepted as a sovereign entity by the Arab world and the international community. Optimism, economic activity, and cultural vibrancy characterize Lebanon today, in the face of continuing violence and instability.

The fate of the Palestinians in Lebanon, inequities in the status of women, urban sprawl, and environmental pollution need to be resolved. Recognizing these problems, however, is the first step toward change.

It is hoped that this volume will help the peoples of Lebanon find a deeper understanding of their heritage and provide a blueprint for the peace that is necessary to Lebanon's renewal.

Notes

1. "Documents: The Constitution of Lebanon after the Amendments of August 21, 1990," *Beirut Review* 1, no. 1 (Spring 1991): 119–60.

2. Saree Makdisi, "Reconstructing History in Central Beirut," *MERIP*, no. 203, 27, no. 2 (Spring 1997): 25.

3. "In the same enormous recess of my mind, thronging with so many great images, I say to myself, 'That's what I will do!' and the action I have envisaged follows. 'Oh if only this or that could be! Pray God this or that may not happen!' I say to myself, and even as I say it the images of all these things of which I speak pass before me, coming from the same treasure house of memory. If they were not there, I would be quite unable to conjure up such possibilities." St. Augustine, *The Confessions*, book X, 14, in *The Works of Saint Augustine*, intro., trans., and notes by Maria Boulding, O.S.B. (Hyde Park, N.Y.: Augustinian Heritage Institute, New City Press, 1997), 246.

4. "Lebanese territory is one for all Lebanese. There shall be no segregation of the people on the basis of any type of belonging, and no fragmentation, partition, or colonization." "Preamble,The New Constitution of Lebanon," sec. i. See *Beirut Review* 1, no. 2 (Spring 1991): 123.

5. *The Post Synodal Apostolic Exhortation*, n. 45.

6. Suad Joseph, "Secularism and Personal Status Codes in Lebanon: Interview with Marie Rose Zalzal, Esquire," *MERIP*, no. 203, 27, no. 2 (Spring 1997): 37.

7. Kamal Salibi, *A House of Many Mansions: The History of Lebanon Reconsidered* (Berkeley: University of California Press, 1989), 195.

8. Ibid., 217–18.

Overview

Lebanon as an Experiment in Multicultural Interdependence

Hafeez Malik

Throughout its history, Lebanon has represented a unique experiment in multicultural and multireligious interdependence. Christians and Muslims have coexisted for centuries within a tradition of *la ghalib wa la maghlub* (there is no conqueror and no vanquished). This experiment has not been easy or peaceful. Exogenous states, including the Ottoman Empire, France, Great Britain, Syria, Israel, and the United States, have exercised great power over Lebanon. Internally, power has shifted in different epochs from one community to the other. No community, however, has ever managed to achieve complete domination. A tenuous equilibrium that reflects the demographic weight of each community has been maintained, and the resulting balance of social forces has been a stabilizing factor for the Lebanese state.

The consciousness of being "Lebanese" is historically associated with the Maronites, who have survived as Christians in the face of Islam. The Maronites have substantially resisted Arabization along with Islamization. However, some Western scholars maintain that the Maronites have been Arabized linguistically, as they speak a dialect of Arabic and share the social traditions of Syrian Arabs.[1] Named after Saint Maron, a legendary fifth-century ascetic monk, the Maronites moved to the Mount of north Lebanon and blended with the Syriac-speaking population "to create in the early eighth century a quasi-nation, defying the ruling Umayyad Caliphate, and holding friendly contacts with Byzantine emperors."[2] The Maronites also joined forces with Christian Mardaites, who came to Lebanon in 666 after having effectively checked the Umayyad caliph Muʿawiyah's policy of expansion in Syria. The Mardaites "became the nucleus around which many fugitives and malcontents, among whom were the Maronites, grouped themselves."[3]

The Maronites first began to forge enduring alliances with the West during the Crusades (1097–1291). In 1099, Crusaders made contact with Maronites in northern Lebanon who provided them "with guides and a limited number of recruits."[4] In the twelfth century, Catholic France established relations with the Maronite patriarch and started to treat the Maronites as special protégés. The Vatican granted open recognition to the Maronite Church's orthodoxy and by the eighteenth century had solid institutional links with the Maronite Church hierarchy.

The era of the Crusades also brought to Lebanon another significant religious minority, the Druzes, a heterodox community from Egypt's Ismaili Fatimids. Subjected to persecution from the Sunni Muslim majority, the Druzes sought refuge in the southern part of Lebanon and developed an exceptionally secret system of religious beliefs that defy precise definition. Consequently, it is impossible to label them as Muslim, Christian, or Jewish. They currently account for 9 percent of the Lebanese population, along with 3 percent of the population of Syria and 1.2 percent of the population of Israel. It was Mount Lebanon, however, that became the center of Druze life; the name Jabal al-Druze refers to Mount Lebanon.

The Druzes had to deal with a variety of political forces that were hostile to them for religious reasons. Consequently, they cultivated the delicate arts of skillful diplomacy and coalition building in order to establish new alliances.[5] During the Crusades, the Druzes repeatedly switched alliances to stay on the winning side. Because they had suffered persecution in Egypt, their relations with the Mamluks were poor. It is not surprising, therefore, that the Druzes supported the fifteenth-century takeover of the region by the Ottoman Turks, putting an end to Egyptian domination.

By 1516, the Ottoman Turks had established in Mount Lebanon their distinctive style of *millet* rule, which allowed religious and cultural autonomy to every community by recognizing the primacy of a single leader within that community. Much of the history of Ottoman Lebanon revolves around the Maronites and Druzes and their feudal lords, the Manis and Shihabis. This period inaugurated the formation of the modern Lebanese state, which has culminated in Lebanon's Second Republic.

Formative Phases of the Modern Lebanese State

The development of the modern Lebanese state can be divided into four formative phases: intersectarianism and modernism (1590–1635); the Maronite and Druze equilibrium (1697–1842); the *mutasarrifiyyah* of Mount Lebanon (1861–1914); and the emergence of the Republic of

Lebanon (1920–present). In each phase, Lebanon maintained a political equilibrium, no matter how strained or difficult, that enabled its major communities to preserve their religious and social identities.

The First Formative Phase: Intersectarianism and Modernism (1590–1635)

After the establishment of *millet* rule in 1516, the Ottoman sultan Salim granted authority to the Druze lord Fakhr al-Din I al-Mani, allowing him and other feudal lords the same privileges that they had had under Mamluk domination. For 180 years, the Manis ruled over a large part of Lebanon. As emirs, they exacted taxes, acted independently in all domestic matters, and transmitted their offices to their descendants.

Mani hegemony reached its apex under the progressive Druze emir Fakhr al-Din II (1590–1635). Fakhr al-Din II relentlessly pursued three major ambitions: building a greater Lebanon, leading Lebanon to "modernity" and progress, and severing links with the Ottoman sultans. To this end, he signed a treaty with a foreign power, the Medicis of Florence. By 1610, Fakhr al-Din had extended his authority over Lebanon from Dog River to Mount Carmel and inland to Tiberias. He took over Tripoli and extended his sway into Syria, Palestine, and Transjordan. Ottoman forces that moved against him from Damascus were defeated by his army. The Ottoman sultan capitulated to Fakhr al-Din's demands by designating him emir of a territory called Arabistan.

In order to modernize the Lebanese economy, Fakhr al-Din brought in engineers, architects, and agronomists from Tuscany and allowed European Catholic missions to carry on their educational and religious work in Lebanon. True to his Druze values of secrecy, mobility, and adaptability, "Fakhr is said to have been baptized (as a Christian) by his Capuchin physician."[6] His rule over Lebanon came to a violent end, however. In 1635, the Ottoman sultan had Fakhr al-Din brought as captive to Constantinople, where he was "strangled in the square of a mosque by two mutes."[7]

Fakhr al-Din II clearly established a precedent for Lebanese self-determination through his policies of acquiring new territory, seeking independence from the Ottoman Turks, and fostering religious tolerance by allowing all confessions freedom of religion without threat of persecution or forced conversion. In 1697, the Mani emirate died out and was replaced by its allies and relatives by marriage, the Shihabis. The Druze Shihabi emirate became officially Christian when Mansur (1754–70), the fourth Shihabi emir, converted to Christianity in its Maronite confession.

The Second Formative Phase: The Maronite and Druze Equilibrium (1697–1842)

For nearly 150 years (1697–1842), the Shihabis preserved Lebanese autonomy and hereditary succession by maintaining an equilibrium of rights between the Maronites and Druzes, the two major elements of population in Mount Lebanon. The friendly Maronite-Druze relationship established by Fakhr al-Din II was described in the late 1600s by the Rome-educated patriarch of the Maronite Church, Istifan al-Duwayhi, as "a local patriotism."[8]

The Shihabis maintained the friendly policy toward Europeans initiated by their predecessors. Capuchins and Jesuits, as well as French traders, became firmly established in Mount Lebanon. These Europeans implemented the policy that Louis XIV (1643–1715) had initiated to promote French trade in the Near East and to protect the Catholics of this region. In this period the Maronites, who had established cordial relations with France in the time of the Crusades, became even closer to that European power.

Shihabi rule ended in the emirate of Bashir al-Shihabi II (1788–1842). Bashir had a harsh temperament and ruled his people sternly. Nonetheless, he attempted to create an autonomous, enlightened, and modernized Mount Lebanon. "Christian by baptism, Muslim by matrimony, and Druze to his subjects, Bashir opened Lebanon's doors wider than ever to Western educational influences and commercial contacts."[9] Bashir's ecumenical spirit is reflected in the beautiful palace he built at Bayt al-Din, which contains both a chapel and a mosque. The palace is still used as a summer residence for the president of the Lebanese republic.

In 1842, Bashir was deposed by the Ottoman sultan and replaced by a renegade Hungarian, Umar Pasha, the first governor to be sent from the Ottoman capital. This direct interference by a foreign power transformed the orientation of Lebanese politics from tribal to religious. The Druze-Maronite equilibrium broke down as both communities sought help from the great European powers. The Maronites secured French patronage, and the Druzes counterbalanced this alliance with British support. The Russians became involved through their support for the Greek Orthodox Christians, whose confession they shared.

Civil wars between Christians and Druzes broke out in 1845. In 1860, after several periods of bloodshed and uneasy truce, the French intervened directly, landing 7,000 troops in Lebanon. An international commission consisting of British, French, and Russian delegates met at the Ottoman capital, and in June 1861 they produced a basic constitutional document for a unified Lebanon, the *Règlement et protocole, relatifs à la réorganisation du Mont Liban.*

The Third Formative Phase: Mount Lebanon: A Mutasarrifiyyah (1861–1914)

With the agreement of the Great Powers, the *Règlement* was promulgated on 9 June 1861 in the form of a *firman* (order) of His Imperial Majesty the Ottoman Sultan. Consequently, Lebanon, stripped of its seaport and the Beqaa plateau, was created as an autonomous region *(mutasarrifiyyah)* under a governor-general *(mutasarrif)*. The area of the *mutasarrifiyyah* was considerably smaller than that of present-day Lebanon (6,500 square kilometers, as opposed to 10,452 square kilometers today), and the population was only 266,487, less than one-tenth of present-day Lebanon's 3.45 million. In 1865, Maronites were in sheer numbers the largest community (171,800), followed by Greek Orthodox (29,326), Druzes (28,560), Greek Catholics (19,370), Shi'a Muslims (9,820), and Sunni Muslims (7,611). By 1895, the population had increased to nearly 400,000, but the sectarian rankings remained the same.[10]

Despite the Maronite majority, the *Règlement* prevented political power from falling solely into Maronite hands. It reestablished political equilibrium, specifying only that the governor should be a Catholic Christian. During the existence of the *mutasarrifiyyah*, seven different governors of Armenian, Italian, Polish, and Levantine origins were appointed by the Ottoman sultans, and they exercised a measure of self-rule. The governor was assisted by an elective administrative council of twelve members, with two representatives from each of the religious communities. The *Règlement* divided Mount Lebanon into six districts, each with a *mudir* appointed by the governor from the dominant sect. The districts were then divided into sectarian cantons. Justice was left entirely in the hands of local courts, and cases of personal status were kept under the jurisdiction of the respective religious authorities.[11]

Economically, the *mutasarrifiyyah* made impressive strides. In 1863, a French company built the Beirut-Damascus highway. In 1895, another French company constructed a Beirut-Damascus railroad, which subsequently connected these two cities with Turkey, Iraq, and Egypt. Mount Lebanon became an open zone for the exercise of Western educational and cultural forces, to which its people reacted with greater spontaneity and enthusiasm than did people of neighboring states. The *mutasarrifiyyah* became a showplace of modern Western culture.

The *Règlement* remained the basic constitution of Mount Lebanon for fifty-three years, until World War I. Despite its successes, its complete disregard of proportional representation became a major Maronite grievance. The Maronites were overwhelmingly aware not only of their numerical superiority over the Druzes, but of their greater educational and material advances as well. They were also, according to one scholarly assessment, imbued with a feeling of cultural superiority over non-Christians.[12] Maronite feelings of cultural and religious superiority became an obstacle to Maronite-Muslim relations when the Lebanese state expanded under the French mandate after World War I.

Emergence of the Republic of Lebanon: Failure of the New Balance and Syrian Irredentism (1920–present)

While Arabs were yearning for the freedom promised after World War I, the Allied Powers were dashing these hopes by dividing up Arab lands. In 1920, Syria and Lebanon were assigned as mandates to France, the Hijaz was recognized as independent, and Iraq and Palestine, along with Transjordan, were assigned to Britain. France greatly increased Lebanon's territory. Lebanon now included the Syrian maritime coast and interior plain, including Beirut, Tripoli in the north, Sidon in the south, southern Lebanon (with its predominantly Shi'a population), and the fertile Beqaa Valley, occupied by a mixture of Muslims and Greek Orthodox. This increase in territory decreased the fraction of Maronites and other Christians to a little more than half the total population, a shift that would have long-term consequences for sectarian relationships and the stability of the state. Lebanon was proclaimed a republic with a constitution of its own in 1926, while still under the French mandate, and was declared an independent and sovereign state in 1943. Despite being repeatedly suspended by the French and amended several times, the 1926 constitution endured until the signing of the Ta'if Agreement in 1989, after which it was further modified to transfer some of the Christian president's powers to the Sunni prime minister.

The loss of the Beqaa Valley and Tripoli to Lebanon was particularly painful for Syria and remained an ongoing source of tension. Without the addition of these areas, Mount Lebanon would have emerged as a Christian state without a militant Muslim population, whose continued demand for union with Syria threatened state unity. Despite these difficulties, both the constitution and the proclamation of the Republic were turning points in Lebanon's history. The National Pact of 1943 committed Christians to abandon their traditional dependence on France, pledged Muslims to forego their aspirations of union with Syria or a larger Arab state, and divided up state powers along sectarian lines. The constitution, proclamation of the Republic, and the National Pact of 1943 represented crucial stages in the transformation of Lebanon into a viable modern state. The National Pact of 1943 also cemented the acceptance of the modern Lebanese state by its Muslim citizens and provided the basis for Christian-Muslim coexistence in an independent Lebanon. Nonetheless, Maronites remained apprehensive about the future of Christians in an Arab-Muslim Middle East. They wondered who would protect Lebanon from Syrian ambitions once the French were gone.

During the 1950s and 1960s, new threats to Lebanon's solidarity were spawned by republican, socialist, and nationalist ideologies, including Gamal Abdel Nasser's revolution in Egypt. After the British-French attack on the Suez Canal in 1956, Nasser became not merely an Egyptian hero, but an Arab hero. Lebanese Muslims made a public statement in support of Arab nationalism, adorning their homes, public places, and vehicles with pictures of Nasser. They also began to think of themselves as second-class citizens and demanded a new census, which they believed would indicate a Muslim majority in Lebanon. Christian, especially Maronite, reaction to this proposal was equally intense: to them a new census would destroy the fundamental promise of the National Pact to acknowledge Christian majority. Christians sought security in the continuation of the status quo. Maronite Christian president Camille Chamoun attempted to have the Lebanese constitution amended so that he could serve another term. In 1958, the Muslims decided to rebel. Chamoun turned for protection to the United States, rather than to France, under the auspices of the Eisenhower Doctrine. U.S. Marines were sent in to calm the tense situation, and General Fouad Chehab was elected president to succeed Chamoun. The status quo suffered a serious jolt but survived as a political system.

However, the Lebanese status quo could not survive the fifteen years of civil war (1975–90), ignited by the struggle of the Palestine Liberation Organization against Israel and the presence of Palestinian refugees in Lebanon, a population that today numbers nearly 400,000. Since 1991, when parliamentary elections were held for the first time in almost twenty years, successive governments have faced the monumental task of Lebanon's reconstruction under the shadow of exogenous Syrian influence and the presence of 30,000–35,000 Syrian troops in Lebanon.

In 1978, Israel established a security zone in south Lebanon, which it reoccupied in 1982 after a brief withdrawal in response to pressure from the United Nations. This security zone, which Israel occupied until May

2000, stretched from the foothills of Mount Hermon to the Mediterranean and occupied 10 percent of Lebanese territory and 150 towns and villages whose population included all of Lebanon's religious communities—Shi'a, Sunni, Muslim, Druze, Maronite, and other Christian sects. Israel used a local proxy, the 2,500-man South Lebanon Army, to provide it with security against Hizballah militants.[13]

The United States has supported Israel and other Arab states at Lebanon's expense as part of a broad and comprehensive foreign policy appropriate to the period of the cold war. States that followed the foreign policy of nonalignment, such as Syria, were seen as unfriendly; the conservative monarchies, including Saudi Arabia, Jordan, and the Gulf states, had to be protected from internal or external threats in order to retain access to and control over Middle Eastern oil, and Israel's security had to be promoted and protected. Israel, which has received more than $90 billion in economic and military aid since 1949—more than one-third of all U.S. foreign aid—is the greatest military power in the Middle East. A steady supply of state-of-the-art weaponry has enabled Israel, according to reliable estimates, to defeat any combination of Arab states in a projected conflict. The United States has also endeavored to break the solidarity of Arab states in encouraging Israel to negotiate with its neighbors bilaterally, rather than in a multilateral peace conference. No major agreement between Israel and an Arab state has been signed without U.S. mediation. Since the signing of the Egyptian-Israeli peace agreement in 1979, the United States has given $50 billion in foreign aid to Egypt, two-thirds of what it gives Israel each year.[14]

Since its withdrawal from Lebanon in 1984, the United States has conceded a "legitimate" hegemony over Lebanon to Syria. This development was brought about by Syria's opposition to the Lebanon-Israel peace agreement, its subsequent abrogation by Lebanon, and the killing by a suicide bomb of 241 U.S. Marines who were in Beirut as part of the Multinational Force (MNF). Southern Lebanon continues to be unstable, due to Syria's desire to maintain pressure on Israel for its continuing occupation of the Golan Heights. The Syrian presence in Lebanon thus leaves Lebanon under an occupation that will not end until Israel reaches a peace settlement with Syria.

Conclusion

Civil war has left Lebanon truncated and occupied by foreign powers. Maronite Christians still regret their lost political powers and demographic majority, mourning a Lebanon that could have been the Switzerland of the Middle East had their own leadership not insisted on adding Syrian territory to Lebanon in 1926. Non-Christians are embittered by the collaboration of the Christian Phalangists (Kata'ib) with Israel, which led to the siege of Beirut in 1982. This wound has not healed despite the termination of hostilities. Finally, the question of whether Syria will withdraw from its former possessions and establish diplomatic relations with the Lebanese state—or gradually establish a commonwealth with Lebanon in which the two states would speak with one voice both economically and militarily—has not yet been resolved. One conclusion, however, is inescapable: The attempts to destroy Lebanon's ethnic-religious balance, which lay at the core of its civil war, have imperiled Lebanon.

Notes

1. Helena Cobban, *The Making of Modern Lebanon* (Boulder, Colo.: Westview Press, 1985), 31.

2. Philip K. Hitti, *The Near East in History* (Princeton, N.J.: D. Van Nostrand Company, 1961), 450.

3. Philip K. Hitti, *History of the Arabs* (London: Macmillan and Co., 1956), 204.

4. Ibid., 638–39.

5. Gabriel Ben-Dor, *The Druzes in Israel: A Political Study* (Jerusalem: Magnes Press, 1979), 37–47.

6. Hitti, *The Near East in History*, 452.

7. Ibid.

8. Abdu1 Rahim Abu Husayn, "Duwayhi as a Historian of Ottoman Syria," *Bulletin of the Royal Institute of Inter-Faith Studies* (Amman, Jordan) 1, no. 1 (Spring 1999): 11–22.

9. Hitti, *The Near East in History*, 454.

10. John P. Spagnolo, *France and Ottoman Lebanon, 1861–1914* (London: Ithaca Press, 1977), 24.

11. Ibid., 41–47.

12. Ibid., 54–55.

13. David Hirst, "South Lebanon: The War that Never Ends," *Journal of Palestine Studies* 28, no. 3 (Spring 1999): 6–9.

14. For further details, see Richard H. Curtis, "U.S. Aid to Israel Now Exceeds $90 Billion," *Washington Report on Middle East Affairs* (September 1999): 45.

Part I

Lebanon and the Middle East Peace Process

The Regional Struggle for Lebanon

Kail C. Ellis

> A small country is rarely involved in an international conflict to
> her advantage. Whatever side such a country may support, her
> real interest in the conflict remains of secondary importance, and
> is likely to be sacrificed should higher interests so dictate. Her al-
> lies will normally keep her uninformed of their ultimate motives,
> leaving her to drift into complex situations which she can little
> understand or control. Finally, as her internal affairs become en-
> tangled in the outside conflict, these affairs themselves get out of
> hand, leaving her at the mercy of whatever forces prevail.
> Kamal Salibi, *The Modern History of Lebanon*

Kamal Salibi's observation concerned the Lebanon of the early nineteenth
century, but it is relevant to an understanding of contemporary Lebanon.
Two destructive civil wars have interrupted Lebanon's struggle to develop
a national identity out of its various social, religious, ethnic, and class
groups. Although the weakness of its intersectarian political system has
allowed outside forces to influence its domestic affairs, its location in a
turbulent, highly symbolic, and culturally significant part of the world has
made entanglements in regional conflicts impossible to avoid. As a result,
the Lebanese see themselves alternately as a people helpless in the face of
more powerful outside forces and as innocent of any responsibility for the
social and political havoc that has racked their country.

Syria, Israel, and the Palestinians have influenced Lebanon's political
system, and each continues to be inextricably involved in Lebanon's internal affairs. Each has fought wars on Lebanon's soil and their conflicts
continue to imperil the future of the region and Lebanon itself.

Syrian-Lebanese Relations

From their inception, Syrian-Lebanese relations have been influenced by
the carving out of Greater Lebanon's new borders in 1920 from provinces
that Arab nationalists regarded as historically belonging to an indepen-

dent Arab Syria. This separation gave rise to an irredentism that was only slightly assuaged by Syria's late president Hafiz al-Asad's reference to *sha'b wahid fi baladayn* (one people in two countries).

After Syria and Lebanon achieved independence in 1943, both countries gradually came to accept their roles as separate national identities: Syria as the heart of pan-Arab nationalism and Lebanon as independent and sovereign but within the Arab world. This understanding was affirmed by Lebanon's Sunni and Maronite communities in the National Pact of 1943 and by the Alexandria Protocol of 1944. Lebanon's independence, sovereignty, and territorial integrity were guaranteed by the Arab League Pact of 22 March 1945.

The Arab-Israeli Conflict

The history of modern Lebanon is roughly contemporary with the Arab-Israeli conflict, and for most of its existence Lebanon has been struggling to contain the effects of that connection.[1] Lebanon's role in the conflict was determined primarily by its sectarian composition. Dominated by a conservative Christian leadership anxious to maintain its connection with the West, the Lebanese government officially opposed the partition plan of the United Nations for Palestine, but it had neither the desire nor the ability to actively participate in the conflict. Its position as a charter member of the Arab League required at least a limited military and political role in support of the Palestinians, and Lebanon did send a token force, estimated at 1,000 to 2,000 men, to its border with Palestine.[2]

Prior to the outbreak of hostilities, Lebanon's position toward the Arab-Israeli conflict was influenced considerably by the minority status of the Christians in the Middle East. Some Maronite Christian leaders, both ecclesiastical and lay, adopted a policy favorable to Zionism in the belief that this would counter pan-Islamic and pan-Arabist movements that saw Lebanon as part of the Syrian Arab hinterland. In July 1947, the Maronite archbishop of Beirut, Monsignor Ignatius Mubarak, presented a memorandum to the United Nations Special Committee on Palestine in which he declared that "to consider Palestine and Lebanon as parts of the Arab world would amount to a denial of history."[3] The archbishop also declared that "Lebanon as well as Palestine should remain as permanent homes for the minorities in the Arab world" and advocated the establishment of a Jewish state in Palestine.[4]

Some influential Lebanese perceived Israel as a useful buffer between themselves and the Arab nationalism of their neighbors. This led some members of the government not only to support a Jewish state in Palestine but also to espouse Western-sponsored defense schemes for the Middle East. In 1951, Dr. Charles Malik, then Lebanon's ambassador to Washington and the United Nations, predicted that in the event of war between the West and the Soviet Union in the Middle East, the Arab states would have to cooperate with Israel. In espousing Arab cooperation with Israel, Malik foreshadowed the alliance of the Lebanese Forces with Israel during the 1975–76 civil war.[5] The emergence in the mid-1950s of Gamal Abdel Nasser as the champion of pan-Arabism and the Palestinian cause gave Lebanon's Muslim and progressive groups added support and complicated the government's pro-Western leanings, especially its embrace of the Eisenhower Doctrine of 1957.

The Palestinian Refugees

The Arab-Israeli war of 1948 left Lebanon as host to an estimated 141,882 Palestinians, mainly from Galilee in northern Palestine.[6] Fifty years later, that number has grown to approximately 400,000, with the result that, for the Lebanese of all confessions, the future of the Palestinians in their country has become the most pressing issue in any regional peace settlement.

Lebanon, like other Arab countries bordering Israel that found themselves hosting Palestinian refugees, absorbed those few that it could, primarily the professional classes, and distributed the rest among camps scattered throughout the country. Unlike its neighbors, Lebanon had unique concerns with the Palestinians. Its capacity to absorb the Palestinians economically, given its proportionally much smaller population, was very limited. In addition, the overwhelming majority of Palestinians were Muslims who could not easily be absorbed into the mainstream of the country without upsetting the delicate communal balance that had been worked out in the National Pact of 1943.

For their part, the Palestinians did not wish to be absorbed by any country. Having never abandoned the quest to return to Palestine, they looked initially to the Arab countries to rectify the injustice that had been done to them. The desire for a national identity found expression in Nasser's pan-Arabist ideology, which during the Lebanese civil war of 1958 caused them to side with the opposition. Their impact on that struggle was minimal since they were not yet organized as a group either militarily or politically. This quiescent stage was soon to change, as the

Palestinians organized both politically and militarily in response to regional events.

The PLO in Lebanon

Lebanon's involvement in the Palestine question entered a new phase with the establishment of the Palestine Liberation Organization (PLO) and its military arm, the Palestine Liberation Army (PLA) by the Arab League in 1964. Whereas the other Arab states sharply restricted the movements of the Palestinians and controlled the resistance through government-sponsored guerrilla groups, Lebanon's laissez-faire political system permitted neither the national consensus nor the authoritarian system necessary to enforce such measures.

The Palestinian movement emerged as the standard bearer of Arab resistance after the Arabs' military defeat in the June 1967 war. This led to the next phase of Lebanon's involvement in the Palestine question. The defeat had so discredited the Arab governments and the Arab masses had become so demoralized that Arab public opinion looked to the skirmishes and commando operations of the Palestinians against Israel for some consolation. The rise of the Palestinian resistance, however, contained within it the seeds of division between the Palestinians and the established Arab governments. The Palestinians recognized this danger from the beginning, but, determined to pursue the cause of their own national identity and develop the organizations necessary for their political and military operations, they ignored the danger.[7] In Lebanon they established guerrilla bases and began recruiting in the refugee camps.

The Palestinian resistance movement accentuated the deep social and political fissures between the Muslim and Christian confessions in Lebanon. The specter of refugee camps being turned into fortified arsenals and of young Palestinians being trained for commando operations threatened most Christian Lebanese and even the more conservative Muslims. When the Lebanese authorities attempted to restrict these activities, the Palestinians took advantage of the social and sectarian cleavages between Christians and Muslims to establish a firm basis of support in the country among Muslims and leftist Lebanese of both confessions.

Israel's Policy of Retaliation

The first consequence of this support was the 28 December 1968 Israeli raid on Beirut International Airport.[8] Israel claimed that the raid was in retaliation for a Palestinian attack and hijacking of one of its airplanes over Italy in July 1968. In fact, it was a harbinger of a future policy of retaliation against Lebanon. Israel's prime minister, Levi Eshkol, announced that "a state cannot harbor and encourage an armed force operating from its territory against a neighboring state and be considered immune from reaction."[9] The incident, in turn, precipitated a series of conflicts between the Lebanese authorities, anxious to put an end to Israeli military actions, and the Palestinian resistance.

Lebanon, now deeply embroiled in the Arab-Israeli conflict, sought to resolve the increasing confrontations with Israel and the Palestinians by defining the conditions under which the Palestinians could operate in Lebanon. Not without some alarm, the government noticed that support for the Palestinians by the radical parties and Lebanese Muslims was increasingly coupled with criticisms of the Lebanese political system and the privileged position of the Christian community. With the Palestinian movement becoming a lever for the Muslim community to effect political change in Lebanon, Christian politicians reacted by criticizing Palestinian activities as an infringement on Lebanese sovereignty. The resulting tensions between the Christians and the Muslim politicians who viewed the Palestinian movement as an essential part of the Arab cause escalated to armed confrontations between the army and the Palestinians.

The 1969 Cairo Agreement

The Lebanese government had three pressing needs: to find a way to disclaim responsibility for the Palestinians' actions in order to ward off Israeli retaliation; to maintain the fig leaf of Lebanese sovereignty in order to satisfy its domestic critics; and to be seen as an advocate of the Palestinian cause to the opposition parties and its Muslim constituencies. In May of 1969, the Sunni prime minister, Rashid Karami, proposed that commando activity on Lebanese territory could be made compatible with Lebanese sovereignty if there was cooperation (tansiq) between the Lebanese army and the Palestinian Armed Struggle Command.[10] Although initially rejected by the Christian politicians, this proposal was eventually incorporated into the Cairo Agreement of October 1969, giving the Palestinians the right of autonomous administrative control over their refugee camps in Lebanon.

The Palestinians in Lebanon were now officially given the right to use the camps as bases, install weapons, and recruit resident Palestinians for the resistance. In return, the Palestinians promised to control the lawless elements in their ranks, to cooperate with Lebanese authorities to ensure noninterference in Lebanese affairs, and to recognize that the "Lebanese civil and military authorities will continue to exercise their full rights and responsibilities in all Lebanese regions in all circumstances."[11]

The Cairo Agreement did not resolve the basic issue of Lebanese sovereignty that the Christian politicians felt was being compromised by the actions of the Palestinians. This sentiment was forcefully expressed by the Kata'ib leader, Pierre Gemayel, who strongly criticized the agreement as a betrayal of Lebanon's sovereignty and who viewed the actions of the Palestinians as "not a Lebanese internal crisis but a difference between two independent and sovereign states in which one is openly attempting to interfere in the affairs of the other. The whole problem is clear: it is no longer the actions of the fid'ayyun; it is our system, our regime, our institutions which are desired under the cover of the Palestinian commandos and the sacred cause of Palestine."[12]

Deterioration of the Security Situation

Israel responded to the Cairo Agreement by intensifying its raids against southern Lebanon. The result was the creation of a Lebanese, primarily Shi'a, refugee problem, in addition to the Palestinian refugee problem.

The situation was further complicated by the subsequent expulsion and transfer of the Palestinian leadership to Lebanon after the 1970 Jordanian civil war. The activities of the Palestinian resistance increased, as did Israeli retaliations against Lebanon. Caught between the Palestinians and the Israelis, the Lebanese security forces were severely criticized by the opposition parties and the Palestinians for their inability to protect the country from Israeli reprisals. In the end, Israel's attempt to force the Lebanese government to become actively involved in suppressing the commandos was based on a gross overestimation of the Lebanese government's abilities and contributed to the breakdown of what authority it actually had.

Prelude to Civil War

Clashes between Kata'ib militia, the army, and the Palestinians in 1970 raised the specter of a sectarian civil war. The Palestinians had come to exert considerable influence on Muslim political circles since the ethnosectarian divisions in the country, already aggravated by economic and social inequalities, had caused the Muslims to look upon the commando movement as an ally in the struggle against what they regarded as a Christian-dominated establishment. The traditional Muslim politicians who were invested in the status quo gradually lost their following and even their armed support. Leftist commandos moved into the Muslim sectors of Beirut, took the law into their own hands, and established control over the city.[13]

The Israeli raid on Beirut in 1973 was a turning point in the spiral of violence. The Israelis' assassination of three Palestinian leaders increased the climate of bitterness, humiliation, mutual fear, and hostility between the Lebanese army and the Palestinians. Although that crisis was temporarily resolved by reaffirming the Cairo Agreement, the Christian leadership girded for the next round, determined, now more than ever, to uphold Lebanese sovereignty and the Christian character of Lebanon. The Palestinians, for their part, did not want to suffer a repeat of the 1970 Jordan debacle that resulted in their expulsion from that country. Lebanon, which had always had a tradition of bearing arms, became even more of an armed camp when the Kata'ib and Chamoun's National Liberal Party established military training camps for their militias. This was justified as a reaction to the Cairo Agreement, which gave the Palestinians freedom to carry arms.[14]

Isolation Step by Step

To the Palestinians, Secretary of State Henry Kissinger's step-by-step strategy to negotiate peace between Israel and the Arab states following the October 1973 war seemed to be based on isolating first Egypt and then Syria from the Arab-Israeli conflict and on studiously ignoring the Palestinians. When it became clear that the PLO was not going to be accepted by Israel as a party to the peace negotiations after the October 1973 war, the Palestinians determined to consolidate their position in Lebanon.

The Palestinians extended the provisions of the 1969 Cairo Agreement to the Lebanese radical parties and to the various Nasserist movements. These included pro-Iraqi and pro-Syrian Ba'thists, the Lebanese Communist Party, other communist factions, the Syrian Socialist Nationalist Party, and various Muslim nationalist Arab parties, who proceeded to arm themselves under the umbrella of the Palestinian movement. Meanwhile, everyday life in Lebanon became marked by bomb explosions, robberies, kidnappings, and political assassinations. The general breakdown of law and order in the country was abetted by the undisciplined and sometimes purposefully lawless behavior of the Palestinian commandos.

The Civil War and Syria's Intervention

Given the intense involvement of the Palestinians in Lebanon's internal affairs, it is not surprising that the incident that touched off the Lebanese civil war in Ain al-Rummaneh on 13 April 1975 began with the massacre of twenty-six Palestinians who were returning from a rally in Beirut. Although preceded by the assassination of Pierre Gemayel's bodyguard and the killing of others by persons unknown at a newly dedicated Maronite church, this incident ignited the conflict that was to engulf Lebanon for the next fifteen years.

Although Syria watched intently the dangerous security situation on its border, over a year of bloodletting and destruction passed before it intervened. Its inaction, due in part to the inherent cautiousness of its Ba'thist leadership and the need for international acceptance of its intervention by Israel, the other Arab countries, and the United States, belied the pressure on Syria from various sources to stop the killings. Syria finally intervened against the Palestinians and their allies on 1 June 1976, in what proved to be the end of the first phase of the Lebanese civil war.

Syria's efforts were officially sanctioned by an Arab summit convened in Riyadh, Saudi Arabia, in October 1976. An Arab Deterrent Force (ADF), a 30,000-strong peacekeeping body, was created to bring security to Lebanon. Nominally under the control of Lebanon's president, the ADF was composed primarily of Syrian troops, and all military action was determined solely by Syria. The ADF imposed an uneasy peace in Lebanon despite continuing skirmishes between the Lebanese factions and fighting in the south between the Palestinians and Israel.

Israel

Israel, too, watched with concern the developments in Lebanon. To the Likud government, the fighting provided an opportunity to weaken the Palestinian resistance. Consequently, Israel increased its military and political involvement with the Lebanese Forces and armed the militia of Saad Haddad, which had formed to protect Christian villages in the south against the leftist and Palestinian guerrillas. Israel also allowed recruits from the Maronite militias to be sent to Israel for training and then used as surrogates in the battle against the Palestinian guerrillas. In an effort to build a favorable position in the south (despite the devastation it was wreaking on the local villages), Israel extended the Good Fence policy it had established in 1976 to allow local Lebanese residents to cross into Israel for medical treatment, jobs, and shopping.

Israel also sought to check Syrian influence in the country. It prevented Syria from extending its pacification efforts southward by establishing its "Red Line," defined as somewhere at a point midway between Sidon and Tyre on the coast to the Syrian border. Although this area was controlled by the PLO-leftist coalition, Israel preferred their presence to having Syrian troops on its northern border.

The 1978 Invasion and Israel's Security Zone

Israel's war against the Palestinian guerrillas and its daily incursions into south Lebanon culminated in its March 1978 invasion and occupation of south Lebanon. Israel's actions raised fears that it intended to annex and settle the area, in the manner of the Golan Heights and the West Bank, in order to guarantee its access to the waters of the Litani. The United Nations Security Council took swift action to counter Israel's invasion. UN Resolution 425 called for the withdrawal of Israeli forces and the restoration of the authority of the Lebanese state. The Security Council also created the UN Interim Force in Lebanon (UNiFiL), with the ultimate mission of confirming the withdrawal of Israeli forces from Lebanon. Israel finally withdrew its forces in June 1979 but gave the vacated territory to Saad Haddad's militia, now constituted as the Army of Free Lebanon (later the Army of South Lebanon). Israel's occupation of Lebanon through its self-proclaimed security zone and its defiance of UN Resolution 425 until its withdrawal in May 2000 have done little to accomplish peace on its northern border.

The Palestinian State within a State

By 1982 the Palestinians had established themselves as the only real military and civil authority in south Lebanon. They had created all the trappings of a state within a state through their extensive network of social services and other institutions that extended to the people the basic services that the Lebanese government had not provided since Israel began its military incursions in 1972. Despite the sympathy with which the Palestinian movement was initially received, the local population soon came to resent the heavy-handedness and corruption that some PLO officials exhibited, as well as the policing action and the restriction of movement that the commandos exercised over the south in the name of the Palestinian resistance. The Shi'a, in particular, galvanized by the political and social movement (Amal) of Imam Musa al-Sadr, turned away from their alliance with the Lebanese Left and the Palestinians to take control of their own affairs. Israel observed this development and decided to capitalize on it in its campaign against the Palestinians.

Invasion Preludes

The withdrawal of Israel from the Sinai in 26 April 1982, as the last phase of the Egyptian-Israeli peace process, increased Syria's isolation in the region and its fear of military vulnerability. The Israeli-Egyptian peace accord had left the Arab world weak and divided. Syria was not only isolated from Egypt, but Israel had forged an alliance with the Lebanese Forces, and the Palestinians had alienated the Shi'a in south Lebanon. Syria sought to compensate for Egypt's defection by reviving its alliance with the Palestinians and the Lebanese opposition. This development, in turn, strengthened those Israelis who believed that with the pacification of its western border, the time was ripe for a military solution to the Palestinian conflict. In the spring of 1981, Israel clashed with Syria over the deployment of missiles in the Beqaa Valley and engaged the Palestinians in south Lebanon. The Israeli government felt that the time was ripe for it to crush, once and for all, the Palestinian resistance.

The Consequences of the 1982 Invasion

On 6 June 1982, Israel invaded Lebanon and began its three-month siege of Beirut. Intense fighting inflicted severe hardships on West Beirut's 600,000 civilian population before the PLO was finally forced to agree to withdraw from Beirut. A Multinational Force (MNF) was established on 1 September to oversee the PLO's withdrawal. The MNF, however, anxious to complete its mission, left Beirut on 10 September, leaving the Palestinian civilians unprotected. The assassination of Lebanon's president-elect, Bashir Gemayel, and a score of other high officials by a massive bomb in the Kata'ib party headquarters on 14 September (reportedly by a young Maronite who had been linked to a pro-Syrian faction of the Syrian Popular Party) had disastrous consequences for the remaining Palestinian civilians.[15] On 15 September, Israeli troops entered West Beirut and around six that evening a massacre of several hundred Palestinians by the Lebanese Forces took place in the camps of Sabra and Shatila.

Israel's continued occupation of a security zone in south Lebanon was regarded by Lebanon as a violation of UN Resolution 425. For a brief moment, after Israel's second invasion in 1982, it seemed that Lebanon and Israel might liquidate the zone and jointly impose a security regime with the Agreement of 17 May 1983. But that agreement, which the Lebanese saw as a means of effecting the withdrawal of all foreign forces from its territory, was regarded by Syria as a threat to its position in the region. The agreement was eventually renounced by the government of Lebanon as a result of Syrian pressure.

The Emergence of Hizballah

Israel's 1982 invasion accomplished the withdrawal of the PLO from Beirut, but it also gave birth to a new resistance movement against Israel. Israel had, with some success, fanned the flames of resentment against the Palestinians among southern Lebanon's majority Shi'a population, and they at first greeted Israel's 1982 invasion with some relief. Their elation, however, quickly soured when the Israelis began to assume the posture of an occupier. The Shi'a, motivated by religious fervor and the desire to liberate their homeland from occupation, fiercely resisted the Israelis.

The emergence of Hizballah received important sources of support and encouragement from Iran and Syria. Iran's revolutionary leaders viewed the Shi'a of southern Lebanon, who already had strong historical connections with Iran, as ideal proponents for their brand of political Islam. And Syria, having survived what it considered to be an Israeli-American military and diplomatic onslaught in Lebanon, found the Iranian connection useful in making Israel's occupation of southern Lebanon as costly as possible. A carefully contained war of attrition developed in south Lebanon and occasionally spilled into northern Israel.

Syria Reasserts Its Role

Israel's 1982 invasion reaffirmed Syria's belief that Lebanon was its first line of defense. Lebanon could never be allowed to separate itself from the conflict with Israel, nor could any single, strong local force in Lebanon be allowed to emerge. It was in pursuit of these goals that Syria blocked the 17 May 1983 agreement that Israel exacted from Lebanon and which was designed to formally terminate the state of war between Lebanon and Israel and open the stage for "normal relations with Israel."[16]

Next, Syria consolidated its position in the Beqaa, provided arms to the

Lebanese groups that opposed the government, principally Amal, and tried to weaken the Lebanese Forces and the Lebanese army units that supported Amin Gemayel. Syria also tried to gain control of the Palestinian movement and drove Yasir Arafat's PLO out of the Beqaa and Tripoli.

According to the Syrian strategy, Lebanon was to remain weak and, above all, was not to be allowed outside support from the United States, Israel, or their allies. Crucial to this strategy was the removal of the Multinational Force that had been established to oversee the PLO evacuation from Beirut in 1982 but which later became active in supporting the Lebanese army in its operations against the Shi'a and Druze opposition. This was accomplished when the bombings of the American embassy and the Marine barracks at Beirut International Airport forced the MNF's "redeployment." Next, Syria intervened to stop the fighting between the rival Amal and Hizballah Shi'a factions, thereby consolidating its position in West Beirut. By 1987, Syria had reestablished control over the Palestinian camps on the edges of the city. With its forces, numbering some 35,000 troops, holding sway over more than 60 percent of Lebanese territory, Syria was once again the dominant force in Lebanon.[17]

The Aoun Interregnum

The end of the discredited Gemayel presidency in September 1988 presented another challenge for Syria. The Lebanese political factions, Syria, and the United States had failed to agree on the election of an acceptable successor. Consequently, in the closing hours of his term, Amin Gemayel created a constitutional crisis by appointing General Michel Aoun as interim prime minister. Aoun's appointment was not recognized by the Lebanese opposition or Syria. Complicating matters, the incumbent Sunni prime minister, Salim al-Hoss, refused to step down and in turn claimed executive power. Lebanon's internal divisions were now mirrored in these two legal authorities.

Initially, General Aoun attempted to broaden his base of support among the Christian and Muslim populations. He appealed to their common sense of Lebanese identity and blamed outside forces for their misery. His goals of national unity, rule of law, sovereignty, and the withdrawal of all foreign forces from Lebanon were greeted enthusiastically by the Christian community and received the cautious support of the Muslims. When provocations by the Lebanese Forces caused the Syrians to shell East Beirut, however, Aoun countered by shelling West Beirut. In the process, he lost any support he might have gained from the Muslim community.

The Document of National Reconciliation

Although Aoun was a threat to Syria's aims in Lebanon, he was unable to muster the necessary support to unify the country or evict the Syrians. As Lebanon's security situation degenerated, Syria stepped in once more. Under the aegis of the Arab League, Syria, with support from Saudi Arabia, summoned the seventy surviving members of Lebanon's Parliament (which had not had an election since the beginning of the civil war) to Ta'if, the Saudi summer capital, to deal with Aoun and the constitutional crisis. With Syrian encouragement, the parliamentarians amended the constitutional system and developed the Document of National Reconciliation, initially approved by the Lebanese Parliament in 1989, and approved with amendments and written into the constitution in August and September 1990.[18]

In addition to guaranteeing the presidency to the Christians and ensuring the sharing of executive power with the prime minister and the speaker of Parliament, Ta'if equalized Muslim-Christian representation in Parliament. Since this arrangement generally extended to high-ranking posts in government and in the public sector, Ta'if enshrined the unwritten confessional arrangement of the 1943 national pact. The agreement was signed on 22 October. On 5 November 1989, the deputies elected René Moawad president of the republic.

The actions of the parliamentarians were not without consequences. Those who signed the document and the newly elected president were subject to numerous death threats and assassination attempts. President Moawad was himself assassinated two and a half weeks later during a celebration of Lebanon's Independence Day, 22 November. The parliamentarians acted swiftly in the face of this new threat, and two days later, Elias Hrawi, a Maronite from Zahle with close ties to Syria, was elected to succeed him.

The Denouement

General Aoun refused to recognize the Hrawi government or the Ta'if Agreement, which left indefinite Syria's continued presence in Lebanon. Seeking to capitalize on the conflict between the Ba'thist regimes in Iraq and Syria, Aoun sought with Iraq's support to drive the Syrians from Lebanon. To prepare for the confrontation, Aoun had to consolidate his position with his Christian constituency. He attempted to wrest control of the small Christian area between Beirut and Jebail but in the process inaugurated a Christian civil war in January 1990. The conflict lasted until July of that year and ended without a clear-cut victory for Aoun. The war did, however, have disastrous human and political consequences for the Christian community, which suffered 1,000 dead, 5,000 casualties, and $1.2 billion in property damages.[19]

Meanwhile, Iraq's invasion of Kuwait on 1 August 1990 provided Syria with the opportunity to remove Aoun by force. Syria had prepared by allying itself with the United States coalition against Iraq, its long-time enemy, and in October 1990 was given permission to move against Aoun and resolve the Lebanese crisis. The presidential palace in Baabda was attacked and Aoun was forced into exile. With Aoun's removal, constitutional authority was reestablished, and the militias, with the exception of Hizballah (which was engaged in the resistance to Israeli occupation in the south), were dismantled. The Lebanese army, with Syria's assistance, proceeded to collect the assault weapons of the militias and the Palestinians and was deployed throughout the country. Syria's suzerainty in Lebanon was once again firmly established.

Grapes of Wrath

The reestablishment of constitutional authority in 1990 allowed Lebanon to experience a slow and painful recovery. This gradual resumption of political and economic life that took place under the auspices of the Ta'if Agreement was again interrupted in April 1996, when Israel launched its third military attack on Lebanon. The ostensible justification for Israel's "Operation Grapes of Wrath" was the need to secure its northern border against attack from Hizballah forces. Israel was reeling from terrorist attacks from Islamist groups opposed to the Israeli-Palestinian peace negotiations, and the government was under strong pressure to take action. The invasion was intended to be a strong message against terrorism that was needed to secure a victory for the Labor government. Its immediate effect, however, was the bombing and destruction of villages, the killing of civilians, and the creation of 400,000 internal refugees. The operation also carried another message to Lebanon. The bombing of electric power plants near Beirut was an implicit warning to the Lebanese authorities that their economic recovery and the rebuilding of the country's infrastructure were at stake if they did not control Hizballah.

Israel's 1996 action served only to reemphasize the weakness of the Lebanese government and strengthen Syria's political role in the country. Hizballah would not be disarmed as long as UNiFiL or its troops were prevented from entering Israel's security zone. The Syrian defense minister, Mustafa Tlass, in an interview with the Beirut weekly *Monday Morning*, stated Syria's position succinctly: "We support the forces of the Arab resistance which are confronting the enemy in armed struggle, especially the Lebanese resistance. . . . It is an important means by which the material strength and morale of the enemy can be weakened."[20]

Lebanon sought the withdrawal of all foreign troops from its territory, in accord with UN Resolution 425, but it could not accomplish this as long as Israel continued to occupy the south. Lebanon's then Foreign Minister, Fares Buwayz, wanted the United States to assist in an Israeli withdrawal.[21] According to Buwayz, Lebanon was not asking for an immediate withdrawal but for a decision to withdraw that would take place under conditions to be decided by a commission composed of Lebanese and Israelis.[22] Former prime minister Ehud Barak actually withdrew Israel's troops from the south in May 2000, but stability in the region is still hostage to an eventual Syrian-Israeli peace agreement and Israeli withdrawal from the Golan Heights.

Implications of Ta'if for Lebanon

The Ta'if Agreement formalized Syria's influence in Lebanon[23] and provided for the development of additional treaties. The Treaty of Brotherhood, Cooperation, and Coordination, signed on 22 May 1991, is a prime example of the new relationship.[24] The treaty established a mixed Higher Council to promote intergovernmental cooperation on economic, defense, culture, and energy issues. The membership of the Higher Council gave it the status of a supraauthority that can negotiate, sign, and enforce bilateral agreements.[25] The treaty also defined the framework for Syrian and Lebanese relations, as its provisions illustrate. Article I provides for "The highest levels of cooperation and coordination in all fields, including political, economic, security, educational, scientific, and others, with the aim of promoting the mutual interests of the two sisterly states within the framework of their respective sovereignty and independence."

Article IV sets the time line for Syria's redeployment of its troops, that is, "after the political reforms have been approved and endorsed in a constitutional manner in line with the provisions of the Lebanese National [Reconciliation] Pact, and after the deadlines fixed in the Pact have expired."

Article V states the principles that should govern the foreign policies of both countries, that is, the commitment to the charter of the Arab League, the Treaty for Arab Defense and Economic Cooperation, and all other agreements signed within the league's framework. Article VI develops the structure, that is, the Syrian-Lebanese Higher Council, that would provide any future confederal relationship between the two countries with a central authority.

Article III establishes the interconnectedness of Syria's and Lebanon's security and has caused the greatest concern among some Lebanese observers. The article provides that "Lebanon shall not become a transit way or a base for any power, state, or organization which seeks to undermine Syria's security, while Syria, keen to preserve Lebanon's security, unity, and independence, shall not allow any action that would constitute a threat to Lebanon's security."

Another statement in Article III says that "Syria's security requires that Lebanon should not be a source of threat to Syria's security and vice versa under any circumstances." This is significant, given Lebanon's recent history and its relations with Israel. This article effectively gives Syria the right, after its own evaluation of an impending threat from "any power, states, or organization which seeks to undermine Syria's security," to preserve Lebanon's security, but there is no mention of the possibility that Syria might become such a transit way or base.[26] It also raises the question of the operation of Syrian security forces within Lebanon and the independent authority these forces exercise over both Lebanese and Palestinian nationals.

Economic Relations

The Treaty of Brotherhood, Cooperation, and Coordination's multiple and binding agreements in virtually all social and economic fields have raised questions about the future of Lebanese-Syrian relations. What effect, for example, will contact with Lebanon have on Syrian society as Syria attempts to liberalize its domestic economy? Conversely, to what degree will Lebanon be able to manage its social and economic cooperation with Syria without becoming subcontracted to the Syrian economy?

One manifestation of this concern is the labor agreement signed on 18 October 1994, which sought to legalize the status of Syrian laborers in Lebanon. Given that an estimated 900,000 Syrians work in Lebanon and that Syrian workers at home earn approximately two thousand Syrian lira ($50) per month—and are willing to work for much less than a Lebanese worker, who averages approximately $200 per month—how much can Lebanon absorb in terms of potential unemployment and social disloca-tion?[27] Added to this is the enormous expense that Syria's presence entails for Lebanon and the millions of dollars that leave Lebanon every day and are added to the Syrian economy. As these statistics indicate, Lebanon is an economic outlet where the Syrian private sector can invest and prosper, while the Syrian public sector remains under the control of the present regime.[28]

The Future of Syrian-Lebanese Relations

Any future regional peace settlement will remain a challenge to Syrian-Lebanese cooperation. Currently, Syria uses Lebanon to put pressure on Israel. The suspension of the Israeli-Syrian peace talks has affected the Lebanese-Israeli track, and Lebanon will not conduct independent nego-tiations with Israel. Syria will continue to consolidate its position in Leba-non, as it did on 19 October 1995, when it judged that the extension for three years of President Hrawi's term was necessary in order to strengthen its negotiating position vis-à-vis Israel.

In addition, an eventual peace agreement between Syria and Israel might have adverse economic and political effects on Syria. The regional balance of power would shift with Syria's diminished status as a confron-tation state with the result that Syria might not be able to retain its suzer-ainty over Lebanon. Studies conducted by the World Bank and other insti-tutions predict that the main communications lines in the Middle East will start from or lead to Israel, not Lebanon.[29] Syria would also note the advantage to Israel, which no doubt would also benefit economically from the opening up of Arab markets and foreign capital investment in Israel, especially in the promised $11.6 billion economic support provided by the 13 September 1993 agreement with the Palestinians.[30]

Given these conditions, Syria will continue to exercise political pre-dominance in Lebanon for the foreseeable future. Lebanon is too impor-tant for Syria's protection and Syria's influence will remain dominant, even after a settlement with Israel. Although some might point with dis-may to the fundamentally unequal relationship between the two coun-tries, rational and direct cooperation will require the continuance of their present relationship as long as both countries are confronted with the exigencies of regional challenges.

The Future of Israeli-Lebanese Relations

Ehud Barak's landslide win over Prime Minister Benjamin Netanyahu in May 1999 was generally regarded as enhancing the prospects for the peace process and, by extension, the future of Lebanon and the region as a whole. Barak's pledge to withdraw Israeli forces from southern Lebanon by July 2000, albeit with a rider that the withdrawal would come about "by agreement"—implying that an overall political understanding with Syria and Lebanon could be secured in the space of a few months—was greeted with cautious optimism in Lebanon. Prime Minister Salim al-Hoss noted that Barak's inauguration speech did not mention UN Security Council Resolution 425 as the basis for the withdrawal, and most Lebanese observers felt that the withdrawal would be conditioned on a freeze of the resistance operations of Hizballah. Given the political climate in Lebanon and the political capital Hizballah achieved as the only resistance force fighting the Israeli occupation, this condition would not be possible.

Previous propositions, such as the Lebanon First proposal put forward in the summer of 1996 by former prime minister Netanyahu, did not involve negotiations with Syria, nor did they link Israeli withdrawal from Lebanon to the future of the Golan Heights. Netanyahu's proposal also had a number of conditions linked to it, such as incorporating members of the SLA into the Lebanese army and disarming Hizballah as a precondition for withdrawal. His proposal was a "nonstarter," as such preconditions had been rejected by Lebanon and Syria many times before. Even more unacceptable for Syria was Netanyahu's expectation that Syria would willingly cooperate in helping Israel disengage from southern Lebanon but not from the Golan Heights.

The initial optimism that Barak's election occasioned soon faded when the departing Netanyahu administration launched its largest and most destructive air raid on Lebanon on the night of 24–25 June 1999. The operation, which killed eight civilians and injured seventy others, caused more damage to the civilian infrastructure than the Grapes of Wrath onslaught of April 1996. This attempt to punish the Lebanese government for supporting the Hizballah resistance by destroying power plants, roads, and bridges was also viewed by some as an attempt by the outgoing government to scuttle the peace process. Although Barak was not deemed to be immediately responsible for the raid, it seemed to be part of a consistent Israeli policy of retaliation going back, in Lebanon's case, to 1968. The realization of this fear was to be borne out a few months later.

Syria and Israel were on the verge of an agreement in 1996 when the

Washington talks were suspended after terrorist bombings in Israel. These negotiations were resumed on 15 December 1999 in Washington when, under the auspices of President Bill Clinton, Prime Minister Barak and Syria's foreign minister Farouk al-Sharaa met at Blair House. The talks were, in Syria's view, to continue where they had left off, namely, with Israel's commitment to withdraw from the Golan Heights. Shortly afterward, the talks recessed with the agreement that they would be continued in January 2000 at Shepherdstown, West Virginia. The Shepherdstown talks broke down, however, over Israel's refusal to commit to full withdrawal from the Golan Heights. When an Israeli newspaper later printed a leaked text of a working paper that seemed to make clear that Israel had already wrung some concessions from Syria on security and the opening of normal relations, while Syria had not even gotten Israel to declare that it would withdraw from the Golan, the third round of talks scheduled for late January was suspended.[31]

Speculation around the suspension of the talks centered on the need for breathing room on the part of the Barak government due to public pressure in Israel against abandoning the Golan Heights and the fact that the situation in south Lebanon seemed to be getting quieter. In late 1999, the Israeli military changed its operational tactics in south Lebanon by abandoning its aggressive search-and-destroy methods against Hizballah forces that often resulted in high casualties. Taking a lesson from NATO's operation in Kosovo, Israeli troops were told to hunker down in fortified areas, leaving active operations against Hizballah to long-range artillery and the air force. The new tactics resulted in fewer Israeli casualties and in increased military confidence that seemed to make the talks on the Syrian track a little less urgent. Indirect communications with Damascus, however, continued.[32]

This apparent complacency ended in late January 2000 when Hizballah inflicted a series of casualties on Israeli forces that resulted in the deaths of several soldiers and a senior commander of the Israeli-allied South Lebanon Army. The publicity surrounding the deaths and the footage of the fighting provoked public anger, raising concerns from Israeli military experts that a unilateral withdrawal would merely shift hostilities to the Israel-Lebanon border and place Israeli civilians in danger. Thus, the familiar sequence of diplomatic deadlock, escalation of Hizballah's armed resistance against Israeli occupation in south Lebanon, and Israeli retaliation designed primarily to inflict pain on Lebanese civilians was set in motion. Foreign Minister David Levy warned that "the soil of Lebanon will burn" if Hizballah launched rocket attacks against northern Israel,[33] while Israeli warplanes on 7–8 February 2000 mounted extensive raids against power plants in Lebanon that were just recovering from the raids of the previous June. Serious damage was once again inflicted on Lebanon's infrastructure and its struggle for economic recovery.

The Lebanese government concluded that Israel would withdraw from southern Lebanon only as part of the resumed negotiations between Israel and Syria. Separate negotiations for an Israeli withdrawal from southern Lebanon were not an option. As the 17 May 1983 agreement demonstrated, any peace agreement between Lebanon and Israel would have to reflect that the ultimate governing authority in Lebanon resided in Damascus. Nor were hopes to be realized that the monitoring group cochaired by the United States and France after Operation Grapes of Wrath would encourage Syria and Israel to interact directly to solve the issues between them. Although such talks might have been useful as confidence-building measures, they would not have addressed the basic issue of an overall settlement of the conflict.

Lebanon's dilemma was that Israel would not withdraw unilaterally from southern Lebanon absent a special security regime, and Syria would not agree to such an arrangement without Israel's withdrawal from the Golan Heights. By March 2000, however, many observers thought it was reasonable to assume that a deal on the Golan was in the offing that could pave the way for an agreement. President Clinton and President Asad had met in Geneva amid optimism that the Israeli leadership had conceded to Syria's major demand of complete withdrawal. The release of a report that Prime Minister Barak had told his cabinet on 27 February 2000 that Yitzhak Rabin had given guarantees that Israel would fully withdraw from the Golan Heights in exchange for security commitments by Syria gave credence to that scenario. Stating that he would "not erase the past," Barak implied that he would honor "the historical record" as understood to mean the complete Israeli withdrawal from the Golan.[34] Tying the withdrawal from southern Lebanon (which was highly popular in Israel) to a withdrawal agreement from the Golan (which Barak's opponents insisted had to be ratified by a national referendum in Israel) would ensure the success of a peace agreement with Syria and Lebanon.

The optimism that the long-sought dream of peace might be fulfilled soon turned to cynicism about Israel's motives. The obstacle turned on Israel's refusal to return to the pre-1967 border with Syria and its insistence that Israel retain the northeastern shore of Lake Tiberias in order to ensure access to its water. When Syria rejected Israel's territorial demands, Israel announced that it was lifting its freeze on settlement construction in the occupied Golan. It also notified the United Nations in mid-April that it intended to withdraw unilaterally from Lebanon. Barak apparently believed this move could strengthen Israel's hold on the Golan by depriving Syria of one of the few ways of pressuring Israel to withdraw from the Golan. By mid-May, Israel began handing over its fortified positions to the SLA. In reality, Israel's unilateral withdrawal from southern Lebanon would leave unresolved the very issues that could result in continued conflict.

Syria would not succumb to such pressure and resolved to maintain its Lebanon card. For their part, the Lebanese insisted that Israel's unilateral withdrawal would not resolve the conflict between their two countries, particularly as long as the status of the 400,000 Palestinians in Lebanon since 1948 remained unresolved. They also stated that they could not be expected to send the army to protect Israel's northern border if, as seemed likely, Israel continued to occupy parts of Lebanese territory.[35]

Israel's 22-year occupation of southern Lebanon finally ended on 24 May 2000. The SLA had collapsed when its militiamen refused to sacrifice themselves to protect Israel's troop withdrawal. The occupation had caused the deaths of 900 Israelis, 1,276 Hizballah fighters, and numerous Palestinians and Lebanese civilians.[36] Ariel Sharon, the mastermind of the 1982 invasion of Lebanon, stated that he had long advocated unilateral withdrawal, but he admonished that the withdrawal should have been preceded by devastating strikes on Lebanon, including "Syrian interests," as a way of "restoring the consciousness of deterrence" to prevent renewed hostilities on the Lebanese border.[37] For its part, Hizballah performed an orderly takeover of the evacuated areas, reassuring the Christian and Druze villagers of their safety and turning over captured SLA militiamen to the Lebanese authorities. The Lebanese government proclaimed 25 May "National Liberation Day."

Israel's withdrawal did not achieve from Syria the required guarantees for its northern border. Although its withdrawal was certified by the United Nations as complete, according to the 1923 boundary, and the UN secretary-general, Kofi Annan, had asked Lebanon to take effective control of the south, Lebanon reiterated its refusal to send its army to the border to protect Israel.[38] Instead, Lebanon insisted that Israel's withdrawal was not complete. Lebanon claimed that Shab'a Farms, occupied by Israel along with the Golan Heights after the 1967 war, was also Lebanese territory and that the Israeli withdrawal was a deployment that did not fulfill the requirements of UN Resolution 425.

Lebanon's claims to Shab'a Farms, a fertile 25-square-kilometer area on the western slopes of Mount Hermon, are based on the cooperative policing arrangement between Lebanon and Syria that existed before the Israeli occupation and the fact that many Lebanese own land there. Lebanon claimed that Syria ceded the region to Lebanon in 1951, a fact that Syria later verified to the United Nations.[39] There is, however, no existing map that the territory was ever under Lebanese sovereignty, and the United Nations' chief cartographer, Milos Pinther, would not certify it as such.[40] Nevertheless, Shabʿa Farms has now become a flash point on the border with Israel. Hizballah launched an operation there on 7 October 2000 in which it captured three Israeli soldiers, ostensibly to use as bargaining chips to obtain the release of Abd al-Karim Obeid, a senior Hizballah figure kidnapped by Israel in 1989, and Mustafa Dirani, a former resistance commando whom Israel had kidnapped in 1994. This was followed by another attack by Hizballah in Shabʿa Farms on 26 November in which one Israeli soldier was killed and two wounded. Israel retaliated by attacking Lebanese villages in the south with helicopter gunships.[41] In light of the numerous violations of Lebanese airspace, the Lebanese government's refusal to deploy its army to the southern border, the uncertainty of Syria's policy following the death of President Hafiz al-Asad on 9 June 2000, and the defeat of Ehud Barak and the election of Ariel Sharon in February 2001 as prime minister of Israel, Lebanon will remain hostage to an eventual Syrian-Israeli peace treaty.

The Palestinians and Lebanon

On 13 September 1993, the PLO and Israel signed a "Declaration of Principles" on Palestinian self-rule in Jericho and the Gaza Strip. The Oslo Accords, however, had no effect on the status of the Palestinians in Lebanon. Indeed, the fitful progress of the Palestinian-Israeli negotiations has had negative ramifications for Lebanon. In September 1995, for example, the Libyan government decided to show its disapproval of the Israeli-Palestinian peace process by expelling 30,000 Palestinian migrant workers, about half of whom were from Lebanon. This action renewed fears that Lebanon would have to pay the price of permanently settling the Palestinians after any Israeli-Palestinian peace settlement.

Conversely, the Palestinian presence in post–civil war Lebanon has served as a rare, if negative, unifying element in the Lebanese national political identity. With few exceptions, Lebanese of all factions agree that the Palestinians should not be resettled permanently in Lebanon. This principle is enshrined in the preamble of the new constitution of Lebanon that states, "Lebanese territory is one for all Lebanese. There shall be no segregation of the people on the basis of any type of belonging, and no fragmentation, partition, or colonization."[42]

The former prime minister of Lebanon, Dr. Salim el-Hoss, has expressed his concern that there is no mention of the Palestinians of 1948 in the Israel-PLO accord. Dr. Hoss believes that the resettlement of Palestinians in Lebanon would upset the sectarian balance in the country. He has pointed out that the Ta'if Agreement said "no" to fragmentation, division and implantation. "Implantation [i.e. colonization]," he said, refers to the Palestinians in Lebanon.[43]

Lebanon's foreign minister, Fares Buwayz, advocates the following measures to resolve the Palestinian issue in Lebanon: (1) Give the Palestinians from the areas covered by the Israeli-PLO agreement the right of return to Gaza and Jericho. The United Nations decided this twenty years ago in UN Resolution 194. (2) Give the Palestinians the right of family unification. "Wherever the majority of a given family is located, whether in Israel, the West Bank, Egypt, the U.S., etc., the members of that family should be allowed to rejoin the family." And, finally, (3) give the Palestinians the right to immigrate to their country of choice. Countries like Canada, according to Buwayz, are accepting numerous immigrants and so should allow the Palestinians to immigrate. According to Buwayz, the "implementation of these measures would solve 30 percent of the Palestinian problem in Lebanon."[44]

Palestinians living in Lebanon not only face physical danger but also suffer the afflictions of poverty, unemployment, and political disenfranchisement. Although a few have been granted Lebanese citizenship, most Palestinians feel marginalized by a peace process that holds out no hope of repatriation.[45] As a result, Palestinians cling to their refugee status because it legitimizes their right of return to Palestine. In the interim, some Palestinians are now seeking to redefine themselves as a legal minority in Lebanon in the hope that this will protect them from further displacement and redefine their place in Lebanese society.[46]

Conclusion

Although Lebanon's involvement in regional crises was not the underlying cause of its civil unrest, it has played an important part in sparking the problems Lebanon has endured since its independence. Lebanon was unable to isolate itself from the chronic Palestinian-Israeli crisis, nor could it find any effective way to deal with the presence of Palestinian refugees.

Today, Lebanon is struggling to recover from the effects of the many conflicts and wars that have plagued the country for almost sixteen years and produced thousands of its own internal refugees. While Lebanon's energies will be occupied with these problems, the future of the Palestinians in Lebanon will continue to be a source of uncertainty and contention.

The uneasy balances within its own constitutional arrangement forced the Lebanese to live with the escalating cycles of Palestinian-Israeli violence. The intense polarization that the Palestinian issue caused among the dissatisfied elements during the civil war has given way to a broad national consensus—at least on the surface—that the Palestinian problem should not be settled at Lebanon's expense. This consensus has been reached despite the continued nonresolution of the underlying causes of the Lebanese conflict: social disparity and issues of political representation and confessionalism.

Lebanon's association with Syria has not been fully defined, and its future relationship with Israel awaits the resumption of the peace negotiations. The broader Arab-Israeli conflict and the slowness of the regional peace process will continue to complicate Lebanon's relations with its neighbors, Syria and Israel, as well as the fate of the Palestinians living in Lebanon. The uncertainty of the border with Israel and the continued presence of armed elements over which it has no control, namely the Hizballah resistance movement in the south and the Syrian peacekeeping force, ensure that Lebanon, its eventual recovery, and its future independence will continue to be hostage to regional events.

Author's note:

I am grateful to *Arab Studies Quarterly* for permission to use material in my article "Lebanon: The Struggle of a Small Country in a Regional Context," which appeared in their issue of Winter 1999.

Notes

1. Ghassan Salame, "Lebanon: How 'National' Is Independence?" *Beirut Review* 6 (Fall 1993): 1–5.

2. Fred J. Khouri, *The Arab Israeli Dilemma* (Syracuse, N.Y.: Syracuse University Press, 1968), 70.

3. Roy Alan, "Lebanon: Israel's Friendliest Neighbor," *Commentary* 13 (June 1952), 551.

4. Labib Zumiyya Yamak, "Party Politics in the Lebanese Political System," in

Politics in Lebanon, ed. Leonard Binder (New York: John Wiley and Sons, 1966), 151. Archbishop Mubarak's memorandum was reported in the Beirut daily *Al-Diyar* on 27 September 1946, with the result that he reportedly was reprimanded for his position by the Maronite patriarch, relieved of his ecclesiastical duties, and exiled to a monastery. See William W. Haddad, "Christian Arab Attitudes toward the Arab-Israeli Conflict," *Muslim World* 67 (April 1977): 130, and Laura Zittrain Eisenberg, *My Enemy's Enemy: Lebanon in the Early Zionist Imagination, 1900–1948* (Detroit: Wayne State University Press, 1994), 142–43.

5. Albion Ross, "Dr. Malik Presses Arab-Turkish Tie," *New York Times*, 11 June 1951.

6. Hussein Sirriyyeh, "The Palestinian Armed Presence in Lebanon since 1967," in *Essays on the Crisis in Lebanon*, ed. Roger Owen (London: Ithaca Press, 1976), 77. Estimates of current numbers vary. The Palestinian Refugee Research Net cites 346,164 UNRWA-registered Palestinian refugees in Lebanon as of June 1995 (www.arts.mcgilt.ca/MEPP/PRRN/proverview.html) (23 March 1999). The often-cited figure of 400,000 would include an estimated 50,000 nonregistered refugees.

7. Michael Hudson, "The Palestinian Arab Resistance Movement: Its Significance in the Middle East Crisis," *Middle East Journal* 23 (Summer 1969): 291.

8. Israel destroyed thirteen Arab civilian airliners and a fuel storage tank; the damage caused by the raid was estimated at $43.1 million. John B. Wolf, "Shadow on Lebanon," *Current History* 58 (January 1970): 25.

9. Ibid.; the Israeli raid was also viewed as a warning to the governments of Saudi Arabia and Kuwait that continued contributions of large sums of money to the commando movement might in the future subject their property to Israeli reprisal.

10. Kamal S. Salibi, *Crossroads to Civil War: Lebanon, 1958–1976* (New York: Caravan Books, 1976), 41.

11. Ibid., 55–56; Sirriyyeh, "The Palestinian Armed Presence," 79.

12. John P. Entellis, "Palestinian Revolutionism in Lebanese Politics: The Christian Response," *Muslim World* 62, no. 4 (October 1972): 341.

13. Salibi, *Crossroads*, 55.

14. Sirriyyeh, "The Palestinian Armed Presence," 81.

15. Helena Cobban, *The Making of Modern Lebanon* (Boulder, Colo.: Westview Press, 1985), 187.

16. For an account of this period see Elie A. Salem, *Violence and Diplomacy in Lebanon: The Troubled Years, 1982–1988* (London: I. B. Tauris Publishers, 1995), 145–56.

17. Elizabeth Picard, *Lebanon: A Shattered Country* (New York and London: Holmes and Meier, 1996), 134.

18. "Documents: The Constitution of Lebanon after the Amendments of August 21, 1990," *Beirut Review* 1, no. 1 (Spring 1991): 119–60.

19. Paul E. Salem, "Two Years of Living Dangerously: General Awn and the

Precarious Rise of Lebanon's 'Second Republic,'" *Beirut Review* 1, no. 1 (Spring 1991): 67.

20. Michael Jensen, "Lebanon: Israel on Top?" *Middle East International* 563 (21 November 1997): 14.

21. Foreign Minister Fares Buwayz to author, 10 December 1993.

22. Ibid.

23. "Lebanon, which is Arab in its belonging and identity, has close filial ties to all the Arab states; there exist between it and Syria distinctive relations which derive their force from the roots of propinquity, history, and common filial interests. This is the foundation on which coordination between the two countries shall be based": "The Ta'if Agreement," *Beirut Review* 1 (Spring 1991): 171.

24. "Treaty of Brotherhood, Cooperation, and Coordination Concluded between Lebanon and Syria on May 22, 1991," *Beirut Review* 1, no. 2 (Fall 1991): 115–19.

25. The Higher Council is made up of the presidents of both states, the speaker of the Lebanese Parliament, the prime minister and deputy prime minister of the Lebanese government, the speaker of the Syrian Parliament, and the prime minister and deputy prime minister of the Syrian government. Simone Ghazi Tinaoui, "An Analysis of the Syrian-Lebanese Economic Cooperation Agreements," *Beirut Review* 3, no. 8 (Fall 1994): 102.

26. Ibid. "Lebanon-Syria Treaty of Cooperation, May 20, 1991 *[sic]*," almarshiq.hiof.no/lebanon/300.social_sciences/320/327/lebanon-syria.txt (21 March 1999).

27. Tinaoui, "Analysis," 108–9.

28. Capital flight from Syria over the past decades has been estimated at some $25 billion. See Volker Perthes, "From Front-Line State to Backyard? Syria and the Economic Risks of Regional Peace," *Beirut Review* 3, no. 8 (Fall 1994): 90.

29. Ibid., 89.

30. Tinaoui, "Analysis," 111.

31. Deborah Sontag, "Dust Settles: Israel-Syria Peace Effort Is Set Back," *New York Times* (http://www.nytimes.com/library/world/mideast021000mideast-rdp.html) (10 February 2000).

32. Peretz Kidron, "Barak's Mixed Fortune," *Middle East International*, no. 618 (11 February 2000): 10.

33. Sontag, "Dust Settles."

34. Deborah Sontag, "Rabin Vowed to Pull Back from Golan, Barak Says," *New York Times*, 28 February 2000.

35. Jim Quilty, "Withdrawal Symptoms," *Middle East International*, no. 624 (5 May 2000): 16.

36. Michael Jensen, "Lebanon's Finest Hour," *Middle East International*, no. 626 (2 June 2000): 4.

37. Peretz Kidron, "Good Riddance," *Middle East International*, no. 626 (2 June 2000): 12.

38. Michael Jensen, "Simmering Pot," *Middle East International*, no. 637 (10 November 2000): 10.

39. Ibid.

40. Jim Quilty, "Cutting Deals," *Middle East International*, no. 625 (19 May 2000): 9.

41. See Quilty, "Withdrawal Symptoms," 16; Michael Jensen, "Tension in the South," *Middle East International*, no. 638 (24 November 2000): 9–10.

42. "Preamble, The New Constitution of Lebanon," Section (i). See *Beirut Review* 1, no. 2 (Spring 1991): 123.

43. Dr. Salim al-Hoss to author, 2 December 1993.

44. Foreign Minister Buwayz to author, 10 December 1993.

45. See article by Julie Peteet, "From Refugees to Minority: Palestinians in Post-War Lebanon," *Middle East Report* (July–September 1996): 27ff.

46. Ibid.; according to Peteet, around 60,000 Palestinians have been naturalized in Lebanon since 1994. The majority of these were Shi'a from border villages who had Palestinian refugee status, while others were "Sunnis who, for reasons not made public, were naturalized in 1995, perhaps to balance out the Shi'a naturalization." Although most Palestinian Christians had already been given Lebanese citizenship, the few who remained, about 10,000, have since been naturalized.

2

Israeli-Lebanese Relations

A Future Imperfect?

Kirsten E. Schulze

With the start of the Middle East peace process in 1991, normalization of relations between Israel and its Arab neighbors became the focus of the quest for regional stability. The 1993 Oslo Accords, the 1994 Jordanian-Israeli peace treaty, and bilateral trade arrangements between Israel and Arab states such as Qatar, Oman, and Morocco raised hopes for an end to conflict and increased regional cooperation. At the same time professional unions have spearheaded the antinormalization campaign in Jordan, Egypt, and Syria, drawing strength from every downturn in the peace process, such as the stalemate during the 1996–99 Netanyahu government and the collapse of Israeli-Palestinian talks into the al-Aqsa intifada in September 2000.

This chapter looks at Israeli-Lebanese relations past, present, and future in the context of normalization and antinormalization. It argues that there are no intrinsic obstacles to normalization of relations between these two states. On the contrary, both Israel and Lebanon would benefit from cooperation in the areas of tourism, infrastructure, transport, and water. However, a number of important issues need to be addressed first. Foremost, Lebanon is unable to sign any agreement with Israel until there is an Israeli-Syrian peace treaty. Once negotiations between Israel and Lebanon begin, there are four main areas of concern: security, Palestinian refugees, water rights, and economic development. Finally, Israel needs to be careful that any normalization is not perceived as again favoring the Christian community as this would undermine not only Lebanon's ability to reciprocate but also Israel's broader integration into the region.

The Israeli Perspective

Lebanon has always occupied a special place in Israeli thinking. From the 1920s, Zionist decision makers in the Yishuv (Jewish settlement in Palestine) perceived Lebanon as the most friendly of their neighbors. Trade relations and tourism between Lebanon and the Yishuv flourished until the border was closed in 1948. During this time, Jews began to develop close ties with segments of the Lebanese Maronite community, founded on the belief that both Jews and Maronites were minorities in a hostile, predominantly Arab-Muslim environment, and that nothing would be more natural than an alliance between the two communities. This belief was underlined by the Yishuv political department's sense that the emerging Lebanese state was similar to the emerging Jewish state, both being Mediterranean, linking the East with the West. In the case of Lebanon, this signified enlightenment, education, French language, Christianity, Phoenician heritage, and Middle Eastern cuisine. In the case of the future Jewish state, this meant democracy, Western culture, biblical heritage, education, science, and progress. The political imagination of many Zionist and later Israeli decision makers cast Lebanon as a Christian state, independent of its Arab-Muslim surroundings. Israel's first prime minister, David Ben-Gurion, called it the "weakest link in the Arab chain." It is therefore not surprising that Lebanon became the focus of Israeli attempts to break out of regional isolation. Indeed, Israeli popular perception was that Lebanon, after Jordan, would be the second state to sign a peace treaty with Israel.

Pre-1948 relations between the Yishuv and individual members of the Maronite community (as well as some Muslims) were interpreted by Zionist decision makers as proof of this friendly image of Lebanon. The fact that treaties were entered into, even if they were in some instances secret, gave Zionist-Maronite relations an air of legitimacy. The 1920 cooperation pact between the Zionist Organization and Maronite Najib Sfeir,[1] the 1933 proposals for a general partnership pursued by Maronite patriarch Antun Arida and proposals for a political and military union suggested by Maronite politician Emile Eddé,[2] the 1936 Treaty of Friendship presented to the Zionist executive, also by Eddé,[3] the May 1946 agreement between the Jewish Agency and the Maronite Church,[4] and the 1947 memorandum to the United Nations in support of the establishment of a Jewish state in Palestine by Maronite archbishop Ignatius Mubarak[5] all supported the Zionist perception that Lebanon was indeed a friendly neighbor.

The closure of the Israeli-Lebanese border and the official state of war did not change this perception to any significant degree. In fact, continuing covert relations between Israel and the Kata'ib (Christian Phalangist Party), as well as relations with representatives of the Chamoun, Gemayel, and Eddé families, served to reinforce the Israeli image of Lebanon. Meetings with Emile Eddé[6] and Maronite requests for Israeli aid in support of a revolt in Beirut in 1948,[7] a secret meeting with emissaries from Archbishop Mubarak in 1949,[8] Israeli financial contributions to the Kata'ib's election campaign in the 1951 parliamentary elections,[9] third-country contacts between 1954 and 1956 with Elias Rababi and Pierre Eddé,[10] and Israeli military aid to Pierre Gemayel and then-president of Lebanon Camille Chamoun during the 1958 civil war[11] provided proof of a special relationship.

By this point, Israeli-Maronite relations had become synonymous with Israeli-Lebanese relations. Even the relatively low-level contacts that the two groups had between 1958 and Lebanon's second civil war in 1975 did not dispel this myth. The move of the PLO to Beirut after its expulsion from Jordan in 1970 served to strengthen the conceptual framework of "minority alliance" described by the adage "my enemy's enemy is my friend." Maronite fears that the Palestinians were undermining the political status quo in Lebanon and Israeli fears of Palestinian attacks from southern Lebanon provided the basis for more intense relations and cooperation. Requests for military aid in 1975,[12] arrangements for a more formal supply relationship in 1976,[13] and regular contacts in the period up to the 1982 Israeli invasion turned the relationship into a full alliance.[14] Israel believed that the Maronites represented Lebanon and could deliver the Lebanese republic as a partner in peace.

How deeply the notion of a friendly Christian Lebanon was ingrained in the minds of Israeli decision makers can be seen from the position of Lebanon in Israeli strategy. In 1954, Ben-Gurion drew up plans to invade Lebanon and push the Maronites into proclaiming a Christian state.[15] In 1955, Israeli chief of staff Moshe Dayan presented a plan to find a Lebanese officer who, supported by Israel, would declare himself the savior of the Maronites. The Israelis then would enter Lebanon, occupy the south, and establish a Christian regime in Beirut.[16] In 1956, Ben-Gurion's plans for the Sinai campaign reached far beyond Egypt. They called for invading Lebanon, reducing its borders to the Christian core, and making Lebanon into an ally of Israel.[17] Elements of these earlier plans were revived under Prime Minister Menachem Begin with the establishment of the south Lebanon security zone in 1978 and Operation Peace for Galilee in 1982. Evident in all these plans, whether or not they were implemented, is the key position Lebanon occupied in Israeli political and military thinking. To Israel, Lebanon was essential to securing its northern border, establishing hegemony over the Levant, and restructuring the Middle East.

Since 1982, Israeli attitudes toward Lebanon have shifted radically. Having had their fingers severely burned through involvement in internal Lebanese affairs, Israeli decision makers have restricted their mandate to security of Israel's northern border. Yet not all Israeli notions about Lebanon were discarded. While the Maronites were no longer considered to represent Lebanon, and the idea of "minority alliance" was shelved, the false notion that Lebanon could act out of tandem with Syria, implied by Israel's numerous Lebanon First proposals particularly from 1996 to 1999, remained intact. Lebanon's geostrategic position, however, dictated that it would be the last country in the Middle East to make peace with Israel, regardless of Lebanese desires for a peaceful relationship.

The Lebanese Perspective

The Israeli image of Lebanon was the product of Israel's sense of regional isolation and ethnoreligious separateness. The Lebanese image of Israel, on the other hand, was the product of the dynamics of internal relationships among Lebanese ethnic and religious communities. As a result, there was no monolithic image of Israel in Lebanon, and even the views that can be loosely attributed to particular ethnic and religious communities are equivocal. In general terms, the Lebanese republic refused to recognize its southern neighbor, while at the same time some of the ethnic communities within Lebanon had covert and even overt relations with the Jewish state.

Lebanon's ethnic composition and its consociational political system made it impossible for any one religious or ethnic community to dominate the others completely. At the same time, mutual mistrust impelled each community to seek outside allies in order to boost its domestic position. Alliances with Israel, Syria, and the Palestinians all served this function. The choice of ally coincided with each community's position on the Arab-Israeli conflict. Sympathy with the Palestinians and Arab nationalist sentiments led the Sunni Muslims to align themselves with the PLO. Fear of being engulfed by Islam and dominated by Syria and resentment of the destabilizing Palestinian presence in Lebanon made Israel the choice of the Maronites.[18] Anti-Zionism turned Syria and the Shi'a Muslims into bedfellows. At the same time, however, the Maronites courted Syria to counterbalance Palestinian forces, while the Sunnis, along with the Shi'a, courted Syria to counterbalance Israeli forces.

The position of the Lebanese Christian community toward Israel is of particular interest because Muslims, on the whole, regarded Israel as a foreign implant with hostile imperialist ambitions. Christian attitudes were far less homogeneous. For example, the Greek Orthodox in Lebanon showed little interest in an alliance with Israel because of their ties to the greater Arab economy and to other Greek Orthodox communities in the Middle East.[19] Trade links were vital to the survival of this community, and any flirtation with the Jewish state would have closed the doors to Arab businesses. In addition, Greek Orthodox Lebanese did not define themselves as ethnically separate; despite being a religious minority, they were clearly in the Arab camp.

The Maronites, on the other hand, had never been comfortable with *dhimmi* status (protected minority status under Islam) and had a strong, independent, national identity that placed them at odds with Arab nationalism.[20] Longing for a state of their own, fearful of second-class citizenship in a Muslim environment, and staunchly pro-Western, they were on a level with Israel.[21] Yet this recognition of similarities (which led Israel to develop its policy of minority alliance) had a divisive effect upon the Maronite community.[22] Some Maronites believed that their similarities and alliance with Israel would secure Maronite independence and strengthen their community's position in Lebanon.[23] Only an Israeli intervention in Lebanon, they thought, would allow the Christian people to fulfill their dreams for a separate state.[24] Patriarch Arida, Archbishop Mubarak, Emile Eddé, Elias Rababi, and Bashir Gemayel were all proponents of this view. Other Maronites, however, maintained that the presence of another non-Muslim minority in Lebanon, especially one that elicited such hostile responses from the Arab world, had to be avoided at all costs. They believed that Israel would only compromise the independent existence of the Maronites and that Maronite survival was best guaranteed by alliance with the dominant Arabist forces. Bashara al-Khoury, Suleiman Franjieh, and Amin Gemayel strongly advocated this view. A third group of Maronites based its alliances on pragmatism and espoused contradictory positions dependent on circumstances. This group is exemplified by Pierre Gemayel, who made secret contacts with Israel while engaging in anti-Zionist rhetoric, and who assigned one of his sons to nurture links with Israel while the other nurtured links with Syria.

Maronite-Israeli relations and Lebanese-Israeli relations remained ambiguous until the 1982 invasion of Lebanon. The death of Bashir Gemayel, the victimization of the Maronite community for its alliance with Israel, Israeli withdrawal to the security zone, and Syrian hegemony clarified Lebanon's position. The Maronites abandoned the notion of alliance with Israel, casting a hopeful eye toward the West for salvation. Moreover, since the end of the Lebanese civil war, Lebanon's position on Israel has become unequivocally tied to Syria, a position cemented by the 1989 Ta'if Agreement and the 1991 Treaty of Brotherhood, Cooperation, and Coordination with Syria.

The Security Dilemma

Israeli policy toward Lebanon has been driven by security concerns. Lebanon's inability to control domestic and foreign militias operating against Israel from Lebanese territory (such as the PLO and Hizballah) and its weak geostrategic position have made it the victim of the Arab-Israeli conflict in general and Israeli-Syrian competition for regional hegemony in particular. This situation is unlikely to change even if a regional peace settlement is reached. Any such settlement would, of course, depend upon a prior Syrian-Israeli agreement. Israel's preoccupation with achieving absolute security would no doubt continue to dominate its relations with Lebanon as it has with Jordan and the Palestinian Authority. Security would thus serve as the litmus test for cooperation on other issues, such as economic development and water rights.

The problem of security emerged with the 1969 Cairo Agreement, which was an attempt to end violent clashes between Palestinian guerrillas and the Lebanese army.[25] Rather than curbing Palestinian activity, however, the agreement formalized the Palestinian military presence, providing it with southern Lebanon as a base from which to attack Israel. The Republic of Lebanon, which had been inconspicuous in every Arab-Israeli war up to that time, became a confrontation state overnight. Palestinian cross-border attacks destabilized Israel's northern border and exacerbated the disintegration of Lebanese central authority. The relocation of the PLO's headquarters to Beirut after its expulsion from Jordan in 1970,[26] the inability of the Lebanese army to control Palestinian actions against Israel, the establishment of a Palestinian "state within a state," and Israel's policy of retaliation set in motion a spiral of violence.

As early as 1972, Israeli officers established contacts with Lebanese Christians living along the Israeli border in order to counter the Palestinian threat.[27] It was not, however, until Operation Litani in March 1978 that Israel partially occupied southern Lebanon and established the security zone. Lebanon was in its third year of civil war and its second year of Syrian intervention. The PLO was becoming increasingly better coordinated, trained, and armed. Israel had lurched to the right in its 1977 elections, and its first Likud government changed Israel's approach to security from one that was reactive to one that was aggressive, an instrument to achieve political goals. Limited military force was replaced with broad military operations aimed at changing the geostrategic composition of the Middle East. Although the previous Labor government had intervened in Lebanon by retaliating against PLO military strikes and attempting to make southern Lebanon a neutral buffer zone, it was driven by defensive strategic objectives. With Operation Litani, Israeli military policy in Lebanon went on the offensive.

The first manifestation of this policy shift was the establishment of the security zone and a proxy relationship with the South Lebanon Army (SLA). The ineffectiveness of this buffer zone in protecting Israel's northern settlements from guerrilla attacks provided the incentive for involvement further into Lebanon in 1982. By the time Israel had invaded Lebanon all the way up to Beirut, "peace for Galilee" had been superseded by much broader goals: to install a Christian government under Bashir Gemayel, to make peace with Lebanon, to defeat Syria, to eliminate the PLO from Lebanon, to destroy Palestinian nationalism in the West Bank and Gaza Strip, and to free Israel from past national traumas such as the 1973 war.[28] It was nothing less than a cure-all operation, and rather than producing peace, it created new enemies, such as Hizballah. Above all, it ensured that Lebanon would be the last of Israel's neighbors to sign an agreement with the Jewish state.

Israel's 1985 decision to return to the security zone instead of withdrawing to the international border prolonged its security problem. Its presence in southern Lebanon until May 2000 and in the area of the Shabʿa Farms thereafter was seen as provocation by Hizballah, as a raison d'être by Syria for its continued military presence in Lebanon, and as an opportunity to exercise influence in Lebanon by Iran. Israeli raids aimed at curbing Hizballah activity, moreover, were counterproductive, creating Lebanese solidarity with the Shiʿa plight and strengthening Hizballah's domestic position, as manifested in the 1992 and 1996 Lebanese elections. The security zone also failed to place Galilee settlements out of reach of Katyusha rockets and ultimately resulted in cumulatively unacceptable Israeli military casualties.

While there was no guarantee that Hizballah would end its attacks against Israel if Israel withdrew from Lebanon, continued Israeli occupation of the security zone would also not end the cycle of violence. Israel's northern border remained insecure because Israel, despite a history of military failures in Lebanon, relied upon the threat or use of force to solve an essentially political problem. Neither Operation Accountability in 1993 nor Operation Grapes of Wrath in 1996 enhanced Israel's security. Yet Israel clung to the belief that they did, as reflected in the Israeli press at the time. After the Israeli bombing of Qana, *Ha'aretz* defense correspondent Ze'ev Schiff asserted that "The right to self-defense stands at the forefront. This means the right to fire to its source with any weapon. If Asad insists on Hizballah's right to continue fighting in the security zone, he must know that this grants the Israel Defense Forces (IDF) the right to pursue them and attack them beforehand even beyond the security zone."[29] Schiff's commentary in *Ma'ariv* following the Agreement of Understanding is even more revealing: "In contrast to the past, the written agreement of understanding that was reached after Operation Grapes of Wrath, gives the communities of Israel and Lebanon—including the security zone—better protection from attack than had existed in the past."[30]

Israel's cabinet communiqués of the period demonstrate a similar position on security. For example, on 14 April 1996, point L of the cabinet communiqué stated that "We did not conquer the security zone. The Lebanese authorities have essentially left it unclaimed, and turned it into a terrorist operating theater."[31]

Hopes for change in the dynamics of Israeli-Lebanese relations were raised with the Netanyahu government's Lebanon First proposal in August 1996, which called for Israeli withdrawal to the international border in exchange for Syrian guarantees to disarm and control Hizballah. Syrian rejection of Lebanon First did not end Israel's consideration of the plan. In a letter to the secretary-general dated 27 January 1998, Israel's permanent representative to the United Nations, Dore Gold, clarified the Jewish state's interpretation of UN Resolution 425:

> Israeli withdrawal from Lebanon was conditional upon restoration of security in the region. Israel is ready to implement the provisions of the Resolution. However, Resolution 425 (1978) does not call for an unconditional withdrawal; Israel is prepared to implement the withdrawal envisaged in the Resolution, but only within a framework that will ensure the implementation of all elements of the Resolution, including implementation of UNIFIL's expressly stated goals of the "restoring of international peace and security" and "assisting the Government of Lebanon in ensuring the effective author-

ity in the area." Such effective authority would obviously have to include, inter alia, arrangements for the protection of all residents of the area.[32]

While Israel's willingness to implement UN Resolution 425, even with conditions, was significant, Israel's belief that it could carry out Lebanon First without Syrian cooperation reveals that Israeli thinking on Lebanon and the Arab-Israeli conflict had changed little since 1982. Apart from the obvious domestic political appeal of reducing the number of Israeli casualties and cutting defense expenditures, this Israeli proposal was yet another attempt to use Lebanon to deal with Syria, aimed at denying Syria its major justification for keeping troops in Lebanon and ultimately forcing Syrian withdrawal. It was further intended to decouple Syria and Lebanon in the peace negotiations, the logic being that once Lebanon had regained the security zone, there would be no remaining obstacles to full peace. Underlying this attempt to shift emphasis from Syria to Lebanon was the lack of progress on Syrian-Israeli relations, highlighted by Israel's unwillingness to relinquish the Golan Heights. A separate peace with Lebanon would cut Syria out of the equation and enable Israel to keep the Golan.

The proposal was also an attempt to use Lebanon to deal with the PLO, as movement in Lebanese-Israeli relations would have relieved some of the pressure on Israel from the United States over the stalled Israeli-Palestinian track. It would have signaled Israeli support for the peace process and driven home the message that the obstacle to progress with the Palestinians was Yasir Arafat's inability to control Palestinian extremists. Yet again, Israeli policy towards Lebanon assumed the status of a grand plan, and yet again, Israel failed to accept the geostrategic reality that Lebanon could not and would not go it alone.

Lebanon's and Syria's response to Lebanon First demonstrated awareness of the larger implications of Israel's proposal. Lebanon welcomed Israel's intention to implement UN Resolution 425 but insisted that such a withdrawal had to be unconditional. Lebanese prime minister Rafik al-Hariri stated that "Israel has to withdraw from our occupied land and we'll do what we have to. We won't be held accountable by anyone but our people and our parliament."[33] But Lebanese politicians also feared that if Lebanon was unable to prevent attacks on Israel, Israel would use this inability as a pretext for another invasion, going far beyond the territory Israeli forces had previously controlled. Syria's position was less equivocal. Syrian troops would remain in Lebanon whether or not Israel pulled out, and only the return of the Golan Heights would produce any movement in the negotiations with either Syria or Lebanon. Lebanon First also failed to produce international absolution for Israel in its difficulties in dealing with the Palestinians.

In the absence of a political solution, Israeli policy continued to define southern Lebanon as purely a security problem, which needed a strong security response. The Israeli arms industry's development of the Nautilus laser system, designed to intercept Katyusha missiles, only underlined the policy of deterrence over dialogue.[34] In August 1998, some Israeli politicians proposed that Israel should hit Lebanese power stations, bridges, and other key points in retaliation for Hizballah attacks,[35] suggesting that future Israeli-Lebanese relations, in the absence of a peace agreement, were likely to include more of the same.

The Peace Process

When the Middle East peace process was initiated in October 1991, Lebanon was still in the process of resolving and reconciling its intercommunal differences. The end of fifteen years of civil war raised hopes for the re-emergence of Lebanon as a state player in regional politics. The 1989 Ta'if Agreement, however, linked Lebanon unequivocally to Syria. The 1991 Treaty of Brotherhood, Coordination, and Cooperation further subordinated Lebanon's foreign and defense policy to that of Damascus. As a result, the Lebanese-Israeli bilateral-negotiation track became subsumed within the Israeli-Syrian track; an Israeli-Lebanese peace agreement would be possible only if it were preceded by an Israeli-Syrian agreement. Following Syria's example, Lebanon decided to boycott the multilateral negotiations "until crucial and substantive progress is achieved on the bilateral track."

Lebanon's dependence upon others in the peace process made the Lebanese suspicious and wary of any final settlement with Israel. Lebanon's greatest fear was that it would be forced into concessions such as territorial compromise or full integration of the Palestinian refugees.[36] The general perception was that any agreement would be at the Lebanese republic's expense,[37] and this was clearly reflected in Lebanon's position on the crucial issues relating to the peace process that Israel and Lebanon needed to resolve: security, Palestinian refugees, water rights, and economic development.

Security

Any Israeli-Lebanese security arrangement for southern Lebanon had to take into account four major elements: the Israel Defense Forces, Hizballah, the South Lebanon Army, and Syrian troops. Until May 2000 Israel maintained that it needed the security zone in order to protect its northern settlements. If the north was quiet, the security zone was hailed as successful and logic dictated that it was foolish to abandon the arrangement. If the north was fired upon, then the need for increased Israeli involvement was seen as even more necessary. In either case, Israel felt incapable of returning the territory to Lebanese sovereignty. It was only in recent years—particularly since the 1997 helicopter accident that claimed the lives of seventy-three Israeli soldiers—that significant numbers of Israelis, both civilian and military, started to question the need for IDF involvement in southern Lebanon.

The official Israeli position in the peace process was that its primary concern was security, not making claims on Lebanese land or resources. Therefore, the initial Israeli settlement proposal requested the following: (1) The Lebanese army would be deployed north of the security zone and, for a period of six months, would prevent any terrorist activities against the security zone and Israel. Three months following that initial period, Israel would be prepared to sign a peace agreement with Lebanon. (2) Prior to any changes in its redeployment on the Lebanese front, Israel had to be convinced that the military organs of all terrorist groups operating out of Lebanon had been irreversibly disbanded. (3) The government of Israel was to receive practical and valid guarantees that no harm would be inflicted upon Lebanese citizens and South Lebanon Army personnel residing in the security zone and that they would be absorbed into the governmental and societal fabric of Lebanon.[38]

In comparison, Lebanon's official position in the peace process centered on the implementation of UN resolutions. Bilateral negotiation with Israel was ruled out because of fears that it would compromise UN Resolution 425.[39] Lebanon's solution to Israeli occupation was that expressed by the international community in UN resolutions 425, 508, and 509, which demanded the complete and unconditional withdrawal of Israel from Lebanese territory, with the assistance of UN forces, under the sovereignty of the Lebanese government.[40] This, however, would happen only if Lebanon and Syria could guarantee that southern Lebanon would no longer be used for attacks on Israel. By itself, Lebanon was militarily incapable of disarming and dissolving Hizballah.

Since Israel's redeployment to the security zone in 1985, dealing with the threat posed by Hizballah became the center of Israel's Lebanon policy.[41] Israeli decision makers started contemplating unilateral withdrawal from Lebanon in the belief that since Hizballah had been established in reaction to the 1982 Israeli invasion of Lebanon, unilateral withdrawal would deprive it of the reason for attacking Israel. This position was supported by Hizballah's own statements, as well as the fact that Hizballah increasingly became a domestic player within the Lebanese state rather than a pan-Islamic regional player.[42] Moreover, within the domestic context, Hizballah would no longer qualify for exemption from disarmament and dissolution under Lebanese legislation. Pressure on Hizballah to cease being a militia and to function solely as a political party had already been increasing.[43] Thus unilateral withdrawal would serve Lebanon's desire to complete its post–civil war process of reconciliation and normalization by removing this last gun from Lebanese politics. It would not, however, secure Israel's northern border.

Opponents of unilateral withdrawal countered these arguments by pointing to Iranian and Syrian patronage of Hizballah and the interest of these states in ongoing conflict. They were convinced that Hizballah did not just want to liberate southern Lebanon but was engaged in *jihad* (holy war) against Israel. Consequently, instead of increased security Israel would be faced with decreased security. The risks appeared to be too great. Withdrawal would thus come only as part of a peace treaty with comprehensive security guarantees.

Another factor of concern was the future of Israel's proxy, the SLA, in either withdrawal scenario. The SLA's alliance with Israel dates back to the establishment of the security zone in 1978, which was formed for protection against the PLO operating from southern Lebanon. Since 1982, the SLA served primarily to protect the security zone and northern Israel from Hizballah attacks. Yet it was never able to function without Israeli ground and air cover, and neither its operations against the PLO nor those against Hizballah were particularly successful.

Until May 2000, the SLA, under the command of Antoine Lahad, comprised an estimated 3,000 soldiers. Its leadership was predominantly Maronite with a Druze minority responsible for the Hasbaya region, while its foot soldiers were Maronite, Greek Catholic, Greek Orthodox, Druze, and Shi'a.[44] The stigma of collaboration with Israel was the main obstacle to the reabsorption of SLA soldiers into Lebanese society. Fear of massacres similar to those that followed the Israeli withdrawal from the Shouf in 1983 made relocation and exile more likely, and Israel repeatedly stated that "it will not abandon its friends under any circumstances."[45] Thus it was always expected that Israel would offer asylum to the SLA leadership and their families.

The biggest obstacle to an Israeli-Lebanese peace and normalization of relations has been the presence of an estimated 35,000–40,000 Syrian troops in Lebanon and the Syrian influence on Lebanese foreign and defense policy. In 1976, Syrian troops crossed the border into Lebanon to intervene in the civil war. Their control of 90 percent of the country at the end of the war ensured that Syria would play a key role in Lebanon's process of reconciliation. Syrian departure, as outlined in the Ta'if Agreement, was envisaged as parallel to Lebanon's social, political, and economic reconstruction. Yet no such withdrawal or disengagement took place. Instead, Syria tied Lebanon even more firmly into treaties of cooperation. As a result, Lebanon became "the only remaining captive nation" after the end of the cold war.[46]

Initially, some Israeli decision makers saw Syria as an asset. If Syria could be persuaded to cooperate in security arrangements, Syria would be a stronger guarantor of Israeli security than Lebanon, and Israel could safely withdraw from Lebanese territory. Hopes for such an arrangement were raised during the 1990–91 Gulf War, when Syria joined the U.S.-led coalition against Iraq and then participated in the Madrid peace conference.[47] Israel's Jezzine First proposal (whereby Israeli forces would begin withdrawal from Lebanon in the town of Jezzine) was to serve as a test case for IDF withdrawal from southern Lebanon. Israeli hopes were quickly dashed, however, when it became clear that Syria would not allow movement with Lebanon without seeing substantive progress with respect to the Golan Heights. Hopes were again raised after the conclusion of the Oslo Accords but plummeted with the assassination of Yitzhak Rabin in November 1995 and the suspension of Israeli-Syrian negotiations in 1996 under the Netanyahu government.

Key to understanding the difficulties of the Israeli-Syrian dynamic are Syria's interest in Lebanon and Syria's lack of interest in the peace process. Syria's control over Lebanon is unprecedented even in Lebanon's long history of foreign interventions. Syria's interests in Lebanon range from the relatively narrow need to have a stable neighbor to the broader fulfillment of Greater Syrian territorial ambitions, in which Lebanon becomes a base from which to project regional hegemony. The Syrian-Lebanese relationship also has economic aspects. Lebanon serves as Syria's window to the world outside and as a market for Syria's surplus labor. Moreover, Lebanese business and financial expertise provide the means for Syria to reform its own economy.[48] Syrian disengagement from Lebanon thus is undesirable from Damascus's perspective.

Fear of economic marginalization if Lebanon made peace with Israel should also not be underestimated as a motivation for Syria's reluctance to embrace Israel. Syria gained its credibility as a regional player through its military strength, placing itself at the heart of the Arab-Israeli conflict by promoting radical Arab nationalism. A move from conflict to normalization would mean a shift of emphasis from a relatively strong military position to a much weaker economic position, which could result in regional marginalization.[49] Syria already had had a taste of this with the opening up of Jordanian-Israeli relations in 1994 and the new Israeli-Turkish strategic relationship in 1996. Despite Asad's concessions to peace, which included allowing Syrian Jews to leave the country, cleaning up the drug traffic in the Beqaa Valley, and an appearance by Syrian foreign minister Farouk al-Sharaa on Israeli television, Syria was unable to shake off its image as a pariah state.

It is thus not surprising that Asad insisted that only after full withdrawal to the 4 June 1967 line could peace be negotiated. After the assassination of Rabin, Israeli-Syrian negotiations were virtually nonexistent. And the slight progress made since 1991 was motivated by Syria's need to have better relations with the United States after the loss of its patron, the USSR. The Netanyahu government, in the meantime, was determined not to give an inch to Syria; Housing Minister Ariel Sharon's project on the Golan Heights was a case in point. Syria's lack of interest in the peace process until December 1999 also dampened Lebanon's enthusiasm and hindered Lebanon's maneuverability. It also ensured that Israelis who had no ideological motivations for holding on to the Golan Heights remained trapped by Israel's security-driven policy.

Palestinian Refugees

The Palestinian issue took on particular significance in Israeli-Lebanese relations because of the 350,000–400,000 Palestinians living in Lebanon.[50] The majority of these Palestinians lived in refugee camps and had not been granted Lebanese citizenship. They were not afforded political rights, could not vote, and were not eligible for employment in public functions.[51] The majority of them wanted to return to Palestine. Lebanon's official position on the refugees was that they could not stay in Lebanon. The process of national reconciliation initiated with the 1989 Ta'if Agreement turned Lebanese opinion against the Palestinians, making them the scapegoats for the civil war.[52] Increasing economic problems in postwar Lebanon such as rising unemployment, the fact that one third of the population was already living below the poverty line, and a budget deficit that in 1996 was just under 50 percent[53] marginalized the refugees. Between 1982 and 1992 no more work permits were issued for Palestinians, and from 1986 onward the socioeconomic situation of the refugees began to deteriorate dramatically.[54] This was further exacerbated by the expulsion of Palestinian workers and the drastic reduction of outside financial support to Palestinian refugees since the 1990–91 Gulf War. Palestinians in Lebanon could no longer obtain construction permits, and those who had built illegally during the civil war were faced with demolition of their houses.[55] Palestinians were forbidden by law to take professional or skilled jobs, and they faced fierce competition from Syrian workers in the construction and manual jobs they were allowed to take.[56]

In Lebanon's view, the Palestinians had become a burden upon Lebanese society and economy. Thus, one of Lebanon's main aims in the peace process was finding a permanent solution to the refugee problem. At the same time, Lebanon greatly feared the possibility that regional and international powers would force it to permanently integrate Palestinian refugees,[57] as emigration to the West had become increasingly difficult and Israel was determined that the return to Palestine was not an option.

The slow progress in the Israeli-Palestinian negotiations exacerbated Lebanon's apprehensions. As refugees since 1948, many Palestinians in Lebanon were excluded from Israeli-Palestinian talks. They did not qualify as "displaced persons" by the Continuing Committee established under the Oslo Accords, which primarily looked at refugees from 1967.[58] The strain of the lack of progress on the refugee question affected Lebanon's domestic politics. In 1992, Shawki Fakhouri, speaker of the Ministerial Committee on Palestinian Affairs, stated that the Palestinians "were a real danger, which must be fought against no matter the costs."[59] This statement was immediately mitigated by Foreign Minister Fares Buwayz's suggestion that Lebanon could absorb 50,000–100,000 Palestinians.[60] Yet in 1995, Labor Minister Abdallah al-Amin stated that "the talk about settling Palestinians in Lebanon does not concern us in any way. We say that the Palestinians must return to Palestine, as we are unable to absorb anyone."[61]

The efforts of the multilateral Refugee Working Group to address the central issues of repatriation, compensation, and resettlement were hindered by Israel's determination to keep the group focused on humanitarian aid, by Lebanon's boycott (along with Syria) of the multilateral negotiations, and by the Lebanese government's outright hostility to the Refugee Working Group.[62] Yet, unless a mutually acceptable answer within a broader regional framework is reached, full normalization on the Israeli-Lebanese front is unlikely. A comprehensive solution of the refugee problem must include repatriation, permanent integration with full citizenship rights, and resettlement, and all parties to the negotiations—Israel, the Palestinian Authority, Jordan, Egypt, Syria, and Lebanon—must share the burden. A number of proposals for such "sharing" have been drafted. For instance, Donna Arzt devised a redistribution plan in 1996 that reduced Lebanon's Palestinian population to 75,000, while increasing Israel's Palestinian population to 1,075,000, Syria's to 400,000, and Jordan's to 2 million.[63] Others, however, have placed the number of Palestinians who will have to be absorbed into Lebanon as high as 200,000.[64]

After the election of Benjamin Netanyahu in 1996, the refugee issue virtually disappeared from the negotiating agenda as Israel maintained that even the return of Palestinians to the area under Palestinian Authority control would threaten Israel's "demographic security."[65] Underlying the security argument, however, was the more complex issue of responsibility: "Israel denies the legality of the Palestinian claim. If it recognizes the 'right' of return it would also be admitting responsibility, and perhaps culpability for creating the problem. But Israel categorically denies any responsibility for the War of 1948. On the contrary, the guilt and responsibility are all Arab-Palestinian."[56]

Neither Israel's hard-line position nor the softer version peddled by Salim Tamari, in which "Israel's acceptance in principle of the right of return" would be exchanged for Palestinian recognition that return cannot be exercised within the 1948 boundaries,[67] helped resolve the precarious situation of Palestinian refugees in Lebanon. The standstill on the refugee issue left Lebanon's Palestinians caught between Lebanon, which seemed determined to rebuild its economy and society excluding the refugees, and Israel, which was determined to move forward on its terms or not at all.

Water Rights

At the heart of the Israeli-Lebanese debate over water resources was the Litani River, with an abundant natural annual flow of 750–920 Mcm.[68] Before the civil war the Litani was never fully developed, its main use being for the production of hydroelectricity. As a result, its constant but variable surplus of water flowing into the Mediterranean had attracted the interest of its comparatively water-scarce southern neighbor, Israel. This interest raised Lebanese suspicions that Israel's presence in southern Lebanon was not solely motivated by security concerns.[69] Indeed, most Lebanese believed that it was unlikely that Israel would relinquish the security zone without having obtained a share of the Litani River.[70] Such fears were all the more believable as Zionist and Israeli history is riddled with plans for comprehensive water distribution schemes that include not only the Litani, but the Awali, Hasbani, and Jordan rivers as well.[71] Zionist leaders such as Chaim Weizmann advocated the inclusion of the Litani into any future Jewish state.[72] Israeli leaders continued to put forward plans for the development of the Litani as part of schemes for the Jordan River such as the 1951 All-Israel Plan, the 1953 Israel Seven-Year Plan, the 1954 Cotton Plan, the 1956 Israel Ten-Year Plan, or the 1956 Israel National Water Plan. The Arab-Israeli conflict, however, ensured that none of these schemes would be realized.

Annexation of southern Lebanon and seizure of the Litani remained frequent subjects of Israeli cabinet debate.[73] In 1978, Israel moved to increase the water flow into the Jordan after gaining control over the Wazzani-Hasbani springs and to capture the runoff in pipelines. In 1982, Israelis were reported to have taken seismic soundings in the lower Litani and Qirwan reservoir, and there have been persistent rumors of water siphoning from the Litani to the Jordan River ever since.[74]

Closer inspection of Israeli actions by UNiFiL, however, revealed that there was in fact no hard evidence that Israel had taken any significant amount of water from the Litani, even when the territory concerned was completely under IDF control. UNiFiL's observations were confirmed by satellite photos, which proved that Israel neither laid pipelines nor dug tunnels to divert water across the border. In short, despite lofty plans and Israeli control over the territory in question, Israel did not lay claim to Lebanese waters.

Nevertheless, given the regional scarcity of water, the issue of water sharing was part of the multilateral negotiations. Israel in the 1990s had reached the point where it was using all of its renewable water sources.[75] This precarious situation was further exacerbated by the fact that an estimated 35 percent of its water supply had traditionally been derived from the West Bank and thus was subject to Israeli-Palestinian negotiations. Moreover, from the perspective of regional water consumption, a systemic approach incorporating waters across national boundaries, including Lebanon's, was considered to be the most rational and effective means of solving the problem of water scarcity.[76]

Water sharing between Israel and Lebanon could evolve in several ways. The least costly option for Lebanon would be for the Litani to be included in a broader regional water-sharing scheme in the context of an overall Middle East peace settlement. The Litani could be integrated into Israeli-Jordanian efforts to maximize the yield and equalize the share of the Jordan River. The second, more contentious option is that of a bilateral arrangement with Israel that, no doubt, would create domestic opposition in Lebanon because such an agreement would be perceived as favoring Israeli needs for water over Shi'a rights to water and development.[77] This problem could be overcome if Lebanon received substantial benefits from the agreement, such as payment for the water and a greater supply of electricity.[78] Provided there is peace and stability and full consideration of regional and domestic interests, there is no reason why Israeli-Lebanese cooperation on water rights should not take place.

Economic Development

Israel viewed the opening of the Israeli-Lebanese border as part of the normalization process associated with peace. Lebanon's position was more ambiguous. On one hand, postwar Lebanon was trying to regain its traditional role as the finance and business center of the Middle East. On the other hand, Lebanon was wary of potential Israeli competition, underlined by general Arab suspicion that Israel ultimately planned to replace military hegemony with economic domination. Many Lebanese bankers and businessmen believed that Israel would be far more dangerous in peace than in war.[79] By the same token, they also feared that sudden progress in the peace process, however unlikely, could also mean that Lebanon's position as an international conference, business, and financial center could be usurped by the Gulf states.[80] Lebanon's reconstruction and economic revitalization faced both domestic and regional problems. In 1991, the first year of intercommunal peace, Lebanon's gross domestic product rose by almost 40 percent. Since then it has averaged around 7 percent per year.[81] Investment, however, did not pour in at the rate initially expected and Lebanon did not quite reach the stability desired by multinational corporations and expatriate Lebanese. As a result Lebanon was not able to recover even its prewar status of first rank in the Third World—a middle-income country, as well off as Portugal and more than twice as rich as Jordan.

The main concern for the international business community until May 2000 was Israeli attacks on Lebanon. The targeting of Beirut's infrastructure during Operation Grapes of Wrath in 1996 made potential investors wary. Expatriate Lebanese, many of whom are Christian, were also waiting for evidence of Syrian withdrawal. In fact, an estimated one million Lebanese who emigrated during the war were not planning to return under the current circumstances, depriving Lebanon of their expertise and commercial connections, as well as $50–$60 billion in overseas assets.[82] As a result, the economic goals embodied in the Horizon 2000 initiative could not be fully realized until greater regional stability had been achieved.

Despite Lebanon's inability to participate in regional economic conferences such as the 1996 Casablanca conference, the country was able to improve its economic standing. Commercial and cultural agreements with France worth $100 million and the 1997 lifting of the U.S. travel ban opened Lebanon to international business regardless of Israeli or Syrian constraints. Regaining its reputation as the Switzerland of the Middle East, however, would ultimately depend upon a Syrian-Israeli and Lebanese-Israeli settlement and whether the character of Israeli-Lebanese economic relations would be cooperative or competitive. In the absence of an agreement and, some would argue, even for the initial peace years, the main economic competitors with Lebanon are the Gulf states, as it is unlikely that Israel would become readily acceptable to the rest of the Middle East. This discomfort factor could enable Lebanon to reemerge as the financial center linking Europe with the Middle East. Lebanon's civil-war disadvantage vis-à-vis the Gulf emirates in this scenario is counterbalanced by its human capital, which is 90 percent literate, entrepreneurial by culture, and fluent in three or more languages.

Israel also is an unlikely competitor in terms of trade. Lebanon's manufactured exports, such as textiles, shoes, and furniture, are low tech in character and have a natural market in neighboring Arab countries. Israel's exports in electronics, computers, communications, medical and scientific equipment, agriculture, and arms technology are high tech in character and aimed at Western markets.[83] Sixty percent of Israel's exports go to the United States and the European Union, resulting in Israel's economic growth. If anything, Lebanon could gain rather than lose from Israeli-Lebanese economic relations, as Lebanon's smaller economy is bound to benefit from trade with Israel.

As fierce Israeli-Lebanese competition in an immediate postconflict scenario is unlikely, the possibility for economic cooperation must be explored. One obvious area for mutual cooperation is tourism. Peace between the two countries would allow for joint promotion of their attractions as well as crossborder tours, similar to Israeli-Jordanian operations since the 1994 peace agreement. The Israeli-Jordanian example raises all kinds of possibilities: joint tours, development of border areas including roads, transportation services, an airport, and hotels, development of nature reserves, training facilities such as a tourism school, and revival of the Haifa-Beirut railway. Beyond tourism, there are possibilities for joint industrial parks, collaborative research in crop and livestock production, joint agricultural training, and professional exchange programs, rail networks, telecommunications networks, and regional energy production. Regional cooperation on environmental issues will provide further opportunities for economic cooperation. Environmental protection schemes, recycling, and resource management have in some European countries become an industry within themselves. A flourishing Israeli-Lebanese economic relationship could result from imagination, good will, and regional stability.

Israel's Unilateral Withdrawal from Lebanon

The May 1999 Israeli elections ushered in a change in government and leadership. The departure of Likud prime minister Netanyahu and the landslide victory of Labor's Ehud Barak raised hopes for a speedy conclusion of the peace process, as Netanyahu's politics of nonnegotiation gave way to a series of election promises that included an Israeli withdrawal from southern Lebanon within a year. In his inaugural speech on 6 July 1999, Barak promised to work simultaneously on peace with all of Israel's Arab neighbors—Syria, Lebanon, and the Palestinians.

Even before Barak formally took office there were grounds for optimism on the Syrian-Lebanese track. The first actual movement on the Israeli-Lebanese front was the withdrawal of the SLA from Jezzine in early June 1999. While the withdrawal was made for local and strategic reasons, it had positive and far-reaching implications for the future withdrawal of Israel from the security zone. First, there was no violent reaction from Hizballah, no celebration, and no targeting or pursuing the retreating SLA or its militiamen who decided to stay behind. In the words of one Jezzine resident: "When the SLA left we feared for the former militiamen. It would have been very easy for people to come in and kill them. But now we have seen what's happening and we're much more at ease."[84] This suggested that Israeli fears of being pursued by Hizballah in the event of withdrawal would not necessarily materialize. It also meant that the SLA would not have to be evacuated from Lebanon in its entirety. The treatment of the 203 SLA militiamen who turned themselves over to the Lebanese authorities revealed that while SLA members would not survive unscathed, they would receive a fair trial rather than be subjected to violent retribution.

The positive tone was further reinforced by developments on the Israeli-Syrian track, which began with the unprecedented phenomenon of Syrian president Asad and Israeli prime-minister-elect Barak praising each other. This was followed by Asad's meeting with Palestinian rejectionists in early July 1999, during which they were effectively ordered to cease military activity, an order that also applied to Hizballah.[85] While Hizballah violated that order, the political message from Damascus to Jerusalem remained: Syria understood Israel's security concerns, and those concerns would be addressed within the context of a regional settlement in which the security arrangements would be equal, mutual, and reciprocal. Clearly, if Barak wanted to fulfill his election promise of withdrawal from Lebanon with the safety net of security guarantees from Syria and Lebanon, then the Israeli-Syrian track of the peace process had to be revived.

Not surprisingly, the Israeli-Syrian negotiations were formally reopened in Washington in December 1999. The substantive talks in Shepherdstown in January–February 2000, however, failed to achieve the hoped-for results. Israel was unable to obtain a full peace treaty with comprehensive security arrangements that would allow for an organized withdrawal from southern Lebanon. Syria was unable to obtain a full withdrawal to its definition of the 4 June 1967 border that would give it access to the Sea of Galilee. Both parties accused the other of intransigence, unwillingness to move from stated positions, and playing political games. In a final attempt to bridge the gap between Israel and Syria on the boundary line, U.S. president Bill Clinton met with Syrian president Asad in Geneva in March 2000. To no avail. While Asad returned to Syria empty-handed and disillusioned, Barak was left to contemplate his dwindling options on southern Lebanon. The possibility of a structured withdrawal within the context of an agreement had vanished. That left unilateral withdrawal or a continuation of the status quo regardless of his election promise. Israeli popular opinion against continued occupation, IDF support for withdrawal, and the erosion of the situation on the ground in the security zone pushed Barak in the direction of unilateral withdrawal. With the withdrawal officially scheduled for completion by 7 July 2000, Israeli troops pulled out overnight on 24 May amid the collapse of the SLA. Some 6,500 SLA members and their families followed the IDF across the border.[86]

Prospects for the Future

At the beginning of the twenty-first century Israel and Syria and, by extension, Lebanon came close to shifting from war to peace. But just as Israeli-Lebanese relations during the Arab-Israeli conflict from 1948 to 1991 were subordinated to the Israeli-Syrian struggle for hegemony, so too were Israeli-Lebanese prospects during the Middle East peace process. Syria, and not Lebanon, remained the key to security, peace, and normalization. Following the March 2000 Geneva summit, however, there was little movement on the Israeli-Syrian track. Indeed, incentives for either side to return to the negotiations seemed to have disappeared as the regional environment changed. The first of these changes came with the death of Hafiz al-Asad and the succession of his son Bashar. As a new leader and a latecomer without his own power base, Bashar al-Asad was not in a position to shift from the positions of his father in the peace process for fear that such shifts might undermine his precarious legitimacy and the process of consolidating his regime. Moreover, as far as Syria was concerned, the ball was clearly in the Israeli court after Geneva. Israel, in turn, believed it was Syria's turn to move after Israel's unilateral withdrawal from southern Lebanon. When such a move failed to materialize, Barak shifted to the Palestinian track of the peace process, which culminated in the Camp David summit in July 2000. This summit, too, failed to produce an agreement, and Palestinian leader Yasir Arafat's need for an exit strategy led directly to the next important change: the al-Aqsa intifada.

The outbreak of the intifada in September 2000 was a major setback not just for the Israeli-Palestinian negotiations but also for Israeli-Syrian-Lebanese negotiations. The intifada provided Hizballah with the opportunity to reengage in the struggle against Israel in solidarity with the intifada, and it provided Bashar al-Asad with a means for regional legitimation through anti-Israeli radicalization. Syria and Lebanon had clearly stepped back from the negotiating table. Israeli reaction to the intifada moved Israel further away as well. Not only was Barak forced to resign, paving the way for Ariel Sharon's election in February 2001; the Israeli people were no longer interested in what had driven the peace process so far: acceptance in the region and normalization of relations.

While Israeli, Syrian, and Lebanese interests in negotiations declined, and while there was no immediate necessity for any of them to move on this front, their long-term interests still remain best served through a peace treaty. The consequent normalization of Israeli-Lebanese relations would not be difficult. Indeed, unlike Syria, which will have difficulties competing economically unless it undergoes rigorous domestic reform, Lebanon and Israel, with their inherently entrepreneurial cultures, are in a position to play leading roles in future regional integration.

Notes

1. Treaty of 26 March 1920, S25/9907, Central Zionist Archives (CZA). See also Neil Caplan, *Futile Diplomacy*, vol. 1 (London: Frank Cass, 1983), 68.

2. See also Neil Caplan and Ian Black, "Israel and Lebanon: Origins of a Relationship," *Jerusalem Quarterly*, no. 27 (Spring 1983): 48–58.

3. "Note of Talk with Emile Eddé," 22 September 1936, S25/5581, Central Zionist Archives (CZA). See also "Shertok to Lourie," 22 September 1936, S25/5476, CZA; "Draft of a Pact submitted the twenty-third of December 1936 to Mr. Eddé," Z4/1702b, CZA.

4. Treaty, May 1946, S25/3269, CZA. For a discussion of the treaty see Laura Zittrain Eisenberg, "Desperate Diplomacy: The Zionist-Maronite Treaty of 1946," *Studies in Zionism* 13, no. 2 (1992).

5. "Rapport concernant le Liban présenté aux membres de l'ONU par Monseigneur Ignace Mubarak, archevêque Maronite de Beyrouth," undated, FM 2563/23, Israel State Archives (ISA).

6. "T. Arazi to E. Sasson, Discussion with Emile Eddé," Paris, 22 May 1948, FM 2565/12, ISA.

7. "S. Seligson to Y. Shimoni," 13 July 1948, FM 3766/6, ISA. See also "R. Shiloah to D. Ben Gurion," 30 May 1948, FM 2570/5, ISA. See further Avi Shlaim, "Israeli Interference in Internal Arab Politics: The Case of Lebanon," in *The Politics of Arab Integration*, eds. Giacomo Luciani and Ghassan Salame (London: Croom Helm, 1988), 236.

8. "Memorandum by Shmuel Yaari," 28 February 1949, FM 2563/23, ISA. See also Bennie Morris, "Israel and the Lebanese Phalange: Birth of a Relationship, 1948–51," *Studies in Zionism* 5, no. 1 (1984): 131.

9. "G. Raphael to W. Eytan," 28 December 1950, FM 2565/12, ISA. See also "E. Sasson to M. Sasson," 18 December 1950, FM 2565/12, ISA. See further "Research Department to Foreign Minister, Aid to the Lebanese Phalange," 28 December 1950, FM 2565/12, ISA; G. Tadmor, "Help for the Lebanese Phalange," 25 January 1951, FM 2408/16, ISA.

10. "T. Arazi to Gideon Rafael," Buenos Aires, 30 August 1954, FM 3766/7, ISA.

11. Interviews by Schulze with David Kimche, Jerusalem, 7 November 1992 and with Uri Lubrani, Tel Aviv, 10 November 1993. See also Benny Morris, "The Phalange Connection," *Jerusalem Post*, 1 July 1983.

12. Kimche, *The Last Option* (London: Weidenfeld and Nicolson, 1991), 130.

13. Interview by Schulze with Joseph Abu Khalil, Beirut, 4 July 1995. See also Joseph Abu Khalil, *Qissat al-Mawarinah fi al harb* (The story of the Maronites in

the war) (Beirut: Sharikat al-Matbu'at li al-Tausi'ah wa al-Nashr, 1990), 54. Interviews by Schulze with Mordechai Gur, Tel Aviv, 8 November 1993, and Rafael Eitan, Jerusalem, 9 November 1993.

14. Interview by Schulze with Joseph Abu Khalil, Beirut, 4 July 1995. Also, Sharon's interview with Oriana Fallaci, *Washington Post*, 21 August 1982; Zeev Schiff and Ehud Yaari, *Israel's Lebanon War* (London: George Allen and Unwin, 1984), 52; Itamar Rabinovich, *The War for Lebanon, 1970–85* (New York: Cornell University Press, 1985), 167.

15. Moshe Sharett, *Yoman ishi* (Personal diary) (Tel Aviv: Sifriyat Maariv, 1980), 398–400.

16. Shlaim, "Israeli Interference in Internal Arab Politics," 241–42.

17. Excerpts from Ben-Gurion's diary, 19 October and 22 October 1956, as quoted in Moshe Shemesh and Selwyn Ilan Troen, *The Suez-Sinai Crisis 1956: Retrospective and Reappraisal* (London: Frank Cass, 1990), 305–6.

18. *Letter from Lebanon*, no. 3 (1 August 1984); *Letter From Lebanon*, no. 5, (1 September 1984).

19. Latif Abul-Husn, *The Lebanese Conflict: Looking Inward* (Boulder, Colo.: Lynne Rienner, 1998), 42.

20. Interview by author with Fuad Abu Nader, Beirut, 4 July 1995.

21. Rabinovich, *The War for Lebanon*, 21.

22. Kirsten E. Schulze, *Israel's Covert Diplomacy in Lebanon* (Basingstoke: St. Antony's/Macmillan, 1998), 14–15.

23. Walid Phares, *Lebanese Christian Nationalism: The Rise and Fall of an Ethnic Resistance* (Boulder, Colo.: Lynne Rienner, 1995), 155. See also *Letter from Lebanon*, no. 7 (1 October 1984).

24. *Minutes of Council Command Meetings* (Beirut: Lebanese Forces, 1986–87). See also Phares, *Lebanese Christian Nationalism*, 193.

25. For the text of the Cairo Agreement see Yehuda Lucacs, *The Israeli-Palestinian Conflict: A Documentary Record, 1967–1990* (Cambridge: Cambridge University Press, 1992), 456.

26. Rabinovich, *The War for Lebanon*, 41.

27. Interview by Schulze with Mordechai Gur, Tel Aviv, November 1993.

28. Ilan Peleg, *Begin's Foreign Policy, 1977–1983: Israel's Move to the Right* (New York: Greenwood Press, 1987), 151. See also Abba Eban, *Personal Witness: Israel through My Eyes* (London: Jonathan Cape, 1992), 604; Rabinovich, *The War for Lebanon*, 122.

29. *Ha'aretz*, 23 April 1996.

30. *Ma'ariv*, 28 April 1996.

31. Cabinet communiqué, 14 April 1996.

32. "Letter from the Permanent Representative of Israel to the UN, Dore Gold, to the Secretary-General," 27 January 1998, S/1998/75, UN Archives.

33. *Daily Star* (Beirut), 9 September 1998.

34. *Ma'ariv*, 30 April 1996.

35. *Jerusalem Post,* 2 September 1998.

36. Kirsten E. Schulze, "Rolle und Perspektives des Libanon in der Region," in *Wege aus dem Labyrinth? Friedenssuche in Nahost: Stationen, Akteure, Probleme des nahöstlichen Friedensprozesses,* eds. Margret Johannsen and Claudia Schmid (Baden-Baden: Nomos, 1997).

37. Carole Dagher, "Lebanon's Political Clouds Were Lifting Prior to Israeli Onslaught," *Washington Report,* May 1996.

38. Ministry of Foreign Affairs, "The Middle East Peace Process: An Overview," pamphlet, Jerusalem, 1996.

39. Fida Nasrallah, *The Questions of South Lebanon* (Oxford: Centre for Lebanese Studies, 1992).

40. "The Official Position of the Lebanese Government, Madrid Peace Conference," 30–31 October 1991, press release from the Lebanese Embassy.

41. Laura Zittrain Eisenberg, "Israel's Lebanon Policy," *MERIA Journal* 1, no. 3 (1997).

42. Augustus Richard Norton, "Hizballah in Transition," *Daily Star* (Beirut), 9 August 1997. See also Magnus Ranstorp, *Hizballah in Lebanon: The Politics of the Western Hostage Crisis* (Basingstoke: Macmillan, 1997), 25–60.

43. *Washington Report,* October 1996.

44. Eisenberg, "Israel's Lebanon Policy."

45. *Voice of Lebanon* (radio), 12 July 1995.

46. Habib Malik, "Is There Still a Lebanon?" *MERIA Journal* 2, no. 1 (1998).

47. Eisenberg, "Israel's Lebanon Policy."

48. Volker Perthes, "Syrian Predominance in Lebanon: Not Immutable," *Lebanon on Hold: Implications for Middle East Peace,* eds. Rosemary Hollis and Nadim Shehadi (London: Royal Institute of International Affairs, 1996), 34.

49. Kirsten E. Schulze, "Peace Progress," *LSE Magazine* (summer 1997).

50. Rosemary Sayigh, "Palestinians in Lebanon," in *Peace for Lebanon? From War to Reconstruction,* ed. Deirdre Collings (Boulder, Colo.: Lynne Rienner, 1994), 99–100.

51. Nawaf Salam, "Between Repatriation and Resettlement: Palestinian Refugees in Lebanon," *Journal of Palestine Studies* 24, no.1 (Autumn 1994): 18.

52. Rex Brynen, "Palestinian-Lebanese Relations: A Political Analysis," in Collings, *Peace for Lebanon?* 91.

53. *Washington Report,* May 1996.

54. Lina Abu-Habib, "Education and the Palestinian Refugees of Lebanon: A Lost Generation?" *Refugee Participation Network* 21 (April 1996).

55. *As Safir,* 8 October 1992.

56. *The Economist,* 24 February 1996.

57. *New York Times,* 23 September 1992.

58. Article VII, Oslo Accords, September 1993.

59. *L'Orient Le Jour,* 29 September 1992.

60. *L'Orient Le Jour,* 2 October 1992.

61. *Al-Majallah*, 9–15 April 1995.

62. Rex Brynen, "Imagining a Solution: Final Status Arrangements and Palestinian Refugees in Lebanon," *Journal of Palestine Studies* 26, no. 2 (Winter 1997): 42–54.

63. Donna Arzt, *Refugees into Citizens: Palestinians and the End of the Arab-Israeli Conflict* (Washington, D.C.: Council on Foreign Relations Press, 1996).

64. *Al-Majallah*, 9–15 April 1995.

65. *Yediot Ahronot*, 4 June 1996.

66. Shlomo Gazit, *The Palestinian Refugee Problem*, Final Status Issues Study no. 2 (Tel Aviv: Jaffee Center for Strategic Studies, 1995), 7.

67. Salim Tamari, *Palestinian Refugee Negotiations: From Madrid to Oslo II* (Washington, D.C.: Institute for Palestine Studies, 1996), 39.

68. Thomas Naff, "Israel and the Waters of South Lebanon," in John Kolars and Thomas Naff, *The Waters of the Litani in Regional Context* (Oxford: Centre for Lebanese Studies, 1993), 3.

69. Naff, "Israel and the Waters of South Lebanon," 1.

70. Nasrallah, *The Questions of South Lebanon*, 9.

71. F. C. Hof, *Galilee Divided: The Israel-Lebanon Frontier, 1916–1984* (Boulder, Colo.: Westview Press, 1985), 11–13.

72. M. W. Weisgal, ed. *The Letters and Papers of Chaim Weizmann*, vol. 9 (Jerusalem, Israel Universities Press, 1977): 267.

73. T. Naff and R. Matson, *Water in the Middle East: Conflict or Cooperation?* (Boulder, Colo.: Westview Press, 1984), 70–71.

74. J. K. Cooley, "The War over Water," *Foreign Policy* 54 (Spring 1984): 22.

75. Hussein A. Amery and Atif A. Kubursi, "The Litani River: The Case against Interbasin Transfer," in Collings, *Peace for Lebanon?* 180.

76. Naff, "Israel and the Waters of South Lebanon," 2.

77. Amery and Kubursi, "The Litani River," 188–89.

78. Elisha Kally, *Options for Solving the Palestinian Water Problem in the Context of Regional Peace, Israel Palestinian Peace Research Project*, Working Paper no. 9 (Jerusalem: Harry Truman Institute, Winter 1991–92).

79. Yusuf Salibi, *Al-Muwajaha al-iqtisadiyya al-murtaqaba bayn Lubnan wa Israil* (The expected economic confrontation between Lebanon and Israel), *al-Mustaqbal al-Arabi*, 16/1993, 66–80.

80. Schulze, "Rolle und Perspektives des Libanon in der Region," 199.

81. *The Economist*, 24 February 1996.

82. *Middle East International*, 12 April 1996.

83. Israeli Ministry of Foreign Affairs, International Division.

84. *Daily Star* (Beirut), 14 June 1999.

85. *Times* (London), 20 July 1999.

86. *Ha'aretz*, 25 May 2000.

3

The Dilemma of the Palestinians in Lebanon

Julie Peteet

I begin this chapter with an ethnographic moment to set a tone. During a recent visit to Ain al-Helwah refugee camp in Saida, a young Palestinian man offered to drive me home. It was past nine P.M., and he warned me that we would have to pass through an army checkpoint. Anyone moving in and out of the camp after nine is stopped by soldiers, who check identity papers and register movements in a logbook. After we passed through this procedure, the young Palestinian commented acerbically that the intent was humiliation more than anything else.

"We are monitored as though we are a political threat, when the real threat comes from elsewhere," he said. "People are organizing in the camps and are soon going to show their weapons, even if symbolically in a parade. They are planning a full military dress parade as a show of power. I am very against this kind of action because it will only bring us more trouble, more controls, and longer waits at the roadblocks.

"We are the *jeel al-shabab* [the new generation] and we have a new sense of what we want," he continued. "We want respect and to leave Lebanon. We are fed up with this treatment at the roadblocks. They shout at us 'Get down!' 'Give me your identity card!' 'What are you looking at?' We just want to be treated with respect."

The fourth generation of Palestinians in Lebanon is indeed a new generation It has known nothing but disempowerment and disrespect. It is a generation that grew up with sieges and assaults, but without the resistance movement that characterized their parents' adolescence. Their sense of what they want is grounded in daily experiences of poverty, marginality, and fear. These young Palestinians do not envision the future as a linear progression toward a better situation. Years of violence have ruptured their sense of trust in the future as a place of safety. The only certain thing about their future is its uncertainty. Trauma, "events outside the range of usual human experience,"[1] has become frequent and predictable. The absence of agency, the sense that nothing one does has meaning or effect, pervades everyday life.

Beneath a veneer of control and containment, years of violence and terror have created a Palestinian-Lebanese relationship with the potential to breed even more violence. This chapter explores the development of the worldview of today's Palestinian refugees in Lebanon and the prospects for Lebanese-Palestinian relations.

Palestinians in Pre–Civil War Lebanon

Ambivalence and ambiguity, along with intermittent hostility, have been consistent features of Lebanese-Palestinian relations for fifty years. The 359,005 Palestinian refugees registered with the United Nations Relief and Works Agency (UNRWA) in mid-1997 in Lebanon are those Palestinians who arrived in the country in 1948–49 and their descendants. They now constitute 10.5 percent of the population of Lebanon and 10.5 percent of all refugees registered with UNRWA in the region.[2] UNRWA figures indicate that 10 percent of these refugees are enrolled in the agency's special hardship program.[3]

From the beginning, Lebanon was adamant about the impossibility of resettling the Palestinians. Lebanon's limited resources and its confessional political and social system, which relies on a delicate balance of power among Christians, Muslims, and Druzes, made it the least able of all the surrounding states to cope with a massive influx of refugees. Yet the Palestinians came and stayed and were an integral part of the Lebanese economy until recent plans to marginalize them were enacted. Before the civil war, there was a modicum of certainty in Lebanese-Palestinian relations, despite the enmity that existed between the refugees and their hosts.

Palestinian refugee rights in Lebanon have never been clear, in contrast to Syria, which endowed refugees with the right to work, and Jordan, which extended citizenship. Pre–civil war Lebanon, however, was still a cosmopolitan site of refuge for the Palestinians, with porous and fluid boundaries between space, communities, and nationalities. Borders of refugee camps were nearly indistinct from surrounding Lebanese communities, underscoring an integration since destroyed.

"The past was better—if you enter the camps now they are not the camps of the 1950s. The 1950s were better," Abu Munir, a middle-aged Palestinian professional, told me. "People were more willing to sacrifice, the standard of living was better—people had work. At least we had rations, and women could go out of the camps and collect wild greens. Now we have no work, no rations, and no plants to gather."

A growing Palestinian militancy, however, was not acceptable to the Lebanese populace or government. It soon became a flash point for mobilizing Lebanese around a host of issues, including Lebanon's regional role, identity, and social organization. The Palestinians became an "other" blamed for the ensuing civil war.

Palestinians and the Lebanese Civil War

If one looks at the meaning of the Lebanese civil war for the Palestinians in an anthropological framework, it was about spatiality. The war redefined space and its meaning. People and communities were sorted out. Space, place, and rights were reclassified, as were social relations. Prior to the war, space and social relations between Lebanese and Palestinians were blurred. The war had the effect of making what had become indistinct clearly visible. Borders of refugee camps such as Shatila became brutally defined, both by a military border and a psychological border created by practices of fear.

If mixed social relations and mixed marriages stand as signs of blurred communal boundaries, the Palestinians and Lebanese have significantly tightened those boundaries. Palestinians visit Lebanese much less often than in the prewar period. Marriages across national lines are increasingly rare. Social interactions are hedged with uncertainty.

As Lebanon continues its recovery from nearly sixteen years of war, there has been little national discussion of why the war occurred and how to prevent another. Reconstruction plans have ignored the question of how to commemorate the war in ways that might inform future generations of their past or the possible perils of their future. Coming to terms with the complex and intricate origins of the war has been bypassed in favor of a simplistic discourse of blame. "Othering" the Palestinians, attributing the war to their presence rather than to indigenous problems, has created a short-term social cohesion for the Lebanese, but it is not sufficient for forging a long-term national consensus.

Recovery from trauma requires a grand narrative of what transpired so as to endow it with shared meaning. The Lebanese need to formulate a narrative of the war that can lead to reconciliation, aside from a displacement of blame onto the Palestinians. In the absence of public remembering, of commemorative monuments or sites, the memory of the war is at the level of individual traumas and nightmares. Psychologists who have written on recovery from trauma argue that recovery and healing require speech rather than silence, and commemoration rather than forgetfulness.[4] Yet it is exceedingly difficult to construct a meaningful narrative of a civil war that divided a nation. In a sense, the Palestinian refugee camps in Lebanon serve as Lebanon's war memorials. Their continued existence is a testimony to the reputed cause of the war, and their recontainment represents a tangible victory for the Lebanese.

In focusing on remembrance, however, it is vital to examine forgetting.[5] We must weigh forgetting that leads to historical amnesia against forgetting that can be productive. Despite its drawbacks, the collective forgetting of the complex causes of the Lebanese civil war both contributes to a sense of Lebanese national identity and provides a means of psychic survival in the period of reconstruction.

Palestinians and Lebanese Policy in the Post–Civil War Era

With the advent of the Israeli-Palestinian peace process in 1991, there has been a dramatic return of attention to the issue of Palestinian refugees. Palestinians have always considered the refugees to be at the heart of the Israeli-Palestinian conflict, although they have resisted attempts to define the Palestine problem solely as a refugee situation. To do so would have been to capitulate to a humanitarian solution based on resettlement, rather than a political solution based on issues of national sovereignty and justice.

The destruction of several refugee camps in the course of the war has left thousands of Palestinians in Lebanon homeless and in dire need of shelter. Palestinians in Lebanon now filter all information and see new developments, including some outside assistance, through the lens of resettlement. Their main fear is of being left behind, a fear spurred by the betrayal of the 1993 Oslo Accords and given human form by their formerly respected leader, Yasir Arafat. Painfully aware that the Lebanese government and populace desire to see them leave the country for resettlement, or at least moved to marginal areas of Lebanon, the refugees live in a situation of suspended time.

Palestinian refugee women, serving as the public voice of their people, vehemently rejected the Oslo Accords. "They took our milk and blood and left us here!" shouted one mother in Shatila camp who lost five sons in the 1982 Sabra-Shatila massacre, and her harsh political commentary was echoed by other camp residents. The maternally grounded metaphor underscores the Palestinians' sense of abandonment. Bitter about the

deaths of their children as well as the financial and social abandonment of
the refugee camps in Lebanon by the PLO, they feel that a fundamental
social and political relationship has been breached. The contractual nature of the relationship—we give you our sons to fight, and to you we
entrust the struggle for our future—was voided by a peace process that
ignored the refugees in Lebanon. The refugees fear they will be asked to
pay the price of a peace settlement, one that trades their future for gains in
the West Bank and Gaza Strip.

Reports of UNRWA's demise run rampant in the refugee community.
The refugees see UNRWA's fate as their fate—a kind of reflexive relationship. If UNRWA is forced to shut down operations, they argue, refugees
will cease to be a major political issue. Cuts in UNRWA services, and
conspiratorial rumors of more to come, have the capacity to politically
mobilize refugee camps. Refugees have protested UNRWA cuts, however
hesitantly. These protests displace anger and frustration at the Lebanese
government, which cannot yet be voiced. Eventually, it is likely that protests aimed at UNRWA will incorporate direct criticisms of Lebanese
policy.

"Strangulation" is the term used by Palestinians to refer to the current
Lebanese policy, which has shifted since the war from violent containment
of the refugees to a spatial, economic, social, and political marginalization
whose goal is "voluntary" resettlement of the refugee population. One
Palestinian intellectual I interviewed put it this way: "The policies from
the Lebanese government are going to feed a new round of violence. They
are using the violence of the law against us. They have already demonstrated that the violence of war did not succeed in eliminating the Palestinians from Lebanon. I wonder if they will succeed by other means."

This "violence of the law" has taken a number of forms. Lebanon has
legislated far-reaching restrictions on Palestinian employment. In Lebanon, where foreigners are required by law to obtain work permits, legislation enacted in 1962 has since been implemented that classifies Palestinians as foreigners. Areas of employment open to Palestinians have been
severely curtailed and now encompass only "construction workers and
workers in ancillary tasks, excluding electrical installations, sanitation
facilities, glass mounting, agricultural workmen, tanning and leather
workers, excavation workers, textile and carpet workmen, smelters, sanitation workers, nannies, nurses, servants and cooks, car wash and lubrica-
tion workers."[6]

UNRWA figures put Palestinian unemployment at 40 percent,[7] and local observers claim it is as high as 90 percent.[8] Lebanon contains the great-

est number of UNRWA hardship cases in the region. The new Lebanese policy continues a downward economic spiral started by the 1982 withdrawal of the PLO from Lebanon. The PLO's once-substantial economic, political, and social infrastructure provided a major source of employment for refugees, and its network of social services—including monthly indemnities, health care, child care, and educational assistance—eased refugee poverty and supplemented UNRWA services. The PLO's demise in Lebanon coincided with an economic downturn in the oil-producing states in the Gulf, which had employed many skilled Palestinians who had benefited from the PLO's vocational training programs. This further reduced the incomes of refugee families.

A middle-aged school teacher gave this contemporary perspective on the situation in Ain al-Helwah camp:

These are the worst days I have ever seen, these past four or five years, and I have been doing this work for over twenty years now. Children are hungry and searching in the garbage for food. We have children in the streets rather than in school. They come to school hungry and without adequate clothing. Some of them do not even have shoes. There is a new generation of illiterates. UNRWA throws out those who do not perform well academically and they are in the streets. We have a Swedish program to take these kids and give them remedial help. We looked at one area and found seventy-five street kids. That's just from one small area in the camp!

Those who pass the brevet are semiliterate—not like in the old days when we studied so hard and were expected to learn. Kids these days are unable to study. Their home environment is lacking. How can they study in a home where no one cares, where there are so many problems! And these days, no one looks out for anyone else!

Other measures designed to reduce the number of registered refugees in Lebanon include a September 1995 decree from the Lebanese Interior Ministry that Palestinian carriers of the Lebanese laissez-passer must obtain a visa to reenter Lebanon. This further complicates travel procedures, making leaving Lebanon a risky choice for Palestinian refugees who intend to return.[9] The Lebanese government also has reduced official refugee numbers through selective naturalization. While official Lebanese government policy and public opinion are fairly unanimous in rejecting naturalization of refugees, in the mid-1990s a number of Muslim refugees were naturalized without fanfare. No precise figures have been made public, but popular estimates put the number at 28,000–30,000. Sectarian considerations were an integral part of this move. The first to be natural-ized were Lebanese Shiʿa from seven border villages, who had formerly been classified as Palestinian refugees. A year later, an unknown number of Sunni refugees were naturalized, as were the few remaining nonnaturalized Palestinian Christians.

Palestinians and "Beirut 2000"

The reconstruction of Beirut in all its manifestations—highways, new tele-communications system, new airport, and new buildings in the city cen-ter—are major features of the plan called "Beirut 2000." This reconstruc-tion will have negative effects on the Palestinian refugee population. The two primary development and reconstruction projects, Elisar and Solidaire (the Lebanese Company for the Development and Reconstruc-tion of Beirut Central District), have generated much debate. Elisar is developing the southern suburbs of Beirut, which involves displacing groups of poor people, many of them Shiʿa immigrants who over the past twenty years had fled to Beirut from war-torn areas of southern Lebanon. As a result of political lobbying and pressure, many of these people have been offered low-income housing in nearby areas to compensate for the loss of their homes, despite the fact that their homes were considered by the government to be illegal.

Elisar is also operating in the area of two refugee camps, Shatila (popu-lation 9,499) and Bourj al-Barajneh (population 16,389),[10] both of which occupy strategic areas around the access road to the airport. The recon-struction of the massive Sports City complex adjacent to Shatila, which residents feared would expand into the camp and heighten calls for its removal, has been accomplished without using camp lands. However, Elisar's reconstruction maps show the camps as blank, unnamed areas.

There are rumors that the new road connecting Beirut International Airport with mountain areas will run straight through Bourj al-Barajneh, displacing anywhere from 100 to 600 families and severing the camp's spatial integrity. Bordered by relatively wide streets that serve as a social and physical boundary between Lebanese and Palestinian communities, the interior of the camp is a maze of intricate alleys easily maneuverable by its inhabitants, less so by outsiders. During the camp wars, it remained impenetrable to the outside, despite prolonged siege and assault. This same spatiality that provided wartime defense also accounts for its contin-ued social cohesion.

Although no official pronouncements have been forthcoming, engineers have visited the camp to survey the terrain and estimate the number of houses to be demolished. This road project contains echoes of Ariel Sharon's infamous 1970s plan to build major roads through refugee camps in Gaza in the name of improvement in the standard of living. In this case, the rubric is not "improvement" but "reconstruction," a term with radically opposed meanings and implications, depending on one's geonational location.

Palestinians were convinced for several years that Beirut 2000 meant the outright demolition of the camps, which would be replaced by shopping malls or sports centers, zones of elite leisure and consumption. When this did not happen, fears of being forcibly loaded onto trucks and buses, as refugees were in 1948, gave way to more nuanced fears of marginalization and displacement, of being driven out too slowly to mount effective opposition against the government. Increasing economic restrictions and hardships, the absence in the camps of services such as water, sewage, and transportation, and governmental measures to reduce the numbers of official refugees are seen by Palestinians as manifestations of this new, more subtle policy.

Shatila Camp: An Evolving Example of Palestinian-Lebanese Relations

The evolution of the relationship between Lebanese and Palestinian refugees is illustrated by the history of Shatila camp, once a center of Palestinian political activity. Before the civil war, Shatila housed a significant number of Lebanese Shi'a along with Palestinians. The conflicts that engulfed the camps along with the rest of the country put an end to this coexistence. Many Lebanese Shi'a, sensing danger, left Shatila voluntarily. Others resisted this violent reassignment of space and identity.

One story of that resistance was reported to me by a middle-aged Palestinian woman of Shatila:

When we were living in that building, we were eleven families, nine of them Shi'a. We were living together—no differences among us. We ate together. On the first floor lived a young Lebanese army officer, Mohammed. When the fighting broke out, we went down to the ground floor. There we stayed in a room where the Norwegian volunteers used to stay. Two Lebanese women went down with us; others, like my neighbor, refused to go. She even had a shell land on her balcony and still she refused to come and be with us. The next day all the Shi'a families gathered and got a car and left the camp. The only Shi'a women who stayed were Um Ali and Um Kamel. Their children were fighting with us. They said either we live together or we die together. The following day Amal came to our building and occupied it. They came and found us on the ground floor. We were all sitting there. Our neighbor—the officer Mohammed—was with them. He was wearing a green headband and brandishing a Kalishnikov, ready to shoot. The children were playing in other rooms, so the women went to fetch them. I approached our neighbor Mohammed and said, "Don't do the wrong thing, I beseech you in the name of neighborliness." He said, "Nobody say a word, you so-and-so, nobody move." He took us all into one room and made us sit there. He was dark and looked darker that day. He called on Um Ali—she lived on his floor. She went to him and knelt at his feet, begging him. He kicked her, throwing her flat on the floor. He asked, "Where is Nasser [her son]?" Nasser was there. He stood up. Mohammed ordered him to get closer and then to stand behind him. Then he asked, "Where is Khalil?" Khalil was the type to scare easily. He fell to the floor. Then he asked, "Where are Ali and Abed? Are they fighting with the dogs?" Um Kamel's sons were carrying arms with us and that is why she did not leave. She wanted to stay and either die with them or live with them. Suddenly we could hear the sounds of very nearby fighting. Mohammed left.

In the early 1990s, after the end of the camp wars and the civil war, no Shi'a would walk through Shatila, although skirting the camp meant a much longer walk to a large central marketplace. The strict borders of the camp were conspicuous indicators of national space. Gradually, Shi'a women began to walk through the camp hurriedly, without stopping to talk or look around, although Shi'a men still did not dare to enter Shatila because of continuing hostilities. Over a period of several years, hostilities lessened, and the lines between Shi'a and Palestinian once again blurred.

Today, a new influx of residents has threatened the spatial and social cohesion of Shatila. Palestinian households within the camp are becoming isolated from one another. Economic and demographic pressures, including the quest for affordable housing for Lebanese as well as Palestinians, has fragmented Shatila, and it is no longer a community with common interests.

One Palestinian resident, Um Khalid, captured the shifting nature of space and community in comments made several years apart. As I sat on Um Khalid's roof with her family soon after the end of the war, she said, "You see, Shatila is our home. . . . I know all these people, we went through the sieges together. We are of one hand. It is like a Palestinian village here. How can we be dispersed again?" By the summer of 1999, when I visited again, the once-quiet, one-story house was engulfed by eight- and ten-story apartment buildings full of non-Palestinians, mostly Lebanese. Um Khalid commented sadly, "We are surrounded by big buildings and lots of strangers."

Before the civil war and the camp conflicts, Lebanese and Palestinians in Shatila and elsewhere shared municipal and social services, social relationships cemented by intermarriage, and political struggles, with many Lebanese active in Palestinian organizations. Now there are distinct lines of division between the communities. There are no shared resources or social services, no shared ideology, and very little socializing.

The Future of Palestinians in Lebanon

Palestinian refugees in Lebanon are making a number of responses, both positive and negative, to the continuing marginalization of their communities by the Lebanese government and populace and their fears of forced resettlement. As mentioned, severe social problems have arisen in the camps. Dysfunctional families and communities created by displacement, uncertainty, poverty, and discrimination in turn breed drug activity, prostitution, and crime.

The Palestinians are, however, developing new forms of association and assistance to meet these needs and fill the void left by the absence of PLO leadership and social services once provided by the PLO, UNRWA, family members outside Lebanon, and nongovernmental organizations. Village associations, insurance companies, and credit unions based on traditional ties have emerged in the camps. These associations bring together people from a pre-1948 village who reside in camps and urban areas in different parts of Lebanon. They are led by middle-aged males from the village, some of whom have come up through the political ranks of the Palestinian resistance movement; others are from well-known and powerful families. These associations attest to the continuing relevance of pre-1948 kinship and village affiliations for the Palestinians, with a new focus of helping "villagers" with contemporary problems, such as unexpected medical expenses, funerals, or school fees for children.

This new style of sociopolitical organization, with its crisis-oriented agenda, is seen by some as a sign of the failure of the Palestinian resistance movement and, on a smaller scale, of the popular committees that once had great influence in the camps. Some complain that smaller, less powerful villages are unable to mobilize the resources to form an association and that this inserts a wedge between Palestinians who live on the margins and those who have recourse to some sort of safety net. Another criticism is that these narrowly based traditional forms of organization undermine the possibilities of collective political organizing.

Proponents argue that these organizations represent a reassertion of Palestinian identity grounded in pre-1948 social relations and spaces. In an atmosphere of "every family for itself" and "no one helps anyone anymore," they bring together Palestinians at some level for mutual assistance. They reaffirm the meaning of place and home in exile, connecting the fourth generation with the past.

Palestinians are also framing discussions with the Lebanese government about their status in terms of civil rights and human rights. Within this political and legal framework, refugees hope to secure rights of residency, along with employment and access to medical care and education for their children. The refugees have not asked for citizenship, aware both of the hostility that this demand arouses in the Lebanese and the prospect that Lebanese citizenship would dilute their national identity and make their eventual return to their homeland even more remote.

If the intifada utilized the fax revolution, the struggle for Palestinian civil and human rights will rely on the revolution in global communications. The Women's Humanitarian Organization, a camp-based group, has a website that "calls on all international humanitarian organizations and supporters of the Palestinian people to help protect the basic human rights of Palestinian refugees."[11]

Despite the absence of overt Palestinian-Lebanese conflict, human rights abuses remain a problem. The terror and violence of the previous years have given way to a pervasive feeling of insecurity and profound uncertainty as to the future. The Syrian practice of abducting both Lebanese and Palestinians continues. Human Rights Watch notes that these abductees are held incommunicado in various places in Lebanon before transfer to Syria. Torture is commonplace, including beatings, electric shocks, and prolonged periods of hanging. Relatives remain in the dark as to the whereabouts of loved ones.[12]

Although a Lebanese ministerial committee has been set up to explore human and civil rights issues vis-à-vis the Palestinians, the results to date have been negligible. Lebanese continue to voice strong opposition to any moves that might suggest "implantation" *(towteen)*, a buzzword for a permanent solution of the refugee crisis by resettlement and naturalization. Yet most Lebanese understand that the return of the Palestinians to their homeland, as specified by UN General Assembly Resolution 194, is a remote possibility. The tension between this realization and public statements that continue to reject settlement of the refugees drives the restrictive and punitive conditions imposed on the refugees by Lebanon.

Within the framework of the peace process, the refugee issue requires coordinated action. In January 1996, the Refugee Working Group (RWG) was to begin dealing with this question. Neither Lebanon nor Syria is participating in these talks, however, and there is a danger for the Palestinians that, in the interests of Israel, the issue of the refugees may simply be abandoned or reframed as one of permanent integration into host countries.

Conclusion

It has been more than fifty years since the Palestinian refugees, now entering their fourth generation, came to Lebanon, making Palestinians one of the oldest refugee groups in the world. During this period, the Palestinian community has undergone enormous transformations. These transformations have been anything but linear. The refugee experience has been one of perpetual crisis, punctuated by brief periods of quiet and a semblance of safety. The initial trauma of dispossession, statelessness, and exile has been followed by war, sieges, and massacres. Today, Palestinian refugees speak of having less hope for the future than in the immediate past. Despite new efforts to form effective social organizations and negotiate with the Lebanese government for human and civil rights, the refugee camps are once again clearly marked spaces of containment and marginalization, making refugees into social outcasts.

Uncertainty pervades thinking about the present and the future. Excessive focus on today's safety and security, what I term "presentism," has become a conceptual means for Palestinians to deal with a future that promises little but the continuation of a nightmare. Is there a future for the Palestinians in Lebanon? Yes, but it may not be the one that either they or the Lebanese desire.

Notes

1. Judith Herman, *Trauma and Recovery* (New York: Basic Books, 1992), 33.

2. UNRWA Public Information Office, *UNRWA in Figures: Figures as of 30 June 1997* (Gaza: UNRWA, September 1997).

3. UN General Assembly, *Report of the Commissioner-General of the United Nations Relief and Works Agency for Palestinian Refugees in the Near East*, 1 July 1995–30 June 1996, A/51/13 (New York: United Nations, 1996), 46, 80.

4. Herman, *Trauma and Recovery*.

5. Deborah Battaglia, "At Play in the Fields (and Borders) of the Imaginary: Melanesian Transformations of Forgetting," *Cultural Anthropology* 8, no. 4: 430–42; Michel-Rolph Trouillet, *Silencing the Past: Power and the Production of History* (Boston: Beacon Press, 1995).

6. Lebanon, Ministry of Labor and Social Affairs, *Decision no. 289/1*, 18 December 1982.

7. UN General Assembly, *Report of the Commissioner-General*, 80.

8. R. Sayigh, "Palestinians in Lebanon: (Dis)solution of the Refugee Problem," *Race and Class* 37, no. 2 (October–December 1995): 38.

9. U.S. Committee for Refugees, *World Refugee Survey, 1997* (Washington, D.C., USCR 1997), 159.

10. UNRWA Public Information Office, *Field Fact Sheet: Fact Sheet Revision June 1997* (Gaza: UNRWA, 1997).

11. The Women's Humanitarian Organization, Bourj al-Barajneh Camp, Beirut, Lebanon, "Beirut Freeway to Demolish Palestinian Refugee Camp," FOFOGNET, 20 July 1998.

12. Human Rights Watch/Middle East, *Syria/Lebanon: An Alliance beyond the Law: Enforced Disappearances in Lebanon* (New York: Human Rights Watch, May 1997), 1, 21.

4

U.S. Policy toward Lebanon

Kail C. Ellis

Since World War II, U.S. policy toward Lebanon has been determined by attempts to balance U.S. support for the security and well-being of Israel with the need to maintain influence in Arab countries in order to have access to and control over Middle Eastern oil. Prior to the collapse of the Soviet Union, U.S. policy also focused on preventing the Soviet Union from achieving power in the Middle East. Throughout the wars and conflicts that have convulsed the Middle East during the past fifty years, these fundamental goals have remained constant.[1]

During the cold war era, American policymakers who viewed the Middle East and its problems in terms of the balance of power between Washington and Moscow and their respective clients gained precedence over those who preferred to focus on regional problems and the stake of the United States in those regions. To this end, the United States fostered the continuation or establishment of conservative Arab regimes whose economic and military dependence on the United States meant that they tolerated U.S. support of Israel. In the process, an independent Arab policy attuned to American interests was practically abandoned. As a result, the United States lost its standing in the Arab world, pro-Western ruling elites and regimes were weakened, the security of Middle East oil was reduced, and the prospects for terrorism were enhanced. These policy decisions had grave consequences for Lebanon.

The First U.S. Intervention: The 1958 Lebanese Civil War

The United States first intervened militarily in Lebanon on 15 July 1958. In his address to the nation announcing the dispatch of American troops to Lebanon, President Dwight Eisenhower stated that the troops would "demonstrate the concern of the United States for the independence and integrity of Lebanon, which we deem vital to the national interest and world peace."[2]

The 1958 American intervention in Lebanon is best understood in the context of the Arab nationalism, anticolonialism, and opposition to Western-sponsored defense organization proposals that had swept the Middle East after the Egyptian revolution of 1952 brought Gamal Abdel Nasser to power. Nasser's policies came to be identified with the objectives of Soviet Communism,[3] particularly after the 1956 Suez crisis and the declaration of the Eisenhower Doctrine, aimed at controlling Soviet influence in the Middle East, in 1957. The U.S. conviction that intervention in Lebanon was a necessary response to Soviet expansionism was strengthened by the July 1958 Iraqi revolution, which overthrew a pro-Western monarchy and removed Iraq from the Western-sponsored Baghdad Pact. President Eisenhower drew a parallel between the civil war in Lebanon, the Iraqi revolution, and the "pattern of [Soviet] conquest with which we became familiar during the period of 1945–50."[4] By intervening in Lebanon, the United States showed the Soviet Union that it would be frustrated in its bid to become a Middle Eastern power, that the United States would aid its allies when necessary, and, furthermore, that the United States had the strategic capability to react swiftly with conventional armed forces in response to small-scale or "brushfire" conflicts.

Before the July 1958 intervention, however, the United States had become involved in Lebanon in the service of U.S. regional interests. In February 1955, when the Baghdad Pact was formed and Israel raided Gaza, setting off the chain reaction that culminated in the 1956 Suez crisis, Lebanon's political leaders began to debate their country's role in the new power relationships in the Middle East. In March 1957, Lebanon's acceptance of the Eisenhower Doctrine evoked a storm of protest in the Lebanese Parliament. Opposition parties called for the neutrality of Lebanon, rejection of foreign military pacts, and close, impartial, and effective cooperation with other Arab states. They also demanded the formation of a caretaker government to supervise the parliamentary elections slated for June 1957.[5] This so alarmed the United States that CIA officials in Beirut decided to funnel funds to President Camille Chamoun's government to ensure the elections' outcome.[6] The elections resulted in a government victory so substantial that even Eisenhower noted that "excellent moderates among the Arab nationalists had been thrown out of office."[7] Massive evidence that the elections were fraudulent caused the downfall of the Chamoun government and provoked the ensuing civil war.

Irene Gendzier's important study on the 1958 U.S. intervention in

Lebanon maintains that these events underlined Lebanon's role as an important link in the commitment of U.S. military and civilian planners "to assure access to petroleum resources, the construction of bases, the acquisition of air transit rights, and the more general consensus on commercial expansion in the region."[8] The 1958 American intervention in Lebanon, however, did little to resolve the regional issues of the Middle East. American troops withdrew from Lebanon in October 1958, and the Middle East drifted into chaos. The festering Palestinian issue gave rise to the Palestinian resistance movement in 1964, while tensions on the borders between Israel, Jordan, Syria, and Egypt erupted in the June 1967 war.

In the aftermath of the 1967 war, American policy in the region continued to be refracted through a cold war prism. Because the Arabs relied on the Soviet Union for arms and diplomatic support, the United States frustrated Arab demands for a return of Israeli-occupied lands. Israel's military superiority over any Arab coalition was also viewed as a strategic necessity to safeguard Western interests in the Middle East. This policy of continued stalemate was fraught with danger, as the Arab-Israeli war of October 1973 demonstrated. The United States and the Soviet Union struggled to come to terms with each other in a world in which, as U.S. Secretary of State Henry Kissinger said, "both superpowers have acquired the capacity to destroy civilized life in a matter of hours."[9] While the United States sought to contain the Middle East conflict, it remained adamant in seeking to exclude the Soviet Union from the substance of the peace process. Kissinger's step-by-step diplomacy concentrated on Egyptian and Israeli disengagement agreements while ignoring Syria and the Palestinians and, by extension, the increasingly tense situation in Lebanon.

The Civil War of 1975

Lebanon's second civil war broke out in the midst of Kissinger's negotiations for a second Egyptian-Israeli disengagement agreement in 1975. Kissinger feared that the Lebanese conflict had the potential for transforming itself into a general Middle East war.[10] Kissinger favored the continuation of the equitable power-sharing relationship between Christians and Muslims established by the Lebanese National Pact of 1943. He noted that the United States had "a traditional policy of supporting the Christian community," but that given the collapse of Vietnam and the abdication in Angola, "direct military support [to the Christians] was out of the question."[11] The numerical superiority of the Muslim population and the presence of the PLO, which had moved to Lebanon after its expulsion from Jordan in 1970, made the old status quo untenable. The United States confined itself to opposing any foreign intervention in the Lebanese conflict while trying to maintain a balance between the various forces. This policy was enunciated by Kissinger at a press conference on 14 January 1976: "We support the independence and sovereignty of Lebanon. . . . Any outside military intervention, from whatever quarter, would involve the gravest threat to peace and stability in the Middle East; and we have left the parties concerned in no doubt that the United States would oppose any military intervention from whatever quarter."[12]

Kissinger feared that Lebanon would become dominated by the PLO and other radical groups and their Lebanese allies, making Lebanon a permanent guerrilla base against Israel. This fear constituted the framework for his policy of adamantly opposing PLO participation in the peace process. In his view, PLO participation would guarantee a prolonged deadlock and "would raise such life-or-death issues for Israel that all other initiatives would have to be deferred."[13] Although Kissinger also opposed Syrian hegemony in Lebanon, he saw a role for Syria in balancing radical Muslim groups, as long as this did not provoke a Syrian-Israeli confrontation over Lebanon. After Israel came to recognize that there was a significant overlap between its objectives and those of Syria, Syria intervened in Lebanon in June 1976 to end the first phase of the Lebanese war. The delay of two months caused by U.S. opposition to Syrian intervention, however, served to prolong the killing in Lebanon and touched off an international debate.[14]

Israel, the United States, and the Lebanese Civil War

At first, Israel viewed Lebanon's civil war as an opportunity to weaken the Palestinian resistance. Its war against the Palestinians was marked by almost daily incursions into southern Lebanon. Israel increased its military and political involvement with the Lebanese Forces in the north and consolidated its position with the militia of Saad Haddad in the south. When the situation in the south continued to deteriorate, Israel invaded southern Lebanon in March 1978. In response, the United Nations Security Council passed Resolution 425, which called for the unconditional withdrawal of Israeli troops from Lebanon. Israel refused, and its maintenance of a "security zone" and its use of a proxy force, the South Lebanon Army (SLA), remained a major point of contention in its relations with Lebanon.

Israel invaded Lebanon again on 6 June 1982, allegedly with the blessing of U.S. Secretary of State Alexander Haig, a move that severely damaged the reputation of the United States in the Arab world. When Haig was replaced by George Shultz after clashes with the White House staff over his autocratic style and the substance of his actions, hopes arose for a different direction in U.S. policy in the Middle East. During his confirmation hearings, Shultz raised the issue of the Palestinians: "The crisis in Lebanon made painfully clear the urgent need to resolve the problems of the Palestinian people. The peace process had collapsed, and a war process continued to gather momentum."[15]

Initially, Shultz's concern was that the Arab-Israeli peace process, started in 1967 by UN Security Council Resolution 242, reborn in the Camp David Accords, and brought to initial reality in 1979 in the Egyptian-Israeli Peace Treaty, had become a casualty of the Israeli invasion.[16] While acknowledging that the legitimate needs and problems of the Palestinian people must be addressed urgently and in all their dimensions, Shultz reaffirmed the basic tenet of the U.S.-Israeli relationship: "No one should question the depth and durability of America's commitment to the security of Israel or of the United States's readiness to assure that Israel has the necessary means to defend itself." Shultz went on to state: "We owe it to Israel in the context of our special relationship to work with her to bring about a comprehensive peace acceptable to all the parties involved, which is the only sure guarantee of true and durable security."[17]

Shultz saw in Israel's invasion an opportunity to attain a cease-fire between Israel and Syria and achieve a diplomatic arrangement that would get all foreign forces out of Lebanon. If Lebanon could get back on its feet, he reasoned, it could reassert its national identity and develop a stable relationship with Israel.[18] In his attempts to create movement on the Israeli-Palestinian front, however, Shultz became enmeshed in the situation in Lebanon.

Israeli forces reached the outskirts of Beirut on 9 June 1982. Their objective was the destruction of the PLO and its leadership of the Palestinians. The U.S. special envoy to the Middle East, Philip Habib, labored relentlessly to accomplish the PLO's evacuation from Beirut and thereby prevent Israel's first occupation of an Arab capital. On 2 July, Habib met with Lebanese intermediaries who informed him that Chairman Arafat would accept, in principle, the U.S. proposal for the PLO's evacuation. Their final destination, however, needed to be determined. Shuttling between Beirut, Washington, and Jerusalem, Habib worked throughout July and August on finalizing the arrangements. He was hampered by the relentless escalation of Israeli military pressure on the PLO, the numerous violations of cease-fire agreements, Israel's steady advancement into the city, the fate of the refugee camps (which Israel regarded as the source of manpower for the PLO), the circumstances under which the evacuation would take place and whether it would be overseen by a multinational force, and concern over what country would host the PLO. Agreement was finally reached that the PLO would relocate to Tunis, and the bulk of its forces, about 15,000 troops, departed Beirut by land and sea. Arafat followed on 30 August.[19]

The Reagan peace plan of 1 September 1982 attempted to reestablish the peace process between Israel and the Palestinians. Shultz began to view the Israeli invasion as a historic opportunity to accomplish two main goals: the destruction of the PLO and the reconstitution of Lebanon as a pro-Western state.[20] Both goals proved inimical to the peace process. As Shultz directed U.S. policy toward helping the central government of Lebanon regain control over its own country so it could "negotiate a meaningful agreement with Israel,"[21] the United States was increasingly perceived as an unwelcome partisan in the civil conflict. The bombing of the U.S. embassy in Beirut in April 1983 was a blow directed at the American presence in Lebanon.

Undeterred by the bombing, Shultz embarked on negotiating a Lebanese-Israeli peace treaty that would formally terminate the state of war between the two countries and open the stage for normal relations with Israel. The 17 May 1983 agreement failed on two counts: Syria, the power broker in Lebanon, was not involved in the negotiations, and the Israelis would settle for nothing less than a full peace treaty with Lebanon, as they had previously achieved with Egypt. "Egypt was large enough, strong enough, and independent enough to withstand this temporary estrangement [from the Arab world]," said a disappointed Shultz. "Lebanon was not and could not; this the Israelis simply would not understand."[22]

The hostilities continued, and the American presence in Lebanon continued to be resented. On 20 September 1983, the U.S. embassy annex in Beirut was destroyed by a bomb. The news awakened President Reagan's fears of Soviet dominance in the Middle East, according to Shultz: "In my private meeting with President Reagan [21 September 1983] I found him preoccupied with Lebanon: 'Are we going to let the Syrians and Soviets take over? Are we just going to let it happen?' he asked. I was, if anything, even more convinced than the president that we must stand firm in Lebanon, for worldwide as well as for Lebanese considerations."[23]

In October, the U.S. Marine barracks at the Beirut airport were bombed, resulting in a loss of 243 lives. American forces responded from the air and sea against Syrian missiles in the Beqaa Valley and the Lebanese militias in the Shouf mountains. These actions only succeeded in arousing deeper anti-American feelings among the Lebanese who lived in those areas. By March 1984, the situation was seen as hopeless, and U.S. forces were withdrawn. Lebanon rescinded the 17 May 1983 agreement with Israel on 5 March 1984.[24] Shultz blamed Syria and the Israelis for the failure of American intervention: "I made a major effort, and President Reagan and I had set out two frameworks—the September 1 Fresh Start peace initiative and the May 17 Agreement—which, if followed by the parties in the region, could have spared Lebanon a decade of anguish and could have put the Palestinians on the road to greater political rights."[25]

Pax Syriana

After the withdrawal of all U.S. forces from Lebanon in 1984, U.S. policy began to focus almost entirely on securing the release of American and European hostages kidnapped by radical Shi'a groups linked to Hizballah. Among the kidnappers' aims were the release of Shi'ite prisoners in Kuwait and a change in U.S. policy toward Israel. On the issue of Lebanon, American policymakers were content to support efforts initiated and sponsored by Syria and the Arab League and to accommodate Syrian interests in Lebanon.

Lebanon's inability to disarm Hizballah ensured the continuation of a partial U.S. boycott of Lebanon. The U.S. government banned Americans from traveling to Lebanon, excluded Middle East Airlines from American territory, and officially defined Lebanon as "unsafe." This situation made many diaspora Lebanese wary of committing funds to Lebanon except in speculative ventures.[26]

The United States assumed a more active diplomatic role in Lebanon in late 1987 in anticipation of the end of President Amin Gemayel's term in September 1988. In February 1988, Assistant Secretary of State for Middle East Affairs Richard Murphy visited Damascus. In March, April Glaspie, a State Department specialist in Syrian and Lebanese affairs, went to Beirut to help the Lebanese reach a consensus on political reforms and on the selection of a successor to the president. Fearing Lebanon's partition (with all the attendant regional implications) if a presidential candidate was not found, the United States supported Akkar deputy Michail Daher, whose program satisfied Syria and West Beirut. This effort failed, and, a few hours before he left office, Gemayel appointed army commander Michel Aoun to head an interim military government as prime minister. This move precipitated a constitutional crisis and the formation of a rival Muslim government in West Beirut, headed by the incumbent prime minister Salim al-Hoss.

The 1989 Ta'if Agreement

Its efforts to resolve the Lebanese constitutional crisis having failed, the United States returned to its stance of viewing Syria as a useful policeman in Lebanon. Syria's role was to exercise military restraint and deliver the foreign hostages held by the Shi'a Hizballah group. The United States, in return, endorsed Syrian primacy in Lebanon and supported Lebanese presidential candidates with programs acceptable to Damascus. Washington also encouraged an initiative aimed at reforming Lebanon's political system and ending the constitutional crisis generated by the appointment of General Aoun as president. Under the aegis of the Arab League, Syria, with support from Saudi Arabia, summoned the seventy surviving members of Lebanon's Parliament to Ta'if, the Saudi summer capital. In September 1989, after intensive efforts, the Document of National Reconciliation, later called the Ta'if Agreement, emerged.

The Ta'if Agreement became the centerpiece of U.S. policy in Lebanon. It was regarded by Washington as the best means available to forge a settlement among Lebanon's contending political and religious factions. Its provisions guaranteed the presidency of Lebanon to the Christians, ensured the sharing of executive power among the president, the Sunni prime minister, and the Shi'a speaker of Parliament, and equalized Muslim-Christian representation in Parliament. In the process, however, the Ta'if Agreement also formalized Syria's role in Lebanon.[27] The United States was severely criticized for ceding dominance over Lebanon's political system to Syria while at the same time claiming to support Lebanon's independence.[28]

Lebanon and U.S. Strategy in the Gulf

Saddam Hussein's bid to become the dominant power in the Gulf by invading Kuwait in August 1990 reinforced the U.S. conviction that in order to achieve stability in the Middle East, the Aoun crisis in Lebanon had to be resolved. Lebanon's instability was seen as a barrier to the resolution of the Israeli-Palestinian conflict, which had been further aggravated by the Palestinian intifada.

Syria's credentials in the Arab world and its animosity toward the Iraqi regime made it in American eyes the logical choice to help settle the Arab-Israeli conflict, in line with the new world order the United States was trying to establish after the downfall of the Soviet Union. In return for Syria's cooperation, the United States would not only give Syria military dominance over Lebanon but also provide increased access to Western financial aid and technology and, most importantly, help to secure Israel's withdrawal from the Golan Heights. The first part of this understanding was fulfilled in October 1990 when General Aoun was removed from the Lebanese presidency by Syrian forces and forced into exile. With constitutional authority reestablished in Lebanon and the militias dismantled—with the exception of Hizballah in the south—the collaboration between the United States and Syria was sealed.

Operation Desert Storm turned back Saddam Hussein's bid to become the dominant power in the Gulf, and the regional balance of power seemed to tilt back toward moderate forces committed to peace and stability. The United States moved to seize the historic opportunity by sponsoring the Middle East peace conference in Madrid in October 1991. The Madrid conference launched a series of bilateral and multilateral talks that proved useful in shattering taboos on political dialogue and helping each side to recognize the concerns of its opponent. These efforts led to the September 1993 signing of the Israel-PLO Declaration of Principles, which established mutual recognition between Israel and the Palestinians, along with a mechanism for resolving differences through negotiations and compromise. Despite Israel's withdrawal from south Lebanon in May 2000, the success of these negotiations is still awaited.

Instability in Southern Lebanon

The lack of progress in the negotiations between Israel and Syria and Israel and Lebanon was aggravated by the cycle of violence in southern Lebanon occasioned by Hizballah's resistance to the Israeli occupation. Israel launched "Operation Accountability" in July 1993, which targeted the Shi'ite towns and villages of southern Lebanon for the purpose of completely disrupting civilian life, turning civilians against Hizballah, and forcing the Lebanese government and Syria to curb the Islamic "resistance." At least 300,000 people fled to Beirut, and 128 Lebanese and two Israelis were killed. The United States deplored the violence but indicated that it would not intervene in the case of another firestorm. Operation

Accountability was the first installment of Israeli retaliation that endangered the economic and political stability that Lebanon was making after Ta'if.

On 11 April 1996, Israel launched another attack, called "Operation Grapes of Wrath," in further retaliation against Hizballah activities in the south. This time the Israelis ordered 400,000 civilians to leave southern Lebanon and emptied the city of Tyre. For the first time since 1982, the Israelis attacked Beirut's main electrical transformer substations as a warning to the Lebanese that unless they restrained Hizballah, Lebanon's reconstruction—including revenue transfers to Syria—would be in danger. Because of the alarm at the increased escalation, a cease-fire was arranged on 26 April and a monitoring group was established, cochaired by the United States and France, that encouraged Syria and Israel to interact directly to solve the issues between them. The cease-fire did not preclude Hizballah from further action against Israeli occupation forces.

Meanwhile, Lebanon continued to be the main battlefield between Syria and Israel. In August 1998, fighting between Hizballah and Israeli forces again produced a dangerous crisis in southern Lebanon. Setting the tone for future Israeli actions, Israel's minister for internal security, Avigdor Kahalani, and the head of the Knesset Foreign Affairs and Defense Committee, Uzi Landau, called for reprisal raids against Lebanon's newly built infrastructure every time an Israeli soldier was killed in Lebanon. This declaration echoed a 1997 proposal by Ariel Sharon that Israel withdraw unilaterally from southern Lebanon but return in the event of an attack on Israel to strike at Lebanese installations such as water reservoirs and power plants.[29] Sharon's threat was viewed as a direct violation of the April 1996 cease-fire agreement. *Tishrin*, the official Damascus daily, said that abrogation of the 1996 understanding would lead to war between Israel and the combined forces of Lebanon and Syria.[30]

On 25 June 1999 Israel launched another operation called "Bank of Targets" and bombarded Lebanese electrical substations and bridges in its worst attack since 1996. The attack followed Hizballah rocket attacks into northern Israel in retaliation for Israeli attacks in southern Lebanon, resulting in the deaths of civilians on both sides. Bank of Targets was ordered by the outgoing government of Benjamin Netanyahu and occurred at the moment when developments for the resumption of peace negotiations seemed promising. Both Israel's prime-minister-elect Ehud Barak and President Hafiz al-Asad of Syria had made public declarations of their mutual intentions to reopen the peace negotiations, and Barak had promised in his electoral campaign to end Israel's occupation of southern

Lebanon by July 2000. The attack was interpreted by Lebanon's speaker of the Parliament, Nabih Berri, as "aimed at abolishing the 1996 April understanding and to keep Lebanon crippled by an economic war that would render it unable to catch up with globalization and embark on peace."[31] Since Barak's spokesperson claimed that Barak was not involved in the decision to launch Bank of Targets, it was hoped that the attack would be only a momentary setback to the peace process.

The optimism generated by Barak's pledge to withdraw Israeli forces from southern Lebanon by July 2000 faded as Israel's negotiations with Syria broke down over the extent of its withdrawal from the Golan Heights. Nor did Israel's decision to play the Lebanon card by withdrawing unilaterally from Lebanon on 24 May 2000 bring peace or stability to its northern border or to Lebanon. Furthermore, the lack of progress on the Syrian front was matched by the breakdown of the negotiations with the Palestinians and the violence of the al-Aqsa intifada (named after Ariel Sharon's 28 September 2000 visit to the site) against the Israeli occupation of the West Bank and Gaza. The subsequent defeat of Ehud Barak and the election of Ariel Sharon in February 2001 as prime minister of Israel left Lebanon hostage to the vagaries of regional events.

Domestic Organizations and U.S. Policy toward Lebanon

Since the 1970s, domestic organizations in the United States have attempted, with varying degrees of success, to influence U.S. policy toward Lebanon. These organizations fall into two categories: those that focus on issues of general concern to the Arab American community and those founded by Lebanese activists to promote a specific political agenda in Lebanon. A few of these organizations are registered lobbying groups, but most exist for charitable, religious, scientific, or literary purposes, in accordance with guidelines established by the U.S. Internal Revenue Service. Section 501(c)(3) of the Internal Revenue Code prohibits all but incidental activity by organizations that enjoy tax-exempt status "to influence legislation," and it categorically prohibits such organizations from participating "to any extent in a political campaign for or against any candidate for public office."[32]

The oldest Arab American organization, the National Association of Arab Americans (NAAA), was founded in 1972 with the stated goals of strengthening U.S. relations with Arab countries and promoting an even-handed American policy in the Middle East. The NAAA positioned itself as the spearhead of the Arab American community's lobbying activities with Congress.[33] One of its earliest challenges was responding to the 1975 Lebanese civil war and the Palestinian presence in Lebanon. NAAA's attempts to weigh the interests of each of the parties involved, however, led the nascent organization to be riven with the same factions that divided the Arab world. In recent years, NAAA has focused on issues that pertain to U.S.-Arab bilateral relations and the Arab-Israeli conflict, seeking a "permanent end to the occupation of Palestine, Lebanon, and the Golan Heights through the achievement of a comprehensive, just and lasting peace in the region."[34]

The American-Arab Anti-Discrimination Committee (ADC), a civil rights organization, was founded in 1980 by former U.S. senator James Abourezk. The largest Arab American civil rights group, it was committed to defending the civil rights of people of Arab descent. Through its Department of Legal Services, ADC offered counseling in cases of discrimination and defamation and selected impact litigation in the area of immigration.[35] Although not a lobbying group, ADC published newsletters, action alerts, issue papers, and special reports on Middle Eastern issues, including Lebanese issues.

In an attempt to increase their political power and influence, the leaders of the NAAA and ADC announced on 24 December 1999 that they would merge their operations. The merger agreement, which took effect on 1 January 2000, was heralded as a "major step in the development of Arab-American political consciousness and organization."[36] The new entity, NAAA-ADC, combined ADC's tax-exempt subsidiary, ADC Research Institute, with NAAA. NAAA-ADC will continue the NAAA's work as a foreign policy lobbying organization as well as ADC's work in defending civil rights.

A third broad-based group, the Arab American Institute (AAI), was founded in 1985 to represent Arab American interests in government and politics. AAI provides leadership training and strategies in electoral politics and policy issues that concern Arab Americans. It also conducts research on the Arab American constituency and sponsors forums to promote consensus positions on pressing domestic and foreign policy issues, particularly Middle Eastern issues.[37] The broad-based groups have had some success, particularly in promoting issues not opposed by pro-Israeli groups, such as the withdrawal of all non-Lebanese forces from Lebanon and the disarming of Hizballah once Israeli troops have withdrawn from southern Lebanon.

Several Lebanese-centered domestic organizations share the general goal of ending the occupation of Lebanon but differ widely in methods, objectives, and political views. With the exception of the American Task Force for Lebanon (ATFL), these groups have a narrow partisan focus and subsequently less influence than broad-based organizations. They include the World Lebanese Organization (WLO), the United States Committee for a Free Lebanon (USCFL), Americans for a Free Lebanon, the National Alliance of Lebanese Americans (NALA), and the Council of Lebanese American Organizations (CLAO).

The World Lebanese Organization, which lists as its founders Lebanese expatriates who belonged to or supported groups such as the Lebanese Forces, the Lebanese Front, and the South Lebanon Army, stands in direct opposition to broad-based Arab American groups. Advocating agendas such as "the liberation of Lebanon from Syrian occupation and Arab-Islamist domination" and "self-determination for the Christian people of Lebanon," its members present themselves as "the heirs of Emile Eddé, Bishop Ignace Mubarak, and Charles Malek [sic],"[38] all of whom shared anti-Arab, pro-Christian sympathies. The WLO is a strong supporter of the state of Israel, whose founding it regards as a major positive development in the Middle East, showing Middle Eastern Christians that they can achieve a similar state. The WLO is critical of Lebanese Americans of Christian descent who have "historically been the leaders of the Arab lobbies in this country," claiming that "these individuals do not represent the causes of their motherland, [and have] perpetuated the interpretation (and sometimes even advocated the demands) of the Arabists, both in the region and in the United States."[39]

The WLO has launched media and political campaigns in the United States to defend the Christians of Lebanon, particularly those in southern Lebanon. In 1992 it sought to organize Middle East Christians into an alliance called the Middle East Christian Committee (MEHRIC), which would advocate "the legitimacy of the Christian cause in the Middle East" and the opening of "an historical alliance between American and Middle East Christians and American Jews and Israelis." In 1994, it broadened its alliance to include Mideastern, American Christian, and Jewish leaders into a new organization called the Leadership Committee For a Free Middle East. In 1999, the WLO supported H.R. 2056, the Lebanon Independence Restoration Act of 1999. This unsuccessful bill, drafted by New York congressman Mike Forbes, called for sanctions against Lebanon and Syria until all Syrian military, intelligence, and security forces and their proxies and all Palestinian and other terrorist forces have withdrawn from Lebanon. The bill also contained the provision that only when the governments of Lebanon and Syria were certified to have been freely elected and wholly democratic in nature would the withdrawal of Israeli forces from Lebanese and Syrian territory ensue.[40]

Similar in views to the WLO is the United States Committee for a Free Lebanon, which claims to be a resource and educational institute disseminating information on human rights abuses in Lebanon by the "post-Ta'if Lebanese regime" and its "Syrian controllers" to institutions and policymakers in the United States and abroad.[41] Its board of directors includes representatives from national Jewish organizations and from organizations such as American Academics for Israel's Future and the Christians' Israel Public Action Campaign (a U.S. Christian organization registered to lobby Congress on laws and policies related to Israel and to advocate a strong U.S.-Israel partnership).[42]

The Council of Lebanese American Organizations is an association of organizations whose bedrock issues are the withdrawal of all foreign forces—especially Syrian forces—from Lebanon and the restoration of a constitutional government represented by the "legal and legitimate authority" of the exiled prime minister General Michel Aoun.[43] CLAO's goals are shared by Americans for a Free Lebanon, founded in 1997, which is dedicated to providing "accurate, detailed information to the American public and international community about the continuing Syrian and Israeli occupation of Lebanon and the tragic impact of this dual occupation upon the fundamental human rights of the Lebanese people."[44]

On the other hand, the National Alliance of Lebanese Americans, while opposed to Syria's presence and influence in Lebanon, presents itself as a humanitarian group that addresses issues on Lebanon within the context of American national interests.[45] It has testified before the House Appropriations Subcommittee on Foreign Operations on behalf of aid to the Lebanese Armed Forces under the Military Education and Training Program, and on behalf of U.S. financial support for the American University of Beirut and the Lebanese American University under the aegis of the United States Agency for International Development's (USAID) American Schools and Hospitals Abroad program. NALA has called for U.S. support for the repair of Lebanon's infrastructure, including electric generating plants, water purification plants, and telephone and other communication and transportation facilities, and for humanitarian relief channeled through such agencies as the International Committee of the Red Cross and the Catholic Near East Welfare Association.[46]

The most effective Lebanese American group is the American Task Force for Lebanon. ATFL's stated goals are to heighten awareness by the

American public and U.S. government officials and policymakers of the social, economic, political, cultural, and educational situation in Lebanon; to promote the national unity, independence, and security of Lebanon; to encourage greater involvement by the United States in efforts to promote a peaceful settlement of the problems in Lebanon; and to help restore the infrastructure of Lebanon's economic, political, educational, and social institutions.

In 1996, the ATFL was instrumental in securing passage of H.R. 209, which called upon the President to formulate U.S. policy within the framework of the American commitment to preserve Lebanon's territorial integrity, unity, sovereignty, and full independence. H.R. 209 also called for the withdrawal of all non-Lebanese forces from Lebanon without the precondition of a comprehensive peace in the region and for the United States to negotiate directly with Lebanese officials on issues pertaining to Lebanon. ATFL efforts also contributed to the decision by Secretary of State Madeleine Albright to lift restrictions on the use of U.S. passports for travel to Lebanon (30 July 1997); to the end of the ban on the purchase of airline tickets to Lebanon in the United States by U.S. citizens (19 June 1998); to the issuance of a new, milder Department of State travel warning for Lebanon that replaced the word "danger" with the word "risks"; and to the restoration of Fulbright fellowships for American academics studying in Lebanon (fall 1999).

Lobbying by domestic groups has produced tangible financial results. Fifteen million dollars in economic aid to Lebanon was earmarked in the 2000 Foreign Operations Appropriations bill, $4 million of which is to be used for scholarships and direct support for American educational institutions in Lebanon, the Lebanese American University, the American University of Beirut, and International College.[47] There have also been increased commercial contacts between Lebanon and the United States. On 13 November 1998, William M. Daley became the first American commerce secretary to visit Beirut. Addressing government and business leaders at the Beirut Forum, Daley announced that, after years of civil war during which American business abandoned Lebanon, "We can finally say Lebanon is open for United States industry. We have not forgotten old friends. We are back."[48] Daley promised to urge U.S. companies to invest in Lebanon, but he admonished against corruption. "When American companies bid on projects, whether they win or lose," he said, "they expect the bidding process to be transparent and fair."[49] The success of American investment in Lebanon, however, depends as much on regional security as on the integrity of the Lebanese business community. During

Secretary of State Albright's second trip to Lebanon on 4 September 1999, her Lebanese hosts made the point that the U.S. government must protect its investors, investments, and projects in Lebanon by restraining Israel from further attacking Lebanon's infrastructure.[50]

The American Catholic Church and U.S. Policy toward Lebanon

The National Council of Catholic Bishops (NCCB) is another domestic organization that has expressed concern over developments in Lebanon and the status of Christians in the Middle East. The bishops of the two Maronite dioceses in the United States are NCCB members and have taken a role in policy making on Middle Eastern issues. In November 1996, the president of the NCCB, Archbishop Anthony Pilla, wrote to Lebanese Maronite patriarch Nasrallah Sfeir to express concern over Israel's Grapes of Wrath bombardment of Lebanon. The archbishop denounced Israeli attacks on innocent civilians in Lebanon, defended the cause of Lebanon's sovereignty, and reaffirmed the NCCB's concern that Lebanon be treated as a full partner in the Middle East peace process. He stated that the American bishops have continued to press the case of Lebanon with representatives of the U.S. government and to make their commitment known to the American people. "At the same time," Archbishop Pilla continued, "conference staff intervened with the National Security Council to reprove the Administration's seeming indifference to Lebanon's suffering, and to assert the centrality of Lebanon's Christians to the survival of the Christian presence in the Middle East."[51]

NCCB statements reflect the ongoing concern of the Vatican about Lebanon's involvement in the Middle East conflict. During the Lebanese civil war, the Vatican opposed the partition of Lebanon to create a Christian ministate, much to the dismay of Lebanese Christians, especially Maronites. Archbishop Jean-Louis Tauran, the Vatican's assistant secretary of state, explained the Vatican's position: "The rallying cry was to some extent 'Let us save Lebanon to save the Christians' (and not 'Let us save the Christians to save Lebanon!')."[52]

In the view of the Holy See, it is only through national and regional coexistence that Lebanese believers—including Jews, Christians, and Muslims—can safeguard the identity of their community. During Pope John Paul II's visit to Lebanon in May 1997, the pope stated that he wished "to declare before the world the importance of Lebanon and its historical mission which has been accomplished down through the centuries. A country of many religious faiths, Lebanon has shown that these

different faiths can live together in peace, brotherhood and cooperation."[53] Archbishop Tauran reiterated this position in 1999, stating that
Lebanon was not merely a country but "rather 'a message,' to use an
expression so dear to Pope John Paul II."[54]

The Future of U.S.-Lebanese Relations

In September 1997, Madeleine Albright became the first secretary of state
to visit Beirut in thirteen years, a visit that signaled a transformation in the
attitude of the United States toward Lebanon (and that had been preceded
by the lifting of restrictions on travel to Lebanon from the United States,
despite opposition within the State Department). Speaking to a group of
Lebanese business leaders, politicians, religious figures, media representatives, and former ambassadors, Secretary Albright repeated President
Clinton's statement that "a stable, independent, and economically vibrant
Lebanon is an important national interest for the United States."[55] Secretary Albright's address outlined the issues that will define the future
of U.S.-Lebanese relations. They included continued assistance to the
Lebanese Armed Forces to help it evolve into a disciplined, unified, and
nationally respected military force, international aid for Lebanon's social
reconstruction and economic reform, encouragement of elimination of
restrictions on freedom of the Lebanese press, and the prosecution of individuals responsible for crimes against Americans during the Lebanese war.

Secretary Albright observed that the failure to negotiate a comprehensive peace in the region continues to limit Lebanon's rightful sovereignty,
and she reiterated the U.S. view that any lasting settlement between Lebanon and Israel must include true security for Israel, full sovereignty for
Lebanon over all its territory, and real peace with normal relations. Absent
a lasting peace settlement, the United States will continue to support the
efforts of the Israel-Lebanon Monitoring Group to protect civilian lives
and reduce the incidences of violence.[56]

Secretary Albright's statements did not anticipate the December 1999
negotiations between Israeli prime minister Ehud Barak and Syrian foreign minister Farouk al-Sharaa on Israeli withdrawal from the Golan
Heights. At the time, it even appeared that Lebanon would be at the negotiating table for the first time since 1993 and that progress could be sought
in Lebanon as a preliminary step toward resolving Lebanon's and Syria's
differences with Israel. Given the lack of progress on that track, Palestinian-Israeli negotiations were to remain the U.S. priority.

During her 1999 visit, Secretary Albright also made it a point to reiterate the U.S. commitment to Lebanon's full independence, sovereignty, and territorial integrity and to the withdrawal of all foreign forces. She stated that she had come to the Middle East to explore the possibilities for a comprehensive peace between Israel and its Arab neighbors, and this included Lebanon. At a joint press conference held with Prime Minister Salim al-Hoss, the prime minister raised the issues of Israeli withdrawal from Lebanon and the legitimate rights of the Palestinians to return to their homeland, stating that "the Lebanese agree unanimously on rejecting Palestinian implantation in Lebanon."[57] Secretary Albright, however, would not affirm his statement, responding that "the refugee issue is a permanent status issue and one that will be discussed in that context."[58] Because prominent Lebanese figures such as the Maronite patriarch and the National Party leader Dory Chamoun have rejected any regional settlement that would include permanently settling the Palestinians in Lebanon,[59] Prime Minister al-Hoss was asked if the American position was clarified during the discussions with Secretary Albright. He replied: "We are directly concerned with the issue of the Palestinian refugees in Lebanon, so we cannot really accept saying that the matter will have to be relegated to the final status talks between Palestinians and Israelis. We think that Lebanon should be a party to any such talks because it is hosting such a large number of refugees."[60]

Israeli occupation of southern Lebanon remained the focal point of Lebanese-Israeli negotiations and, by extension, of U.S. policy. On 1 April 1998, following several months of debate, the Israeli cabinet formally accepted the 20-year-old UN Security Council Resolution 425 calling for Israel to withdraw from Lebanese territory. Prime Minister Netanyahu stated that "The meaning of this decision is that Israel is expressing formally here for the first time, in a detailed and organized fashion, its seriousness and determination to leave Lebanon linked to the required security arrangements."[61] Israel's conditional acceptance of Resolution 425, however, was not acceptable to Lebanon, which feared renewed Israeli incursions should "required security arrangements" prove impossible to maintain.

U.S. Secretary of Defense William Cohen agreed with Lebanon that Resolution 425 is not conditional. However, he also stated that Lebanon should take the Israeli proposal seriously. Secretary of State Albright concurred. According to Albright, it was only by progress in the Arab-Israeli peace negotiations that Lebanon's full independence, sovereignty, and territorial integrity would be promoted.[62]

The election of Ehud Barak as Israel's prime minister in early 1999 and Barak's commitment to withdraw Israeli troops from southern Lebanon by July 2000 had contradictory effects. While it accelerated hopes for peace in the region, it also raised fears that the withdrawal would be linked to the continued Israeli presence on the Golan Heights. When, through the efforts of the Clinton administration, peace talks between Israel and Syria resumed in December 1999, after a hiatus of three years, there was renewed hope that talks would resume between Israel and Lebanon. On a visit to Beirut on 20 December 1999, Syrian foreign minister al-Sharaa stated that Syria would not be negotiating with Israel on Lebanon's behalf, opening the way for Lebanon to negotiate directly with Israel. On 24 December Israel announced that a five-man committee had been appointed to direct forthcoming peace talks with Lebanon. All of these efforts, however, failed with the breakdown of the Israeli-Syrian negotiations, the death of President Hafez al-Asad, on 9 June 2000, and the election of Ariel Sharon in February 2001 as Israel's prime minister.

Conclusion

For the foreseeable future, the United States will continue to pursue a pragmatic policy in Lebanon, grounded in fifty years of regional policy objectives. While it will continue to call for a Lebanon that is fully independent, unified, and sovereign and free of all foreign forces, U.S. policy will acknowledge Lebanon's close connection to Syria as stated in the Document of National Reconciliation: "There exist between Lebanon and Syria distinctive relations which derive their force from the roots of propinquity, history, and common filial interests. This is the foundation on which coordination between the two countries shall be based."[63]

For Lebanon and its supporters in the United States, the linkage of Lebanon's involvement in any peace process with Syria and Israel will be problematic. Before the failure of the Syrian-Israeli peace negotiations, the United States urged Lebanese officials to negotiate directly with Israel on issues pertaining to Lebanon. The prospect of Lebanon negotiating independently, however, conflicted with Syria's interest that progress on the Syrian and Lebanese fronts be simultaneous. Each of the two countries has promised not to make peace without the other and not to compromise on basic demands for the full withdrawal of Israeli forces from Lebanon and Syria. If Lebanon is to assert an independent stance, high-level meetings between U.S. and Lebanese officials will be essential to provide a measure of diplomatic cover and support for Lebanese officials, even as the United States continues to balance Lebanese interests with those of Syria and Israel.

An Israeli-Palestinian agreement and an Israeli-Syrian agreement are essential for stable peace in the region. Lebanon's stake in the agreement is that it not be required to "implant" hundreds of thousands of Palestinians. Both Palestinians and Lebanese reject naturalization as a solution to the status of the Palestinian refugees. For Palestinians it would endanger their claim to the right of return to Israel/Palestine. For Lebanon, it would compromise its delicate demographic balance. Given that Israel has refused to accept the right of return of the Palestinians and the remoteness of an Israeli-Palestinian peace agreement, there is a pressing need for a modus vivendi that will address the economic, social, educational, and political situation of the Palestinians who remain in Lebanon. Increased U.S. involvement in the peace process will be necessary to achieve a solution. More immediately, the United States must provide more incentives for U.S. companies who commit to doing business with Lebanon. U.S. investments in reconstruction projects and other humanitarian aid that directly improve the condition of the Lebanese and the Palestinians will be the minimum necessary to foster stability and prosperity in Lebanon.

Notes

1. For a list of eight policy goals in the Middle East, see "U.S. Policy toward the Middle East: Steering a Steady Course," address by Assistant Secretary of State Robert H. Pelletreau before the Chautauqua Institution, Chautauqua, New York, 21 August 1996, 2. U.S. Department of State, Dispatch, Bureau of Public Affairs, 7, no. 35 (26 August 1996).

2. U.S. Department of State, "Statement by President Eisenhower, White House Press Release dated July 15, 1958," *Department of State Bulletin* 39 (4 August 1958): 181.

3. Dwight D. Eisenhower, *Waging Peace, 1956–1961* (New York: Doubleday and Company, 1965), 177.

4. "Statement by President Eisenhower following the Landing of United States Marines at Beirut, July 15, 1958," cited in Robert L. Brayon and Lawrence H. Larsen, *The Eisenhower Administration, 1953–1961: A Documentary History*, vol. 2 (New York: Random House, 1971), 725–26.

5. Fahim I. Qubain, *Crisis in Lebanon* (Washington, D.C.: Middle East Institute, 1961), 53–54.

6. Wilbur Carne Eveland, *Ropes of Sand* (New York: Norton, 1980), 252.

7. Eisenhower, *Waging Peace*, 265.

8. Irene L. Gendzier, *Notes from the Minefield: United States Intervention in Lebanon and the Middle East, 1945–1958* (New York: Columbia University Press, 1997), 6.

9. "Global Peace, the Middle East, and the United States," address by Secretary Henry Kissinger, *Department of State Bulletin* 73 (6 October 1975), 496.

10. Henry Kissinger, *Years of Renewal* (New York: Simon and Schuster, 1999), 1027.

11. Ibid., 1024.

12. "Press conference, 14 January 1976," in *Department of State Bulletin* 74, no. 1910 (2 February 1976): 132.

13. Kissinger, *Years of Renewal,* 1029.

14. Special Envoy to Lebanon Dean Brown said that the U.S. government had "made a mistake" in discouraging Syria from sending troops into Beirut in April. "We reined in the Syrians too much to please the Israelis and it resulted in a lot more killing," said Brown. See David Binder, "Envoy Says U.S. Erred in Beirut Policy," *New York Times*, 27 May 1976, 3.

15. George Shultz, *Turmoil and Triumph* (New York: Charles Scribner's Sons, 1993), 43.

16. Ibid., 85.

17. Ibid., 22.

18. Ibid., 44.

19. Ibid., 62–84.

20. Michael C. Hudson, *From Lebanon to "Irongate": A Review of Recent American Middle East Policy* (Washington, D.C.: Center for Contemporary Arab Studies, Georgetown University, 1987), 8.

21. Shultz, *Turmoil and Triumph,* 109.

22. Ibid., 225.

23. Ibid., 226–27.

24. Elie A. Salem, *Violence and Diplomacy in Lebanon: The Troubled Years, 1982–1988* (London: I. B. Tauris Publishers, 1995), 138–42.

25. Shultz, 227.

26. William W. Harris, *Faces of Lebanon: Sects, Wars, and Global Extensions* (Princeton, N.J.: Markus Wiener Publishers, 1997), 284.

27. "Lebanon, which is Arab in its belonging and identity, has close filial ties to all the Arab states. There exist between it and Syria distinctive relations which derive their force from the roots of propinquity, history, and common filial interests. This is the foundation on which coordination between the two countries shall be based" ("The Ta'if Agreement," *Beirut Review* 1 (Spring 1991): 171).

28. "Treaty of Brotherhood, Cooperation, and Coordination Concluded between Lebanon and Syria on May 22, 1991," *Beirut Review* 1, no. 2 (Fall 1991): 115–19.

29. Serge Schmemann, "Israel Offers Pullout If Lebanon Bars Raids," *New York Times*, 2 April 1998.

30. Michael Jensen, "Violence in the South," *Middle East International* (4 September 1998): 13–14.

31. Zeina Abu Rizk, "Differences Set Aside as Politicians Unite," *Daily Star* (Beirut), 26 June 1999 (http://www.dailystar.com.lb/26_06_99/art5.html).

32. Internal Revenue Service, "Tax Exempt Status for Your Organization," Publication 557, rev. November 1999, cat. no. 46573C, 14 (http://ftp.fedworld.gov/pub/irs-pdf/p557.pdf).

33. The National Association of Arab Americans (http://www.cafearabica.com/organizations/orgnaa.html).

34. Ibid.

35. "ADC Mission Statement" (http://www.adc.org/mission.html).

36. *New York Times*, 25 December 1999.

37. "AAI Mission Statement" (http://www.arab-aai.org.aboutaai/index.html).

38. "WLO Founding" (http://www.wlo-usa.org/founding.html). Emile Eddé was a Francophone president of Lebanon, known for his anti-Arab sentiments; Ignatius Mubarak was the Maronite archbishop of Beirut. In 1947 Monsignor Mubarak presented a memorandum to the United Nations Special Committee on Palestine in which he declared that "to consider Palestine and Lebanon as parts of the Arab world would amount to a denial of history." The archbishop also declared that Lebanon as well as Palestine should remain as permanent homes for the Christian minorities of the Arab world. See Labib Zumiyya Yamak, "Party Politics in the Lebanese Political System," *Politics in Lebanon*, ed. Leonard Binder (New York: John Wiley and Sons, 1966), 151. Archbishop Mubarak's letter was reported in the Beirut daily *Al-Diyar* on 27 September 1946, with the result that he was, reportedly, reprimanded for his position by the Maronite patriarch, relieved of his ecclesiastical duties, and exiled to a monastery. See William W. Haddad, "Christian Arab Attitudes toward the Arab-Israeli Conflict," *Muslim World* 67 (April 1977): 130; Laura Zittrain Eisenberg, *My Enemy's Enemy: Lebanon in the Early Zionist Imagination: 1900–1948* (Detroit: Wayne State University Press, 1994), 142–43. Charles Malik was Lebanon's foreign minister during the 1958 crisis, ambassador to the United States, and secretary-general of the United Nations.

39. Walid Phares, "The Oppression of Middle East Christians: A Forgotten Tragedy" (http://www.foigm.org/IMG/phares1.html).

40. "The Full Test of HR 2056 'Lebanon Independence Restoration Act of 1999' Syria out of Lebanon, U.S. Sanctions until full withdrawal," published by the World Lebanese Organization (WLO) (http://www.wlo-usa.org/ALPAC/HR2056_6_15_99.html).

41. USCFL Board of Directors (http://www.freelebanon.org/board.html).

42. Ibid.

43. Council of Lebanese American Organizations, "Membership Criteria and CLAO Bedrock Issues" (http://www.clao.com/membership.html).

44. "About AFL" (http://www.aflnet.com/information/).

45. "NALA as an Organization" (http://www.nala.com/nala/NALAORG.html).

46. "Testimony of the National Alliance of Lebanese Americans Submitted to the House Appropriations Subcommittee on Foreign Operations," 24 April 1997 (http://www.nala.com/Editorial/TEST97.html), and "Testimony of the National Alliance of Lebanese Americans Submitted to the House Appropriations Subcommittee on Foreign Operations," 31 March 1998 (http://www.nala.com/Editorial/H033198.html).

47. 106th Cong., 1st sess., 2000, calendar no. 159, *Foreign Operations, Export Financing, and Related Programs, Appropriations Bill, 2000, S. 1234 and H.R. 2606* (http://thomas.loc.gov/cgi-bin/query/C?c106:./temp/~c1067uHhzG; http://thomas.loc.gov.cgi-bin/query/D?c196:6:./temp/~c106Mer5j0:e17039): "The Committee is aware of the vital work being done at the local level by existing AID programs in Lebanon. It is also aware of the long-term benefits derived from ongoing support for American institutions of learning in Lebanon such as the American University of Beirut, the Lebanese American University, and International College. The Committee urges the Administration to provide an increase for scholarships and other direct support to these institutions through appropriate funding mechanisms."

48. "Remarks by U.S. Commerce Secretary William M. Daley to the Beirut Forum, Beirut, Lebanon, November 13, 1998" (http://www.doc.gov./OPA/Speeches/beirut.html).

49. Ibid.

50. "Secretary of State Madeline K. Albright and Lebanese Prime Minister Salim al-Hoss, joint press conference, Beirut, Lebanon, 4 September 1999" (http://secretary.state.gov/www/statements/1999/990904d.html).

51. "Anthony M. Pilla, Bishop of Cleveland, President NCCB/USCC, letter of 13 November 1996, to Nasrallah-Peter Sfeir, Patriarch of Antioch and the Whole East," National Conference of Catholic Bishops, Office of the President (http://www.eparchyla.org/bishops.html).

52. Archbishop Tauran, "The Church's Approach to the Middle East," *Origins* (CNS documentary service), 28, no. 39 (18 March 1999): 686.

53. "John Paul II in Lebanon: Going Forward Together on the Path of Peace and Friendliness," *Origins,* (CNS documentary service) 27, no. 1 (22 May 1997): 15.

54. Tauran, "The Church's Approach," 685–86.

55. Secretary of State Madeleine K. Albright, "Remarks at the Beirut Forum, Beirut, Lebanon, 15 September 1997," as released by the Office of the Spokesman in Larnaca, Cyprus, U.S. Department of State (http://secretary.state.gov/www/statements/970915.html).

56. Ibid. After Israel's Operation Grapes of Wrath attack in April 1996, a monitoring group, including the United States, France, Lebanon, Syria, and Israel, was established to supervise implementation of the agreement and to receive com-

plaints of violations in south Lebanon. In addition, the withdrawal agreement called for the establishment of a consultative group, including the United States, France, the European Union, Russia, and other interested parties, to help Lebanon in its reconstruction efforts. *Lebanon Report* 2 (Summer 1996): 9.

57. "Secretary of State Madeleine K. Albright and Lebanese Prime Minister Salim al-Hoss, joint press conference, Beirut, Lebanon, 4 September 1999" (http://secretary.state.gov/www/statements/1999/990904d.html).

58. Ibid.

59. Patriarch Sfeir stated in a interview with the Kuwaiti newspaper *Al-Rai al-Am* that "We call on the United Nations to solve the refugee issue as quickly as possible, but not at Lebanon's expense" (*The Daily Star on line*) (http://www/dailystar.com.lb/14_08_99/art7.html).

60. "Secretary of State Madeleine K. Albright and Lebanese Prime Minister Salim al-Hoss, joint press conference, Beirut, Lebanon, 4 September 1999" (http://secretary.state.gov/www/statements/1999/990904d.html).

61. Serge Schmemann, "Israel Offers Pullout If Lebanon Bars Raids," *New York Times*, 2 April 1998.

62. "Secretary of State Madeleine K. Albright and Lebanese Prime Minister Rafiq Al-Hariri, Press Availability Prior to Their Meeting Washington D.C., June 16, 1998," as released by the Office of the Spokesman, United States Department of State (http://secretary.state.gov/www/statements/1998/980616.html).

63. "The Ta'if Agreement," *Beirut Review* 1 (Spring 1991): 171.

Part II

Religion, Culture, and Gender

5

Muslim-Christian Relations in Lebanon

A Christian Perspective

Paul Nabil Sayah

Muslims and Christians have lived together in Lebanon since the beginning of Islam, often sharing the same villages and honoring each other's religious festivities. Their coexistence has been marked by cooperation as well as by conflict, by trust as well as by suspicion. To a greater degree than in neighboring countries, Christians and Muslims in Lebanon have shared a mutual sense of freedom, prosperity, and security.

Since Lebanon first became a republic in the 1920s, the ability of Lebanese to act as citizens rather than as members of a particular religious confession has been a fundamental issue of Lebanese democracy, an issue reflected in Lebanon's confessional system of government. Muslim-Christian relations continue to have a major influence on the country's culture, politics, and economic development.

The weakness of Lebanon's confessional system of government, which divides political and administrative responsibilities among Lebanon's religious communities, is that it has encouraged in its citizens the sense of belonging to a particular community rather than to the country at large. Its strength is that it has prevented the total subordination of the minority to the majority that can occur in a pluralistic society, as Jean-Pierre Valognes affirms: "If political confessionalism does deprive some communities of access to positions that they could democratically reach, it allows them all to live in a free and pluralistic system which exists nowhere in the area. And unfortunately one finds nowhere an example which could reassure the Lebanese Christians in case they are ruled by a Muslim head of state."[1]

In the broadest sense, Christians in Lebanon have traditionally identified themselves as "Lebanese" and Muslims as "Arabs," but both groups have striven to set aside these differences in order to forge a mutual national identity. In the 1989 Ta'if Agreement, which marked the end of fifteen years of civil war and set the stage for Lebanon's Second Republic, the Muslims renounced unity with Syria in exchange for the Christian concession that "the Lebanese agreed . . . to commit themselves to Lebanon as the definitive country for all its people, in its internationally recognized borders, with its Arab identity and membership of the Arab League."[2]

This chapter analyzes the past, present, and future of Muslim-Christian relations in Lebanon from the point of view of a Christian striving for peaceful coexistence with Muslim fellow citizens and neighbors.

Relationships among Lebanon's Religious Communities

Lebanon recognizes eighteen official religious communities. Primary among these are two Muslim communities, the Sunni and the Shi'a; two Christian communities, the Maronite and the Orthodox; and the Druzes, a heterodox community with Egyptian roots.

Relations within and among these communities are intricate. In Islam, there is no clear distinction between *din wa dawlat* (religion and state). In Christianity, though, the two are not synonymous, with the result that in Lebanon there is confusion between the Church as a spiritual entity and the religious community as a political reality. The Orthodox differ from the Maronites in their relations with the Sunnis, and the Maronites differ from the Orthodox in their dealing with the Druzes and Shi'a. The Muslim communities themselves have different political agendas and inclinations, agendas that are open to change.

On the interaction between the Maronites and the two Muslim communities, Georges Corm wrote, "If the Maronite culture is auto-centered, rooted in the Lebanese mountain, with a long history of openness and friendly relations with the West, this is not the case for the Shi'a or Sunni cultures; the latter is basically motivated by its relations with the great centers of Islamic religious culture in Cairo or Damascus for the Sunni, and in Iran or Iraq for the Shi'a. However there has been recently a greater openness to the West, peaceful at times and problematic at other times."[3]

The Sunni

The Sunni traditionally are an urban community and had more exposure to Orthodox Christians than to Maronites prior to Lebanese independence. Although the Sunni agreed to renounce external attachments and enter into power sharing with the Maronites as part of the National Pact of 1943, which granted the position of Lebanese prime minister to a Sunni, they have repeatedly been drawn to alliances with other groups. Sunni allegiance to Egypt's Gamal Abdel Nasser and Arab nationalism in the 1950s was a factor in the 1958 Lebanese civil war. In 1969, the Sunni openly declared themselves on the side of the Palestinians, and the Sunni prime minister opposed the deployment of the Lebanese army to deal with the PLO. During the civil war that began in 1975, the Sunnis created an alliance with Islamic-progressive forces, in the hope of making the PLO the army that would fight their battle for the domination of Lebanese politics over the Maronites, whose numbers and influence were in decline.

The Sunni political establishment has continually reassessed the Lebanese political situation, shifting its allegiances when necessary. In the words of Valognes: "Hence a hesitant march watching the evolution of the war. In 1982 when the Israeli intervention appeared, for a little while, to give an advantage to the Maronites, the Sunnis voted for Bashir Gemayel in the presidential elections, and when he was assassinated they backed his brother Amin and then cooperated with him for a few months after his election."[4]

The Sunni public, however, responded readily to Arab-Islamicist appeals, including calls for the implementation of Muslim Sharia law in Lebanon. In this they were supported by some of their religious leaders. Other Sunni religious leaders, including the mufti of the republic, Hassan Khaled, denounced such extremism. Khaled established rapprochement with the Maronite patriarch, a decision that sadly led to Khaled's 1986 assassination. In response, the patriarch opened a book of condolences for the mufti at his residence in Bkerke, which was signed by many people unable to pay their respects to the mufti in West Beirut because of travel restrictions imposed by the war.

Because the Sunni relied mainly on the PLO in their military battles with the Christians, their own military force was quickly neutralized by the Druzes and Shi'a (with Syrian approval), after the PLO left Beirut in 1982. At this point, Sunni support for a new national pact with the Maronites increased, and with this support the Ta'if Agreement became a reality. There is still much work to be done, however, before the principles set forth by Ta'if are widely accepted by the Sunni public.

The Shi'a

The Shi'a are traditionally a rural community that has lived side by side with Christians in many parts of Lebanon, continuing to do so throughout the civil war. Their interactions with Christians, however, have been limited. Shi'a wealth is concentrated in the hands of a few powerful feudal families, and the majority of Shi'a are economically underprivileged, a situation compounded by their high rate of demographic growth. The Shi'a are not Arab nationalists but rather allies of Iran and its brand of Islamic fundamentalism. They did not favor the establishment of Greater Lebanon in the 1920s but found it preferable to a Sunni-dominated state. (The National Pact of 1943 granted the Shi'a the presidency of the Lebanese Parliament, putting them in a subordinate position to the Sunni.)

In December 1967, the Lebanese Parliament voted to establish the "Supreme Islamic Shi'a Council," whose mission was to look after the interests of the community and to establish a distinctive Shi'a identity. This coincided with increased migration of Shi'a to urban areas, particularly the southern suburbs of Beirut. Urban migration, however, did not result in economic improvement for the Shi'a.

A new Shi'a leader, Sayyed Musa al-Sadr, emerged in the 1960s but disappeared in 1978 and is presumed dead. The Amal movement tried to continue his work. Shi'a fundamentalism, however, came to be associated with Hizballah under the leadership of Sayyed Mohammad Hussein Fadlallah. Fadlallah openly asserts that he intends to make Lebanon an Islamic state in which minority nonbelievers will have three options: adopt Islam; pay *jiziah* (the poll tax) while "utterly subdued"; or face war.[5] Shi'a fundamentalism in Lebanon has been nourished by the indifference of its own leaders to Shi'a poverty, as well as by the support of Iran.

There are many moderates in the Shi'a community, however, and the Supreme Islamic Shi'a Council has an agenda opposed to that of Hizballah. Its representative, Dr. Seoud al-Mawla, states, "We wish to have a pact which would organize the co-existence of Muslims and Christians in Lebanon, creating a unified society respecting the diversity of its citizens, based on mutual respect, equality and justice for all. . . . The basis for true and sound co-living is knowledge and freedom. True knowledge of the others (as they wish to be known) is a prelude for the respect of their rights and especially the right to be different."[6]

Shi'a support for the abolition of the Lebanese confessional system, however, paves the way for the dominance of a Muslim majority. The Shi'a are increasingly influential in Lebanon. After the departure of the PLO from Beirut in 1982, the Shi'a gained control of the western part of the city. Encouraged not only by Iran but also by Syria, the Shi'a increased their resistance against Israel in southern Lebanon.

The Druzes

The Druzes have lived in the mountain regions of Lebanon since fleeing Egypt in the tenth century. Although the Ottomans considered the Druzes to be Muslims, "the Druze faith is syncretistic . . . it has some basis in Greek philosophy and Hinduism, both foreign to Islam."[7] The Druzes closely guard the rituals of their faith, whose details are revealed only to those initiated within the community.

The Druzes were traditionally aligned with the Maronites, with whom they shared mountain life, a religion looked on with suspicion by Islam, and a strong feudal tradition. The Druzes and Maronites worked cooperatively under the *millet* rule established by the Ottoman Turks in the sixteenth century, and by the eighteenth century the Druze emirate had officially converted to Christianity in the Maronite confession. This alliance, however, was shattered by the bloody Maronite-Druze civil wars of 1845–60. The Maronites found it hard to forget massacres at the hands of the Druzes, and the Druzes never forgave the French and other Europeans for their intervention in favor of the Maronites.

In the 1950s, the Druzes joined the wave of Arab nationalism that was sweeping Lebanon along with the rest of the Middle East. The Druze leader, Kamal Jumblat, became a strong opponent of the Maronites. During the 1975–90 civil war, the Druzes shifted allegiances several times. At first they maneuvered between the Palestinians, whom they supported in the name of progressive Arab nationalism, and the Syrians; their troubled alliance with the Syrians led to the 1977 assassination of Jumblat. After the assassination, the Druzes tried to reestablish good relations with the Maronites in the Shouf mountains. In 1982, they made an arrangement with the invading Israeli forces. When the Israelis withdrew, however, Maronite-Druze animosities erupted in some of the worst massacres of the war, and Druzes expelled Christians from the Shouf.

Recently, the Druzes allied themselves with the Maronite Chamoun family in the Shouf municipal elections, which could be read as a sign of future Druze-Maronite cooperation. Druze relations with the Palestinians and the Sunnis are in decline. Whether the progressive Druzes can manage an alliance with the religious fundamentalist Shi'a, as well as a future relationship with Syria, remains unclear.

The Maronites

The largest Christian community in Lebanon is that of the mountain-dwelling Maronites, named for a legendary fifth-century ascetic monk. The Maronites have drawn strength from their Christian traditions and their strong ties, dating to the Crusades, with the Vatican, France, and other European powers. The Maronite emphasis on education and freedom has been a source of Maronite political and cultural power. (The National Pact of 1943 granted the presidency of Lebanon to the Maronites.) Maronites also contributed greatly to the culture of the Arab Renaissance, despite their preference for a Lebanese identity rather than Arab.

Maronite alliances with Zionists and Israel, fostered by the pro-Western outsider status of both groups, date to the 1920s. These alliances were strengthened by the mutual opposition of Israel and the Maronites to the Palestinians during the 1975–90 Lebanese civil war. The Maronites, however, realize the pitfalls of their relationship with the Israelis; even pro-Israeli Lebanese president Bashir Gemayel was aware that a full alliance with Israel could render national reconciliation impossible.

Early in their struggle with the Palestinians, the Maronites looked to Syria for support. When they realized that Syrian occupation of Lebanon compromised the sovereignty and independence of their country, however, the Maronites turned against Syria.

In the midst of sectarian struggles, the Maronite Church has continued to call for the safeguarding of Lebanese freedom, independence, democracy, human rights, and territorial integrity. The Maronite patriarch has remained open to dialogue with the Muslims, sometimes against the wishes of Maronite political leaders.

The Orthodox

The second largest Christian community in Lebanon, the Orthodox, has been a predominantly urban community since the days of the Byzantine Empire, living side by side with Muslims in Tripoli and Beirut and making its living in commerce and finance. There is also an Orthodox presence in rural areas, particularly Mount Lebanon, where Orthodox have lived in the same villages as Druzes and Maronites.

Unlike the Maronites, the Orthodox have traditionally favored Arab nationalism and a policy of Christian integration into the Arab world. The Orthodox have strong ties with Syria; many are members of the Syrian National Social Party, founded by the Orthodox Antoun Saade. (The founder of the Syrian Ba'th Party, Michael Aflak, was also an Orthodox Christian.) The Orthodox patriarchate is based in Damascus, and Syria may make use of this to counteract the influence of Christian religious leaders in Lebanon.

The Orthodox political elite, however, has been very much part of the Lebanese political establishment, serving in key positions in various governments. Orthodox politicians such as Charles Malik have played significant roles locally and internationally. The first president of Lebanon in 1926 was an Orthodox Christian, and since the signing of the National Pact of 1943, the deputy prime minister has usually been Orthodox.

During the civil war of 1975–90, the Orthodox did not enter the armed conflict as a community, although some individual Orthodox engaged in the struggle on the side of the Palestinian forces or as members of leftist political parties. The Orthodox political elite has inclined toward political conservatism, however, and the Orthodox Church has continued to promote Christian-Muslim entente.

Despite its moderate stance, the Orthodox community suffered equally with Maronites during the civil war, as no distinction was made between one Christian and another in West Beirut or in the Shouf mountains. This experience has led some Orthodox intellectuals to reverse their stance on Arab nationalism, as continuing Muslim-Christian conflict casts doubts on the peaceful integration of Christians into a Muslim-dominated state.

The Future of Muslim-Christian Relations

An examination of some recent documents issued by various Christian gatherings or official councils demonstrates the nuances of how Christians see the future. The most significant among the documents are the three pastoral letters issued by the Catholic Patriarchs of the Orient;[8] the *Post Synodal Apostolic Exhortation (PSAE)*;[9] the pastoral letter issued by the Heads of Churches in the Middle East;[10] and the memorandum handed to the prime minister of Lebanon by the Maronite patriarch during his visit on 6 March 1998, titled "The Truth about the Crisis."[11]

Christian Self-Perception

Christians are called upon to become conscious of their identity and to be guided not by their own private interests but by authentic Christian principles. The Catholic patriarchs, in their Easter 1992 pastoral letter, stated: "Our Christian presence in this part of the world does not intend to be only for ourselves, because Christ did not institute the Church to serve its own children only, but to serve others as well and be a witness to all."[12] The same principle was stated in the *Post Synodal Apostolic Exhortation*.[13] Christians perceive themselves not only as an integral part of the area but also as important contributors to its cultural development. The Orthodox patriarch of Antioch, Ignatius IV Hazim, went so far as to say that "the Christians in this part of the world are the hosts of the Muslims" because Christians were here for centuries before the Muslims arrived. Christians and Muslims have worked together since the early days of Islam to build a common Arab culture. In the nineteenth century, Christians, the Maronites in particular, played a fundamental role in the Arab Renaissance. This role was underlined by the Catholic patriarchs in their 1992 pastoral letter: "We Muslims and Christians share in a unique heritage in a civilization that we have both enriched by bringing to it our own contributions. The Arab Christians are an integral part of the cultural identity of Muslims just as Muslims are an integral part of the cultural identity of Christians. We are responsible for each other before God and humanity."[14]

Unity in Diversity

Despite common cultural factors, Christians are conscious of their own identity and are very eager to preserve it and be able to develop it freely. A future environment must take into consideration their aspirations to live and develop freely according to their beliefs and traditions. Developing one's own identity means bringing in whatever is unique in each community to add to the total heritage enjoyed by all. This was affirmed by the Catholic patriarchs in their statement: "Muslims and Christians together we can enrich each other and each country of the region. . . . If we are divided our countries will be all the poorer."[15]

In order to be able to enrich each other, it is very important that each community be able to be itself, accepted as different, and known by the other as it wishes to be understood. The *Post Synodal Apostolic Exhorta-*

tion stated: "When the Lebanese learn to know each other and fully accept their diversity, then they will have realized the necessary condition for a true dialogue and the respect of persons as well as families and religious communities."[16]

Freedom, Equality, and Justice for All

Christians feel that, unless freedom of conscience and belief are secure, the very existence of Lebanon will be threatened. This is a basic condition to secure human dignity and basic human rights. The *Post Synodal Apostolic Exhortation* is very clear on this point: "No one ought to be subjected to coercion by individuals, groups or social authorities, nor should anyone be alienated from social life because of his/her opinions or prevented from practicing religious beliefs or voicing what his/her conscience dictates."[17]

Christians look forward to a society in which all citizens are equal before the law and able to exercise their full rights and assume their responsibilities. Whenever people, and especially the younger generations, are deprived of their rights and are not allowed to assume their individual or social responsibilities, they are liable to develop a feeling of alienation and lose their sense of belonging. Moreover, experiences of injustice and deprivation of basic rights can often lead to mistrust, withdrawal, or violent behavior. It is understood that the way of life the Christians are seeking to establish is not for themselves only, but for all Lebanese citizens.[18]

Obstacles to Peaceful Christian-Muslim Coexistence

There are a number of obstacles to peaceful Christian-Muslim coexistence in Lebanon. Chief among these are the continuing presence of Syrian and Israeli troops, Palestinian refugees, and illegal Syrian workers; the unresolved displacement of Lebanese citizens, including many Christians, by the civil war; and the precarious position of Christians in Lebanese political life since the signing of the Ta'if Agreement.

The Foreign Presence in Lebanon

In order to secure freedom and independence for Lebanon, all foreign troops must withdraw in accordance with UN resolutions 425 and 520.[19] The Israeli invasion of southern Lebanon caused considerable suffering and hardship, and the 26-year presence of more than 40,000 Syrian troops has neither prevented repeated Israeli invasions nor helped Lebanon to manage its own affairs. On the contrary, the Syrians have made Lebanon totally dependent on their military presence.[20]

The Maronite patriarch and bishops have repeatedly called for Syrian withdrawal from Lebanon on the grounds that Syrian occupation threatens Lebanese democracy and the fair and peaceful coexistence of Lebanon's religious communities. "When will we put an end," they ask, "to the reliance of the Lebanese government on foreign support which is used by one faction to gain the upper hand over the other (i.e., mainly on the Christians)? Why are the relations with Syria not established upon the principle of fidelity to our country and the equal safeguard of the interests of both Lebanon and Syria?"[21]

There are one million illegal Syrian workers in Lebanon, whose cheap labor compromises the Lebanese economy and amounts to an economic invasion, costing Lebanon millions of dollars a day in foreign currency. The presence of 400,000 Palestinian refugees in Lebanon also compromises Lebanon's economy and security. When other foreign workers are added to these figures, it becomes clear that Lebanon's 3.5 million citizens are living in the shadow of 2.5 million foreigners.

Displacement of Lebanese Citizens by the Civil War

Eighty percent of the Lebanese citizens displaced by the war were Christian, but only 20 percent of these have been able to return to their homes. Government assistance to Christians was under 30 percent of the total assistance distributed, and some assistance went to citizens who did not qualify as displaced. The government admitted that justice had not been done. Fifteen percent of the assistance money was simply wasted, and a disproportionate amount went to people that the Solidaire Company needed to evacuate from downtown Beirut.

The Catholic Church has attempted to remedy the situation by giving, through Caritas Liban, about $12 million in U.S. dollars for reconstruction and rehabilitation projects.[22] It has been aided in this effort by the Middle East Council of Churches. Neither organization bases its assistance on religious affiliation.

No real reconciliation between Christians and Muslims can take place as long as displaced persons feel cheated out of their right to return to their homes. If the displaced Christians do not return, religious segregation will become a fact of Lebanese life, undoing a centuries-old tradition of side-by-side coexistence.

Christians in Lebanese Political Life after Ta'if

Many Christians feel that the Ta'if Agreement has been violated by a government that gives political precedence to Lebanese Muslims.[23] The Maronite patriarch and bishops made these feelings plain in a memorandum to Prime Minister Rafik al-Hariri: "National reconciliation could be realized through the implementation of the Ta'if Agreement both in its letter and spirit. Otherwise there is a risk that the attempt at national reconciliation could degenerate into an entente among those in government to serve their own individual interests, with the backing of foreign forces, more eager still to serve their own interests. National reconciliation can be brought about only through an agreement on the common values of freedom, democracy and independence . . . and an equitable sharing in government between Muslims and Christians."[24]

In the 1992 elections, the majority of Lebanese (87 percent) did not vote. The Christians called for a boycott of the elections because they felt that their candidates were disadvantaged by "a selective method . . . employed with the aim of influencing election results in favor of some politicians or communities over others."[25] In the wake of the elections, the country was divided into electoral constituencies of unequal sizes, a grave violation of the Ta'if Agreement. In the 1996 elections, Christians were once again discriminated against.[26] This was confirmed by the Constitutional Council, which judged the electoral law, as applied, to be unconstitutional.[27] The Christians, particularly the Maronites, felt that they were being alienated from public life, with administrative posts being allocated on the basis of political allegiance to the current government. This generated a feeling of injustice, lack of trust in the government, and lack of confidence in the future.[28]

Lebanon's demographic balance has also shifted since the civil war. Increased emigration rates for Christians and the grant of nationality to Muslim immigrants have resulted in a Muslim majority. This imbalance will become more profound if the 400,000 Palestinians refugees, 90 percent of whom are Muslim, become de facto Lebanese citizens. Christian resentment has been provoked by the fact that some recently naturalized Muslim families were registered to vote in the Maronite villages of Matn and Kesrowan, where they have neither homes nor property, at the same time that displaced Christians have been unable to return to their homes.[29]

When the Christian Party of the Lebanese Forces was dissolved and its leader imprisoned because of his alleged role in the bombing of a church (a charge of which he was acquitted), some government officials acknowledged that his prosecution was politically motivated. At the same time, other leaders who participated in the war were given ministerial posts in the government. Christians who lived in the former Israeli security zone in southern Lebanon felt abandoned by the government and lived in constant fear and under great pressure to emigrate.[30]

Despite their fears that Lebanon is losing an important part of its national character, the majority of Christians feel that they must face their difficulties with hope and determination. "Hope urges them," as stated in the Post Synodal Apostolic Exhortation, "to assume their responsibilities, without hesitation, in Spirit and Truth, trusting in God and in their fellow citizens, in order to make their social and national life increasingly more just and friendly."[31] This same attitude is recommended by the Catholic patriarchs in their 1991 pastoral letter: "The difficult circumstances we are facing should not make us run away, withdraw or melt into the larger environment, but rather go back to the roots of our faith where we will find new strength and greater self confidence."[32]

The Role of Christian-Muslim Dialogue in Promoting Peace

Christian-Muslim dialogue is essential to removing the obstacles to peace in Lebanon. True dialogue means an attitude of willingness to advance together. True dialogue fosters reconciliation, mutual trust, and respect for each other's identity and differences. Dialogue presupposes a practice of active listening and honest expression of ideas and feelings, along with a sincere willingness to know the other and to understand how the other's thought and behavior have been shaped by experiences and environment. Finally, dialogue presupposes an openness to meet the other at the deepest possible level in order to discover truth and good.[33]

Christians and Muslims must establish a positive and receptive attitude in their dealings with one another. "Christians face many problems today," wrote the Heads of Churches in the Middle East in their January 1998 pastoral letter, "but they are not alone in being aware of problems and the things which stimulate fear. Many Muslims also see that what causes Christians anxiety should be a concern for all citizens in society."[34]

Muslim and Druze delegates at the Synod for Lebanon stated repeatedly that Lebanon needs the cooperation of all its sons and daughters in order to build its own identity. "No religious group can survive unless it is accepted and recognized by the others. If it is put in an insecure position, it will find it very difficult to share in the life of the nation."[35] Many Lebanese Muslims share the belief that the Christian presence in their

country has given it a special character. In 1986, Moshen Slim, a prominent Muslim attorney in Beirut, wrote the following to Pope John Paul II:
"If the Christians of Lebanon were to leave the country permanently, or
submit to the law of numbers, Lebanon would not be itself any longer; it
would become like any other Arab or Muslim country of the region and
would then lose its *raison d'être*."[36]

The unity of Lebanon and the rebuilding of good relations among its
citizens remains the responsibility of all. In 1994, the Catholic patriarchs
called for Muslim support in this effort. "Muslims," they wrote, "bear a
heavy responsibility in this matter. They are all called upon to make the
Christians feel secure, which means making them feel an integral part of
society, full members with equal rights and duties."[37] Without Muslim
acknowledgment and respect for Christian rights, the patriarchs continued, Lebanon cannot be a free republic: "Any national project which does
not take into consideration the pluralistic character of the society, or is
unable to deal with this plurality in a positive way is doomed to failure."[38]

Conclusion

What will relations among the Muslim and Christian communities of
Lebanon be like in the twenty-first century? A hopeful note was sounded
by a 1997 study of 17- and 18-year-old Christians and Muslims in Beirut,
conducted by the Institute for Educational Development. Over 85 percent
of the young people surveyed said that they would like to make friends
with Lebanese of the other religion. Despite the conflict, violence, and
hatred fostered by the years of civil war, it seems that Christians and
Muslims in Lebanon remain open to dialogue and the possibility of peaceful coexistence in a free republic.

Much has been said and written recently about the renewed eagerness
to bring Lebanon back to its special vocation, a privileged space of Christian-Muslim encounter—in the words of the pope, not merely a country
but a message for the world. The Islamic-Christian Committee for National Dialogue reiterated this vocation in its *Unified Working Paper:*

> Lebanon, as a state and an entity, is based on a formula of coexist-
> ence. This is a formula of human entente which unites around it the
> Lebanese in their various spiritual families. It was expressed in the
> National Pact (1943) and the Document of National Entente (1989),
> and embodied in the Constitution of the Lebanese Republic (1990)
> which states in its Preamble that "there is no legitimacy for any

authority that contradicts the Charter of coexistence." This charter provides scope for all citizens to fulfill themselves completely, in authentic diversity and harmonious integration with each other, in the framework of a unified state based on law.[39]

Written agreements, no matter how valid, cannot automatically change deep-seated memories, attitudes, and suspicions. In the new century, all Lebanese must recognize that peaceful coexistence is not a finite commodity but an ongoing process. The willingness to engage in this process will determine whether Lebanon can ensure justice, equality, and freedom for all its citizens. If the Lebanese want to preserve the uniqueness of Lebanon and continue its development as stated in its constitution, both Christians and Muslims must focus on the country as a whole rather than on their individual communities.

Notes

1. Jean-Pierre Valognes, *Vie et mort des Chrétiens d'Orient, des origines à nos jours* (Paris: Fayard, 1994), 655.

2. Islamic-Christian Committee for National Dialogue, "A Working Paper," n. 1.

3. Georges Corm, *Geópolitique du conflit Libanais* (Paris: La Découverte, 1986), 68, quoted by Valognes, *Vie et mort*, 673.

4. Valognes, *Vie et mort*, 675.

5. Mohammad Hussein Fadlallah, "Islamic Reflections on Minority Status," *Al-Muntalak*, nos. 81–82 (July 1991): 10.

6. Seoud al-Mawla, "Christian Muslim Dialogue and the New World Order," *An-Nahar*, 12 August 1994.

7. Georges Kodr, "Le Liban religieux," *Proche Orient 5* (1994).

8. The three pastoral letters are "The Message of the Catholic Patriarchs of the Orient," Easter 1991; "The Christian Presence in the Orient, Mission and Witness," Easter 1992; and "Together before God for the Good of the Person and Society," Easter 1994.

9. "New Hope for Lebanon," *Post Synodal Apostolic Exhortation (PSAE)*, n. 92. This is a document of about 200 pages (in its Arabic edition) issued on 10 May 1997, on the occasion of the pope's visit to Lebanon. It is the final document resulting from the Special Synod for Lebanon.

10. This is a short pastoral letter (two-and-a-half pages), issued by nineteen heads of churches from all four Christian families: Eastern Orthodox, Oriental Orthodox, Evangelical, and the Roman Catholic Church. All the churches are members of the Middle East Council of Churches, and their statement was issued

at the end of a meeting held in Cyprus on 24 January 1998, upon the convocation of the Middle East Council of Churches.

11. "The Truth about the Crisis," n. 6. This is a 12-page memorandum in Arabic, handed to the prime minister, Mr. Rafik al-Hariri, on the occasion of his meeting with the Maronite patriarch and some bishops on 6 March 1998. In it is stated the opinion of the Maronite Church on the performance of Mr. Hariri's government in general terms and more specifically in the economic, social, administrative, and political spheres.

12. "The Christian Presence in the Orient, Mission and Witness," n. 92.

13. *PSAE*, n. 45.

14. "The Christian Presence in the Orient, Mission and Witness," n. 92.

15. "Together before God for the Good of the Person and Society," n. 14.

16. *PSAE*, n. 92.

17. Ibid., n. 116.

18. Ibid., nn. 96 and 115.

19. In 1978, after the Israeli invasion of parts of Lebanon, the United Nations Security Council issued Resolution 425 calling on Israel to withdraw from areas occupied in Lebanon. Israel withdrew partially to what has come to be called the security zone. After the 1982 Israeli invasion, the Security Council issued, in 1982, Resolution 520 calling on all foreign forces to withdraw from Lebanon. Israeli forces withdrew up to the security zone, but Syrian forces gradually reoccupied the areas they had evacuated under pressure from the invading Israeli army.

20. Archbishop Yousef Bechara, "What the Christians Require from the Civil Society," *An-Nahar Supplement*, 7 March 1998.

21. "The Truth about the Crisis," n. 6.

22. *Report of Caritas Liban*, 12 March 1998.

23. The Ta'if Agreement is a new national pact signed by the Lebanese deputies in Ta'if, Saudi Arabia, in October 1989. It adopts the basic principles of the 1943 version, including a clear statement that Lebanon is a country explicitly for all its citizens. It also places in the hands of the government some of the executive powers that had hitherto belonged to the president of the republic.

24. "The Truth about the Crisis," n. 6.

25. For a thorough study of the Lebanese elections of 1992, see Farid Khazen, *Lebanon's First Postwar Parliamentary Election, 1992: An Imposed Choice* (Oxford: Center for Lebanese Studies, February 1998). On the 1996 parliamentary elections, see Farid Khazen, "The 1996 Elections: The Extension of Imbalance," in *The 1996 Parliamentary Elections and the Crisis of Democracy in Lebanon*, 269–306, unpublished paper.

26. "The Truth about the Crisis," n. 6.

27. "Ruling of the Constitutional Council," *An-Nahar*, 9 August 1996.

28. Ibid., n. 5.

29. "The Truth about the Crisis," n. 6.

30. Ibid.

31. *PSAE*, n. 32.

32. "The Message of the Catholic Patriarchs of the Orient," Easter 1992, quoted in *PSAE*, n. 33.

33. *PSAE*, n. 36.

34. Pastoral letter issued by nineteen leaders of churches from all four Christian families, Cyprus, 24 January 1998. See note 10.

35. *PSAE*, n. 12.

36. Quoted in Valognes, *Vie et mort*, 674.

37. "Together before God for the Good of the Person and Society," n. 15.

38. Ibid., n. 25.

39. Islamic-Christian Committee for National Dialogue, "A Working Paper," n. 3.

6

Religion and Politics

The Case of Lebanon

Mohammad Sammak

The relationship between religion and politics can be defined in many different ways and embraces two mutually contradictory ideas. The first is that there is a strict divide between a person's religious convictions and his or her political actions. The second is that there is a strong connection between a person's religious convictions and political actions, that is, that religion is a force that unites daily life with a global moral order. The second idea has been reinforced by the globalization of economics and technology, not merely as a result of impersonal market forces but as a result of a vast social transformation. Cultural relativism, the notion that morality is specific to individual cultures, is now widely reviled.

A third idea of religious-political conviction, however, rejects the claim of universality of moral values as a continuation of Western dominance, a form of colonialism that attempts to impose Judeo-Christian and Enlightenment principles on the non-Western world. It would be oversimplifying a delicate issue to say that this view is held only in the Islamic Middle East. Even in secularized Europe, as Bosnia, Kosovo, and Northern Ireland demonstrate, questions of political dominance and religion are entwined. In the Islamic world, however, a revolt against decay and humiliation has led to a return to Muslim roots.

Only time will determine the depth of this Islamic revolt and revival. It may prove to be superficial, lasting no longer than the Christian revival in Victorian England (although that revival spanned two-thirds of a century and helped to build the British Empire). Or it may be as inexorable as the Protestant Reformation, which survived despite the attempt of the Council of Constance to stamp it out in 1415 and caught fire in 1517 when Martin Luther nailed his Ninety-five Theses to the church door at

Wittenberg. Nonetheless, its consequences are being felt in every country with a Muslim population. This is true whether Muslims greatly outnumber non-Muslims, as in Egypt, whether Muslims are greatly outnumbered by non-Muslims, as in India, or whether Muslims enjoy a slight majority over non-Muslims, as in Lebanon.

What makes religious politics dangerous is the idea that political decisions are perceived as orders from God, that is, religious leaders act not as representatives of the people but as representatives of God, and opposing them becomes an opposition to the sacred and the holy. In Lebanon, where there are eighteen religious communities, each with its own leader, opposition to the sacred and the holy also comes from the sacred and the holy. This chapter argues that the real differences among these communities stem not from disputes about religious doctrine but from long-standing disputes of history and power sharing, disputes that affect day-to-day political decisions. It also contends that dialogue between Muslims and Christians is key to resolving the differences among these communities.

Religious Diversity and Political Conflict in Lebanon

The Middle East has several characteristics that make it susceptible to foreign intervention: its strategic location between East and West; its abundance of gas and oil; the fact that it contains important Jewish, Christian, and Muslim shrines; and its ethnic and religious diversity.

The region's ethnic and religious diversity became a liability when the European powers tried to use minorities as a wedge to conquer and dominate the Middle East. History demonstrates how European (and later American) missionaries used Christianity to draw non-Muslim minorities to Western interests, even at a time when the Church was being isolated from public life in Western democracies. Western interests exploited the legitimate sufferings of religious and ethnic minorities for political reasons, not religious or humanitarian reasons.

Since the early 1950s, Israel has attempted to create a Christian ministate in Lebanon (or in a part of Lebanon) with the expectation that its creation would be a catalyst for other religious and ethnic communities to establish ministates of their own, thus accomplishing Israel's strategic objective of conquering Lebanon by dividing it. This struggle was at the heart of Lebanon's 1975–90 civil war.

The civil war was manipulated and funded by regional and international powers and fought by proxies. During the war, hard currency and advanced armaments and ammunition poured into Lebanon from different sources: Israel, the Arab countries, and non-Arab countries. Immediately after the cease-fire, foreign assistance stopped and the Lebanese economy almost collapsed. Financing a war of fifteen years' duration would have been impossible for the Lebanese alone, just as it would have been impossible for any of the country's religious communities to sustain or end the conflict.

During the civil war, Lebanese religious leaders kept a distance between themselves and the local militias. They never approved the military actions of any side nor gave their blessings to any of the warlords. When the national entente, embodied in the Ta'if Agreement of 1989, was approved by members of the Lebanese Parliament, the support of religious leaders was urgently needed to help its implementation, a process of reconciliation that balances religious and confessional interests rather than eradicating them.

This policy of national reconciliation seeks to soothe without conquest, to indoctrinate without force, to accomplish social evolution without a common historical memory. The Lebanese have to get to know one another better and to discuss their disagreements with civility, although in politics, civility is an inflated virtue. It is desirable that political debate be conducted in a spirit of mutual respect rather than enmity. The plea for more civility in politics, however, is often a high-minded way of pleading for less-critical scrutiny of illicit campaign contributions or other misdeeds.

Thus, a healthy civil society is important not only because it promotes civility (although this may be a welcome by-product) but also because it generates the habits, skills, and qualities of character that create effective democratic citizens. The institutions of civil society draw individuals out of their private, self-centered concerns and create in them the habit of attending to the common good. Today, these institutions are under siege in every democratic country, but even more so in Lebanon. From families and neighborhoods to cities and towns, from schools to congregations and trade unions, the structures that traditionally provided people with a moral anchor and a sense of belonging have become exceedingly strained.

A century and a half ago, Alexis de Tocqueville praised America's vibrant civil society for producing the "habits of the heart" on which democracy depends. If families, neighborhoods, and schools are in ill repair, they will fail to produce the active, public-spirited citizens a successful democracy requires, regardless of the citizen's religion.

Rebuilding Lebanon's national unity, in addition to its other advantages, will serve as a necessary spur to increased foreign aid and economic investment. Both governmental and nongovernmental agencies, for example, are urging the return to their homes of Lebanese displaced by the civil war. This issue demonstrates the difficulties in achieving national unity. Although most displaced Lebanese want to return to their original homes, some displaced families are hesitant due to the traumas they have suffered, while those who are now living in the areas affected by the displacement are apprehensive about the return of those who were displaced.

Christianity, Islam, and the Quran

Islam does not differentiate ethnically between Arabs and non-Arabs; it recognizes Judaism and Christianity as having the same roots as Islam, which is grounded in the Abrahamic faith. Messages of religious tolerance found in the Quran have provided theological underpinning for policies of tolerance that allowed ethnic and religious minorities to flourish and preserve their identities throughout the periods of Islamic rule.

In Islamic theology, Islam starts with Abraham and ends with Muhammad (peace be upon them). Islamic theology emanates from a series of prophets, including Moses and Jesus. Thus, Muhammad is not the first Muslim, but the last Muslim prophet.

The Holy Quran speaks highly of Jesus and his mother, the Virgin Mary. One verse of the Quran says, "[N]earest among them in love to the believers wilt thou find those who say 'we are Christians,' because amongst these are men devoted to learning, and men who have renounced the world, and they are not arrogant" (al-Ma'ida, 73). This verse provides a theological basis for Christian-Muslim understanding and brotherhood, one that has fostered Arab-Christian-Muslim nationality and Lebanese national reconciliation.

Islamic belief in Christianity as a revealed message from God is deeply rooted in Islamic teachings. The Quran says, "The same religion has He established for you as that which He enjoined on Noah, that which we have sent by inspiration to thee and that which we enjoined on Abraham, Moses and Jesus: Namely, that ye should remain steadfast in religion, and make no division therein" (al-Shura, 130).

This Quranic dictum, in Imam Abu Hanifah's interpretation, is that "religion is One, and religious laws are different" (wahdat al-din wa ikhtalaf al-shara'ia). The Quran states the same idea in slightly different words: "To each among you has He prescribed a Law and an open way. If Allah had so willed, He would have made you a single people, but (His plan is) to test you in what He hath given you. So strive as in a race in all virtues" (*al-Ma'ida*, 47).

Although a religion of absolute truth, Islam respects and preserves the right of individual belief, as the following verses from the Quran demonstrate:

I showed him the way: whether he be grateful or ungrateful. (*Younas*, 99)

If it had been by the Lord's will, they would all have believed, all who are on earth. Wilt thou then compel humankind against their will to believe? (*al-Insar*, 30)

One of the prominent followers of the prophet Muhammad, Ibn al-Abbas, told a story about Abu Hussein, a Christian in al-Madina, who became a Muslim and tried unsuccessfully to convince his two sons to believe in Islam. He threatened them with all his means, but they insisted on remaining Christians. Abu Hussein then sought the prophet Muhammad's advice. At that moment, a revelation came to the Prophet, which established the majesty of religious freedom:

La ikrahah fi ad-din gad tabi'ayn al-rushd min al-ghi.

[Let there be no compulsion in religion: truth stands out clearly from error.]
(*al-Bagrah,* 256)

It is important to note that the Quran is a scripture revealed by God, and as such, it is not only sacred but absolute. Its understanding and interpretation, however, are a human process, and everything human is relative. Human interpretation becomes like any other human thought; it is mobile, that is, open to change and reconsideration. This is *ijtahad* (innovation).

The Islamic-Christian Committee for National Dialogue

In August 1993, the Islamic-Christian Committee for National Dialogue was established in Lebanon. The committee's objective is to preempt any imbalance that endangers the coexistence of Christians and Muslims, including that caused by international events that have sectarian or confessional dimensions. The committee is called upon to emphasize civic spirit, eliminate sectarian fanaticism, rewrite the history of unified Lebanon in a way that accords with these trends, and create a permanent dialogue between the state and the people, as well as between Christians and Muslims of different confessions. Through this dialogue, the committee hopes that Lebanon may take part in other dialogues on the future of the Middle East. As part of its program, the committee organizes seminars and conferences and issues media statements.

Muslim-Christian dialogue in Lebanon has many dimensions but is rooted in the search for truth in the point of view of the other. Truth is not one sided. Even if one side believes it is right, that does not mean that the other side is wrong.

The forms of Muslim-Christian dialogue fostered by the committee are defined as follows:

- A "Dialogue of Life," meaning to understand and recognize the other's background and special characteristics. This helps to build a common life as neighbor or friend with a person of a different religious community.
- A "Dialogue of Action," meaning to work together socially, economically, and educationally. This helps to build relationships based on common interests.
- A "Dialogue of Discussion," meaning to explore commonalities in morals and ethics among different religious communities. This helps to encourage understanding and respect of other faiths.
- A "Dialogue of Experiences," including religious experiences, meaning to recognize that it is possible to worship God, the same God, differently.

The Lebanese do not want Lebanon to be simply an additional Arab state in the Arab world. Lebanon is, in the core of its being, a quintessential message of tolerance, mutual respect, and coexistence. Any harm to this message, either from within or without, harms humanity. Dialogue not only safeguards Lebanese national unity but provides a basis for Arab-Muslim-Christian dialogue and better Christian-Muslim understanding on the international level.

Conclusion

The future of humanity should not be based on the conflict of civilizations but rather on the complementary dialogue of civilizations, the core of which is contained in both Islam and Christianity. The Quran sets forth an unequivocal message of harmony for humankind:

"O humankind! We created you from a single (pair) of a male and female, and made you into nations and tribes, that ye may know each other (not that ye may despise each other). Verily the most honored of you in the sight of Allah (He who is) is the most righteous of you, and Allah has full knowledge and is well acquainted (with all things). (*al-Haqrat*, 130)

7

Lebanon as a Regional Educational and Cultural Center

Nabeel F. Haidar

Many countries have adopted ideologies and pedagogies that regulate education. Some of these systems are open and permissive, while others are rigid. All hold two fundamental principles in common: that the goal of education is the formation of children into responsible citizens and that the state should have a decisive say in education.

Like other countries, Lebanon has a free public school system with a prescribed curriculum, along with a thriving network of private schools. Until the severe disruptions of the 1975–90 civil war, Lebanese universities and colleges attracted students from all over the world and made Lebanon the cultural and educational center of the Middle East. With its vibrant secular society, Lebanon remains unique and uniquely attractive among Arab countries.

Lebanon now faces two profound educational challenges: to regain its position as a regional cultural and educational center and to forge the identity of the Lebanese citizen, particularly in the wake of constitutional agreements that pledge Lebanese of all religious communities to commit to a national affiliation and purpose. This chapter explores the prospects for Lebanon's educational system in the new century.

Lebanon's Private and Public Schools

Less than 35 percent of Lebanon's children attend public school. The majority are enrolled in private Christian and Islamic schools, whose fees range from moderate to high in comparison with family income. In 1997–98, 576,000 Lebanese children attended private schools, while 303,000 attended public schools. Clearly, many Lebanese families feel that private schools have a distinct advantage over public schools, both in quality of education and availability of religious instruction.

There are two types of private schools in Lebanon: schools conceived, administered, and supported by religious organizations, either Christian or Islamic, and lay schools that have no religious affiliation. Both types of schools implement the basic curriculum prescribed by the Lebanese government as a minimum requirement, then supplement this curriculum with subjects pertinent to the aims and purposes of the individual school. Private Christian and Islamic schools add religious history and instruction to their curricula. Private schools established by foreign organizations add the founding country's languages, history, and culture to their curricula; Lebanon contains private schools established by French, German, British, and American entities. Schools established by foreign organizations and schools established by indigenous lay organizations supplement the basic government curriculum with courses in higher mathematics, the sciences, and the humanities. In short, the Lebanese private school offers a public school curriculum plus a curriculum that reflects the values of the school's founders.

The supplemental curriculum provided by private Christian and Islamic schools has come under fire from Lebanese who believe that these schools are building the good Christian or Muslim citizen rather than the good Lebanese citizen. Private lay schools have been subjected to criticism that they promote cultural indoctrination or that they are operating simply from a profit motive. The years of civil war have fueled demands that private schools be closed or that their "suspicious" activities be closely monitored.

As in other countries, Lebanese public schools suffer from poor management and resources, ill-prepared teachers, and outmoded educational methodology, making private schools an attractive choice for many families. Attendance in private religious schools cuts across sectarian lines: many Christian schools have a high percentage of Muslims among their students, and in south Lebanon and north Lebanon, Christian schools serve a predominantly Muslim population.

Despite the claims of critics, the success of Lebanon's private schools has not contributed to the weakness of its public schools. If courses in culture and foreign languages were added to the public school curriculum, public school education would be more competitive with private school education, preparing students for an increasingly global marketplace.

All public and private schools in Lebanon are bilingual, with Arabic as the first language and French or English as the second language. This makes even Lebanese public schools superior to the public schools of other Arab countries, whose curricula do not stress foreign languages. Instruction in the foreign language starts along with Arabic in nursery school and kindergarten. In middle school and senior high school, the foreign language becomes the language of instruction in mathematics and sciences. In the first year of middle school, a third language is added as an elective course.

Lebanese private schools are far ahead of the public schools in the quality of language instruction. Currently, public schools graduate "bilingual" students who usually have only a weak knowledge of the second language, while private schools graduate students who are proficient in three languages. Fluency in two, three, and four languages gives Lebanese students and citizens a definite economic edge. Multinational corporations are recruiting Lebanese university students over students from other Arab countries because of their language proficiency.

Although Lebanon's educational system has had solid academic successes, it has failed in forging the identity of the Lebanese citizen. Part of the solution is to focus on the common values held by all communities regarding the education of children. All education, including religious education, should include the teaching of tolerance and acceptance of differences. The diversity of Lebanese culture should not only be respected but celebrated for the many benefits it brings to Lebanese society.

Recent efforts to rewrite and unify the Lebanese history curriculum and to develop a civic education curriculum are positive but will fall short if the methodology is restricted to lecturing and sermonizing. Practical methods through which students learn democratic practices, including peaceful conflict resolution, should become central to the curriculum. New information technologies that emphasize analysis and communication have revolutionized modern education and created ample time and space in the curriculum to explore issues of citizenship and national identity.

Lebanese schools have long been distinguished by their independent spirit, a spirit that reflects the essence of the Lebanese people. In many Lebanese schools, freedom of expression is encouraged as an integral part of the educational process. In Lebanon, rather than memorizing the speeches of their country's leaders, students are taught to analyze them. Dissent is encouraged over passive acceptance of official political dogma. This spirit can provide the basis for the formation of the new Lebanese citizen.

Lebanon's Public and Private Universities

Lebanon has one large public university, the Lebanese University, which has a full-time faculty of 2,000 and over 50,000 students enrolled in six branches. The Lebanese University offers a wide variety of majors and very low tuition (250,000 LL or $165 per year). Lebanon's eight private universities, in contrast, charge tuition ranging from $3,000 per year to $20,000 per year, depending on the university and the subject of study. The oldest of these universities is the American University of Beirut (established in 1866), followed by the University of Saint Joseph (established in 1875) and the Lebanese American University (established in 1924).

Private Lebanese universities were the pride of the Middle East until 1975, when the Lebanese civil war began. These universities made Lebanon the educational center of the region, producing many leaders, including businessmen, statesmen, engineers, and doctors. Students from countries such as Syria, Jordan, Egypt, Palestine, Kuwait, Iraq, the United Arab Emirates, Saudi Arabia, Cyprus, Greece, Pakistan, Iran, Afghanistan, India, and Yemen were drawn by the reputation of Lebanese universities as well as by the lack of educational opportunities in some of their own societies. The Lebanese American University had as its special mission the education of hundreds of women, many of whom in turn contributed to the development of their own societies. Prior to 1975, both the American University of Beirut and the Lebanese American University conducted thriving junior-year-abroad programs with American institutions, and the number of American students exceeded 50 percent of total enrollment in many years.

The rich history of these universities will be a major factor in their revival in the new century, as Lebanon strives to regain its position as a cultural and educational center. Despite the devastation wrought during the years of Lebanon's civil war, students from other Arab countries continue to seek a Lebanese education. Some have parents nostalgic for their own days as students in Lebanon, or parents who value the long-standing academic traditions of Lebanese educational institutions. Others have parents who fear the Islamic fundamentalism that permeates some of the new universities in Arab countries, despite the advantages of fine buildings, libraries, laboratories, and faculties.

Universities may have beautiful buildings, rich laboratories, and faculty and staff with excellent credentials, but if they do not have the essential catalyst of academic freedom, they will merely distribute information. Only an atmosphere of freedom can nurture new ideas and generate unfettered creative spirits, and Lebanon is unique in the region in providing such an atmosphere. Unlike other Arab countries, Lebanon has no state religion. Although some may argue that countries with a state religion can practice tolerance, discrimination on the basis of religion—whether conscious or unconscious—remains an unpleasant reality. Lebanon also has a free press and is the only Arab country with private television and radio stations. Even its government television and radio stations air opposing views. I once asked a friend from a neighboring Arab country, "Why do you come to Lebanon so often?" His answer: "In Lebanon I can breathe freedom."

Lebanon pulsates with intellectual and artistic activity. Every season, Lebanese theaters show at least five or six plays, art galleries exhibit the works of local and international artists, and Lebanese institutions organize respected international academic conferences. Lebanon's printing industry has been rejuvenated and modernized since the end of the civil war, making Lebanon once again the print capital of the Arab world. In other Arab countries, such activities are heavily censored or curtailed by customs that prevent full artistic expression. All of these benefits will continue to draw foreign students to Lebanon.

The challenge of forging the identity of the new Lebanese citizen has been taken up by some Lebanese universities. The Lebanese American University has established the Center for Peace and Justice Education, the Center for Civic Responsibility and Leadership, and the Institute for Women's Studies in the Arab World, conducting not only academic courses but also workshops, conferences, and community action programs. The university's objective is to reinvent Lebanese citizenship, or perhaps to invent it, since at no time in modern Lebanese history has citizenship and allegiance to the nation been put into practice, despite being approved and blessed by the Lebanese constitution.

The Lebanese American University has also created a special center for the documentation of Lebanese identity. Although a shared heritage provides the tie that binds Lebanon's diverse communities into a nation, this heritage has never been sufficiently documented. The books and papers that the Lebanese National Library succeeded in collecting disappeared when the library was vandalized and ransacked during the civil war.

Conclusion

Every nation uses its educational system to forge an identity for its citizens that protects the nation from internal strife, gives all citizens a strong sense of belonging, and enables citizens to develop a common view of their history, a common language, and a common geographical space. Lebanon's national life has been marked by the tenacious and fierce attempts of each of its religious communities—including Maronite Christians, Orthodox Christians, Sunni Muslims, Shi'a Muslims, and Druzes—to preserve its singular traditions, customs, and history. Although these groups share a common culture and have coexisted in peace throughout much of their history, they have also endured turbulent and bloody times, especially when outside forces have played one group against the other. Interaction between the Lebanese citizen and the government is still based on confessional affiliation, and the average citizen views his or her religious leader as a political mediator. Successive governments have not yet convinced Lebanese citizens that the state can impart directly what the Church offers, without the tribute the Church exacts.

The Lebanese educational system continues to work to regain the preeminence shaken by the years of civil war and to forge a strong national identity for its citizens. It is aided in this struggle by its multicultural and multilingual society, which acts as a bridge between East and West, and its traditions of freedom of speech and freedom of expression. Lebanon will remain a cultural and educational force in the Middle East in the new century.

8

Women in Postwar Lebanon

Mona Chemali Khalaf

Once you started—no matter how scared you got, how dangerous it became—you were not allowed to turn back. . . . We, too,
cannot turn back. We, too, must keep going in our commitment
to the dignity of every individual, to women's rights as well as
human rights.
Hilary Rodham Clinton, Remarks, 150th anniversary of
the first Women's Rights Convention

The last half of the twentieth century has witnessed an unprecedented and
significant focus on women's issues that highlighted all types of discrimination to which women are subjected. At the level of international organizations, attempts were made to redress these injustices by the Charter of
the United Nations, which embodied the principle of full equality between
men and women, the adoption of a series of more specific conventions
related to women's economic, political, and educational rights, and the
organization by the United Nations of four world conferences on women
between 1975 and 1995.

Despite these advances, in the twenty-first century there remain huge
discrepancies in the status of men and women worldwide. Women constitute 70 percent of the world's poor and two-thirds of its illiterate, working
at the lowest paying jobs and earning only 50 to 75 percent of the wages
paid to men for similar work. Half of all new cases of HIV infection are in
women, and the majority of women are subject to violence both inside and
outside their homes. Women are vastly underrepresented in the political
life of nations, occupying only 10 percent of parliamentary seats and 6
percent of cabinet positions.[1]

In Lebanon, the disheartening differences in the status of men and
women have been further aggravated by the 1975–90 civil war. Even before the conflict began, the impressive growth of the Lebanese economy

was tempered by disparities in income levels and standards of living of rural and urban Lebanese. Despite economic surpluses, prewar Lebanon provided its citizens with few social services, particularly in the areas of health and education. The war shattered the country's infrastructure, segmented its labor and goods markets, and caused a huge outflow of capital from Lebanon. Thousands of Lebanese were displaced from their homes and thousands of others emigrated, resulting in a brain drain that reduced the population of the Lebanese middle class and created a growing gap between income and expenditures. Lebanese women were forced to manage their households with fewer resources, and many had to sustain families without assistance from husbands. This dire situation forced Lebanese women's organizations to shift their emphasis from women's rights to social services and relief work, filling the gap left by a weakened government.

This chapter assesses the impact of the Lebanese civil war on family life, women's participation in the labor force, and the feminization of poverty; surveys discrimination against women in Lebanon's laws and legislation; and makes recommendations for the empowerment of Lebanese women in the hope that they can become full-fledged participants in the political, social, and economic life of their country.

The Civil War and Family Life

Statistics support the contention that the civil war has had a major impact on Lebanese family life. Generally poor economic conditions and the emigration of young men seeking better work opportunities have led to a sharp decline in the number of marriages, although the deferral of marriage until the completion of a woman's education also is a factor in this decline. In 1970, the number of unmarried Lebanese women over fourteen years of age was 29.3 percent. It rose to 35.1 percent in 1986 and to 38.3 percent in 1997. There has been an increase in the number of unmarried women in all age brackets. In the 25–29 age bracket, when the majority of women marry, the percentage of unmarried women jumped from 25 percent in 1970 to around 50 percent in 1997. These figures can be correlated with findings from the 1995–96 Household and Population Survey, carried out by the Lebanese Ministry of Social Affairs and the UN Population Fund, showing that between July 1993 and December 1995, 85 percent of the 23,500 emigrants from Lebanese resident households were males in the 20–24 and 25–29 age brackets.

The decrease in the number of marriages has contributed to a decrease in the Lebanese fertility rate,[2] from an average of 5.2 children per woman in 1970 to 4.1 children in 1995. At the same time, the number of children living with their parents has increased, from an average of 2.7 in 1970 to 3.1 in 1997. This can be attributed to young adults remaining in the parental home because of financial difficulties. More women, both widowed and unmarried, are heads of households, whether they are caring for dependent children, being cared for by adult children, living alone, or supporting parents and siblings. The percentage of Lebanese women heading households rose from 11.2 percent in 1970 to 14.2 percent in 1995, although it dropped to 12.6 percent in 1997.

The Civil War and Women's Participation in the Labor Force

Economic need and marital status have long been determining factors in Lebanese women's participation in the paid labor force. In the early twentieth century, uneducated and poor women were employed in large numbers by the Lebanese silk industry, where they earned half the wages of men. The famine that ensued after World War I led Lebanese women to emigrate to countries such as the United States, where they worked in factories. The married women among these émigrés left their husbands behind to care for land and children.

Upper-middle-class women were discouraged from working outside the home and urged to use their energies and education in the domestic sphere. In 1928, Mohammad Jamil Beyhum concluded a women's conference in Beirut with these telling remarks: "Ladies, I do not want to educate girls to take over the labor market or compete with men in that market, but rather to enable them to manage more efficiently their households and give their children a better education. A lot of activities could take place within the household setting and could be resorted to in case of economic need."[3]

Economic need has driven the increase of women in the labor force following the outbreak of the civil war. A 1998 study by the Institute for Women's Studies in the Arab World (IWSAW) at the Lebanese American University reported that 35 percent of working women stated economic need as their primary reason for being in the labor force.[4] This is corroborated by the results of a textile industry study showing that 81 percent of women workers were motivated by economic need. Over 50 percent of the women in this study worked overtime and took fewer holidays than stipu-

Table 8.1. Enrollment of women in the Lebanese labor force by marital status (in percentages)

Age	Single				Married			
	1970	1985	1993	1997	1970	1985	1993	1997
20–24	39.4	30.4	39.3	28.4	6.8	5.6	7.6	7.5
25–29	51.9	50.3	67.1	52	8.9	10.4	10.4	10.9
30–34	48.0	53	66.5	56.3	9.9	12.8	14.9	12.9
35–39	36.3	48.2	68.1	56.6	9.6	10.8	17.8	15.4
40–44	40.2	40.7	61.1	52.3	9.0	8.8	17.0	18.5
45–49	36.9	34.0	48.3	51.0	8.4	5.4	13.2	12.9
50–54	26.0	37.6	41.4	40.6	7.2	5.0	11.2	10.2
55–59	28.4	27.7	43.8	43.2	5.5	3.0	7.0	8.4
60–64	29.9	22.2	22.6	27.0	5.4	2.1	3.6	4.8
15+	28.4	25.9	36.5	28.7	7.9	7.6	11.9	11.4

Source: Comité National de la Femme, La femme Libanaise 1996–1997, chiffres et sens, vol. 3 (1998), 65.

lated by Lebanese law in order to earn additional income. Interestingly, the ratio of married women doing extra work was higher than that of single women, reflecting not only the pressing need for extra family income but the responsibility that married women often feel in securing it.[5]

Despite increases in the number of married women working outside the home, the majority of Lebanese working women are single (see table 8.1).

Tradition demands that for Lebanese women, children and family responsibilities take precedence over work. In the textile industry study, 53.1 percent of married women said they were willing to give up their jobs if their husbands asked them to do so. In Lebanon as elsewhere, married women who work outside the home bear a heavy dual responsibility as both workers and homemakers, a responsibility not currently being shared by their husbands.

One striking change in the status of all working Lebanese women since the civil war is in their level of education (see table 8.2). In 1970, the majority of working women were illiterate (40.6 percent) or barely knew how to read (17.2 percent). By 1997, only 7.1 percent of working women were illiterate, and the majority had a secondary school education or better. In August 1998, a study by the Lebanese Central Administration of Statistics revealed that most young women enter the labor force at age twenty, after completing their education; in contrast, 36.6 percent of boys between fifteen and nineteen are already part of the labor force. The same

Table 8.2. Distribution of women in the Lebanese labor force by level of education (in percentages)

Level	1970	1986	1993	1995	1997
Illiterate	40.6	9.8	5.3	9.2	7.1
Less than primary	17.2	4.2	4.5	7.0	3.3
Primary	13.2	15.0	14.5	13.5	14.5
Complementary	17.1	17.5	18.2	17.1	18.2
Secondary	8.6	26.9	31.0	28.6	27.3
University	3.4	26.6	26.6	24.6	29.6

Source: Comité National de la Femme, *La femme Libanaise, 1996–1997, chiffres et sens*, vol. 3 (1998), 74.

study ranked the total percentage of women in the labor force at 21.7 percent.

The increase in the level of education of Lebanese working women is the direct result of the rapid growth in the number of girls and women in schools and universities. Females now represent 49.7 percent of the students in Lebanese schools and 51 percent of students in Lebanese universities. There is also a relationship between a woman's level of education and her level of economic activity. Despite a tradition of Lebanese upper-middle-class women not participating in the paid labor force, the percentage of university graduates among working women is now higher than the percentage of university graduates among working men.[6]

Although most women university students still major in the humanities (77.4 percent in 1995), the number of women in the field of business administration increased from 2.9 percent in 1970 to 18 percent in 1995. In mathematics, physics, and chemistry, however, the number of women students decreased from 15.4 percent in 1970 to 6.8 percent in 1995. The total number of professional women in Lebanon, although low, has steadily increased, and the majority of these women are young: in 1997, their average age was less than thirty-eight. At that time, professional registers listed 1,747 women engineers, 1,328 medical doctors, 634 dentists, 1,605 pharmacists, and 123 accountants.

Increases in levels of education have not yet enabled Lebanese women to break through the "glass ceiling" that keeps working women from positions of power. Over 66 percent of Lebanese working women are in the service sector, and women represent only 9.2 percent of the managerial class. Only three women are members of the Lebanese Parliament, a position they occupy either because of inheritance or kinship, and no woman has ever held a governmental ministry or cabinet post. Education, although a necessary condition for women's advancement in Lebanon, does not appear to be a sufficient one.

The Civil War and the Feminization of Poverty

The growth of women's participation in the Lebanese labor force since the civil war has not translated into an improvement in the standard of living for women or their families. Unfortunately, Lebanon today is an example not only of the "feminization of poverty," in which there is "an increase in the number of women among the poor," but of the "impoverishment of women," where "women in general, and poorer women in particular, are getting even poorer."[7] In this chapter, the discussion of women and poverty is limited to women heads of households, women self-employed in the informal sector, and rural women.

As previously mentioned, the number of households headed by women increased as a result of the civil war. Eighty percent of these heads of households are widows, and 12.7 percent are unmarried. Their incomes are usually lower than those of households headed by men. Fifty-nine percent of households headed by women have a monthly income of less than LL 800,000 ($528), compared to 40 percent of total households, and 18.2 percent have a monthly income of less than LL 300,000 ($198), compared to only 5.8 percent of total households. In 1997, the average annual income for households headed by women was LL 8,659,000 ($5,715), significantly lower than the national average of LL 15,241,000 ($10,059). This gap is compounded by the fact that only 23 percent of women heads of households have salaried jobs; the others rely on the financial support of children or other relatives.

Women who are self-employed in the informal sector, unlike other contemporary Lebanese working women, are still poorly educated. Forty percent are illiterate or barely able to read. Their income is low and unstable, and they lack access to adequate credit, marketing, and vocational training that could increase their productivity and economic status.

Rural women are undervalued; their contribution to agricultural labor is often unpaid, considered an extension of their role as homemakers. Even when salaried, rural women receive half of men's wages for the same type of work.[8] They often lack access to productive assets, including land, capital, and technology. Although Lebanese women have the right to inherit land, that land is traditionally registered in their brothers' names to ensure that it remains within the family. The Lebanese National Report to the Beijing Conference indicates that very few land transactions are carried out and registered under women's names.[9] Even in the rural households headed by women (10 percent), major decisions are usually made by male relatives, either a brother-in-law or adult son.

Discrimination against Women in Lebanese Laws and Legislation

Lebanon has ratified a number of international conventions that protect the rights of women. The amended preamble to its 1990 Constitution states that "Lebanon is committed to apply the Universal Declaration of Human Rights in all domains, without exception." Other important international conventions ratified by Lebanon include the 1955 Convention concerning Women's Political Rights; the 1964 UNESCO Convention against Discrimination in Education; the 1976 International Covenant on Economic, Social, and Cultural Rights and the International Covenant on Civil and Political Rights; the 1977 International Labor Organization (ILO) Conventions concerning Equal Remuneration for Men and Women Workers for Work of Equal Value and Discrimination with Respect to Employment and Occupation; and the 1996 Convention on the Elimination of All Forms of Discrimination against Women, with reservations regarding Articles 9, 16, and 29.

The reservations regarding the 1996 Convention on the Elimination of All Forms of Discrimination against Women highlight discriminatory aspects of Lebanese law and the barriers to implementing international conventions, despite their ratification. Article 9 enables mothers to pass on their nationality to their husbands and children; in Lebanon, this privilege is granted only to fathers. Article 16 states the equality of rights and duties in marriage and family relations; this is considered an infringement of Lebanon's personal status laws, which are specific to Lebanon's eighteen religious communities, each of which has its own tribunals to deal with issues related to marriage, divorce, custody, inheritance, guardianship, and adoption. Article 29 makes provisions for arbitration regarding the interpretation and implementation of the convention and refers disputes to the International Court of Justice. This article was flatly rejected by Lebanon.

The Lebanese Constitution does not clearly state that men and women are equal, nor does it include clauses related to the social and economic rights of the Lebanese citizens. The rights and privileges of working men and women are regulated by an antiquated 1946 labor law. The labor law, however, was in the process of being amended when this chapter was written.

There are clauses in Lebanese legislation that actively discriminate against working women. In the public sector, a salaried male employee is entitled to a family allowance, without conditions. A salaried female employee, however, only receives the allowance if (1) her husband is incapacitated, (2) she is financially responsible for her children, or (3) she is divorced and there is evidence that her ex-husband cannot pay her the agreed-upon alimony. Although all salaried public sector employees are entitled to a medical allowance for their families, salaried women receive a fraction of the full amount, unless they have also been approved to receive a family allowance. Employees in the private sector are subject to similar restrictions with regard to family and medical allowances.

The maternity leave as stipulated in the labor law is forty days, with full pay for thirty days after delivery, and prohibits the termination of a woman employee either during the maternity leave period or after her fifth month of pregnancy. The actual length of the leave, however, varies not only between the private and public sectors but between different government institutions.

In the private sector, equal pay for men and women is secured only at minimum wage, and there is no provision for opportunities for equal work. Above minimum wage, pay differentials between men and women are substantial; the discrepancy in some sectors (such as agriculture, as mentioned) is 50 percent.[10] Agricultural workers and domestic workers of both sexes are not covered by the labor law. As a result, they are not entitled to any of its benefits, including paid vacation, indemnity, or a 40-hour work week.

As previously mentioned, Lebanon's personal status laws give jurisdiction over marriage and family relations to the country's religious communities, making application of a universal code of rights impossible. The Lebanese penal code also reflects religious prejudice and discrimination against women. It condemns women who have committed adultery more severely than men, meting out jail sentences from between three months and two years for a wife and one month to one year for a husband. Crimes of honor, in which a woman is killed by "her father or brother for engaging in, or being suspected of engaging in sexual practices before or outside marriage," could remain unpunished; even if the perpetrators were sentenced to capital punishment, the law allowed the sentence to be commuted to imprisonment that need not last for more than one year.[11] The article of the penal code relating to crimes of honor, however, was being amended by the Lebanese Ministry of Justice as this chapter was being written.

Conclusion

The "century of women" is over, and a new century has begun. The fight for international women's rights and the rights of women in Lebanon must shift to what Betty Friedan called "the second stage": "The second stage is where we must move, women and men together. We need a new and politically active consciousness to get us beyond the polarized and destructive male model of work and decision-making and the undervalued women's model of life—the model that takes it as inevitable that having children is a woman's free individual choice to short circuit permanently her earning power and her professional future."[12]

In this spirit, Lebanese women and men should work together to achieve the following advances in women's rights:

- Remove from Lebanese legislation all clauses and texts that discriminate against women.
- Adopt a unified personal status law, which would initially be optional. The vehement opposition of religious dignitaries to former Lebanese president Hrawi's proposal for optional civil marriage makes a step-by-step approach necessary. Young Lebanese women and men should lead the fight for this change.
- Increase the awareness of women—particularly less educated and traditional women—on their value, not just in terms of their relationships to men, but in terms of their own strengths and achievements.
- Work to establish equitable distribution of home and child care responsibilities, without guilt on the part of Lebanese women. Raise children in a egalitarian manner, with the hope of changing the ingrained belief that a working man "always has a wife at home to handle life for him."[13]

These recommendations may sound utopian. At a recent Arab regional conference on population and development in Beirut, several women pressed for improvements in women's status in the Arab countries. The president of the Kuwait delegation, who was also the chairperson of the Drafting Committee, protested vehemently and said while leaving the room: "Where do you think you are, in Europe or in the States? None of your recommendations will be included in the final draft." This anecdote points out how tough the battle remains to achieve equal rights for women in Lebanon. Once having started, however, no matter how scared we get, how dangerous it becomes, we are not allowed to turn back.

It is to be hoped that Lebanese men and women, when looking back at the progress that has been made, will share Betty Friedan's sentiments when she reminisced on the gigantic work achieved by her and her colleagues within the feminist movement on the occasion of the 150th anniversary of the first women's convention in Seneca Falls: "It was very hard; but Oh! It was fun, it was lots of fun!"[14]

Notes

1. United Nations Development Program, *Human Development Report 1995* (Oxford: Oxford University Press, 1995).

2. All figures quoted in this chapter, unless otherwise specified, are taken from Comité National de la Femme, *La femme Libanaise, 1996–1997, chiffres et sens*, vols. 3 and 4 (La Source Research Center, Beirut: Joseph D. Raidy Printing Press, 1998).

3. Gladys Saadeh, "Education et travail feminin au Liban," Ph.D. diss., Paris, 1984.

4. "Female Labor Force in Lebanon, 1998," unpublished study, Lebanese American University, Institute for Women's Studies in the Arab World.

5. Mona C. Khalaf, *The Arab Woman and Work: Facts and Prospects: The Lebanese Case Study* (in Arabic) (Tunis: Center of Arab Women for Training and Research, 1998).

6. République Libanaise, Administration Centrale de la Statistique, "La population active en 1997," *Etudes Statistiques*, no. 12 (August 1998).

7. T. Allen, "Economic Development and the Feminization of Poverty," in *Women's Work in the World Economy*, eds. Folbre, Bergman, Agarwal, and Floro (New York: New York University Press, 1992).

8. The Lebanese Republic, Ministry of Agriculture, and FAO, *Women in Agriculture in Lebanon*, National Report, in preparation for the "Policy Framework and Regional Program of Action for Women in Agriculture in the Near East," 1995.

9. Ibid.

10. Ibid.

11. Alia Berti Zein, "Women's Rights in the Lebanese Personal Law" (paper

presented at the conference *Women in Lebanon*, Washington D.C., 7 November 1997).

12. Betty Friedan, *The Second Stage*, with a new introduction (Cambridge: Harvard University Press, 1998), xvi.

13. Ibid., xvii.

14. Ibid.

Part III

Problems of Urbanization, Ecology, and the Economy

9

The Emerging Urban Landscape of Lebanon

Michael F. Davie

Living in a Lebanese city in the twenty-first century is not a rosy prospect, despite optimistic projections that Lebanon is in a period of recovery. The 1990s slogan *al-balad macheh* (the country is moving) expressed a collective will to rebuild the country after years of civil war and economic hardship and to reestablish Beirut as the financial and cultural capital of the Middle East. Lebanese politicians heralded Lebanon's return to democracy; state institutions proclaimed their intention to modernize; economists lauded the widespread benefits of rebuilding Beirut's city center; and small private businesses were confident of their ability to rescue the Lebanese economy.

The difficulties of survival in postwar Beirut, however, are many. Lebanon's political uncertainties and mismanagement, the consequences of the failures of the Middle East peace process, the glaring destruction of the country's rural and urban environments, and increasing opposition to the reconstruction of Beirut all have contributed to a feeling of helplessness in the face of a threatening future.

This chapter explores the ways in which Lebanese cities have evolved since the 1920s and predicts development trends for the next twenty-five years, basing its analysis on historical research and current fieldwork. The destruction of traditional social forces in the creation of the Lebanese republic led to the emergence of new elites. It also meant the end of policies that regulated development, resulting in uncontrolled urbanization and urban disorder. The Lebanese civil war damaged these elites and shredded the urban fabric, allowing new actors, the militias, to redefine Beirut in a national and regional context.

Today, the reconstruction of Beirut is attempting to reshape the city in the context of a new global economy, bringing different elites to the fore. The continued growth of Beirut and other Lebanese cities is part of a trend toward 100 percent urban population, which will require new strategies for urban planning and governance. Lebanon's ability to meet these challenges will determine the future of the Lebanese metropolis.

The Urban Landscape and the Ottoman Empire

Prior to 1920, Lebanese cities developed under the aegis of the Ottoman Empire. The Ottoman urbanization period was marked by strict city planning, the building of roads and squares by municipalities, the imposition of building and aesthetic norms, the planned linkage of road, rail, and port infrastructures in a coherent regional vision, and the participation of large portions of the local population in decision-making processes.

This last point is perhaps most important. Through a sophisticated system of urban representation, most residents of the city, as well as all religious groups, were part of various *majlis*. This inclusive system prevented governmental representatives from making widely unpopular decisions and ensured the protection of common interests. It recognized the city as a living instrument that required continual fine tuning.

The local Beiruti elite headed the municipality and was instrumental in building the city's port, introducing gas and electricity, modernizing the Sahat al Burj as a business center with a distinctive architecture, and making plans to link the Damascus Road to the port with new wide streets (a plan that was partially completed by the end of World War I). The Ottoman urbanization period also encompassed the opening of public gardens and the construction of new and imposing public buildings, a railway station, schools, universities, and hospitals. The quintessential Beiruti invention, the family house with three arches and a red tile roof, became a common sight in the city during this time.

In retrospect, this period was one of harmonious urbanization directed by a self-regulating local government, a situation shared by most cities of the Ottoman Empire. There was enough work for almost everyone, and there was always room on the ships for those who contemplated emigration. Immigrants from Mount Lebanon, who had suffered from chronic insecurity, economic crises, and feudal conflicts since the 1840s, were absorbed into the city and did not upset its socioeconomic balance.

The Urban Landscape and the Lebanese Republic

The situation changed radically in 1920, when France became the political power in the Levant. Almost overnight, the old *millet* system was abolished and a new country invented (Greater Lebanon, or *état du Grand-Liban*). Beirut, a city with only limited economic links and no political links to Mount Lebanon, was annexed to this new state made up of rural areas and was declared its capital. The French military authorities reconfigured Beirut in the manner of a North African colony. Their first step was to surround it with barracks, then to link the port to these defensive points. Their second step was to destroy the heart of the city and reorganize the road system, mimicking the Place de l'Etoile in Paris. They extended the port to accommodate the French Mediterranean fleet and large cargo vessels and built a landing field for airplanes on the city's outskirts.

The most important transformations were political and demographic. The old Beiruti elite was supplanted first by direct French rule, then in 1926 by a Lebanese republic under French mandate. In Lebanon's confessional system of government, officials are elected through a one-man, one-vote system, but the major religious communities—most importantly, Maronite Christian, Orthodox Christian, Sunni Muslim, Shi'a Muslim, and Druze—agree to share power by dividing government positions on the basis of religion. Lebanon's first (and, to date, only) census in 1932 gave Christians a slight numerical majority over the other religious communities in this delicately balanced system. Lebanon became an independent sovereign state in 1943.

This political shift is key to understanding Lebanon's urban morphology. The religious communities did not have the know-how, means, or inclination to manage a city according to clear-cut rules or shared urban interests. Because of a heavy-handed French presence, the Beirut municipal government was reduced to simply managing basic urban services, while real decisions were made elsewhere. At the same time, Beirut was perceived by the new elites as a source of wealth for their impoverished mountain communities. The city and its port provided new jobs for extended family and village neighbors. Direct and indirect corruption became rampant, as the new elites used their access to the workings of the city and port to buy political favors.

Many rural Lebanese migrated to the cities. There they were joined by a significant number of foreign immigrants. French authorities resettled survivors of the Armenian genocide in Beirut because as Christians, their presence would give the demographic edge to the Maronites, strongly allied with the French. Other settlers included French military staff and their families, Kurdish laborers from eastern Anatolia, Syria, and Iraq, Palestin-

ian bourgeois, Syrians from the now Turkish-annexed *sanjaq* of Alex-
andretta, merchants from all over the Mediterranean, White Russians,
and Assyrian and Chaldean refugees from Iraq.

The result was urban sprawl, as Beirut rapidly and haphazardly expanded toward the coast and the sand dunes to the south, and new neighborhoods (such as Burj-Hammoud and Karm al-Zeitoun for the Arme-
nians) were created. The new cityscape, unlike that of the Ottoman
period, had no master plan, no regulating bodies, and, most importantly,
no clear economic goals. Instead of a relatively well planned city, the new
suburbs (today's outer municipal periphery) were a sum of individual,
low-quality buildings whose footprint often matched the irregular plots
on which they were built. Their architectural style contrasted sharply with
the buildings of the old city. Cement and concrete replaced sandstone
ramleh. Tall apartment buildings replaced one-family houses. The new
buildings first spread along the main roads, then beyond them into fields
whose land patterns determined the shape of the new neighborhoods. The
composition of old neighborhoods also changed. Traditionally Greek
Orthodox quarters (such as Achrafiyyeh) had an influx of Maronites;
Basta, a typically Sunni urban area, received Kurds of rural origin; Ras
Beirut, which had been mainly bourgeois Sunni and Orthodox, saw an
increase in the numbers of foreigners and Lebanese of other religious communities.

The expansion of Beirut was mirrored by the expansion of Lebanon's
secondary cities, Tripoli and Sidon, as well as of its small mountain villages. These communities spread from an original nucleus toward abandoned terrace farms or small subsistence farms operated by a declining
number of farmers. Revenues from Beirut and abroad not only fostered
this expansion but modified traditional land-property structures. In many
villages, church land was sold to the new town-based bourgeoisie, consolidating their semifeudal political power. New wealth also brought tourism
as city dwellers returned to the mountain for summer vacations, frequent-
ing growing communities with service-oriented economies such as Aley,
Bhamdoun, Sofar, Beit-Meri, and Broummana. Expansion of secondary
coastal cities and villages was spurred by the widespread use of the auto-
mobile: Jounieh, Jebail, Batroun, and Chtaura in the Beqaa Valley were
among the communities that profited from an increasingly mobile population. The result was a radical transformation of the Lebanese country-
side as well as the Lebanese urban landscape.

The Urban Landscape in the Post–World War II Era

The next major change in Lebanon's urban development came in the wake of World War II and the 1948 war in Palestine. Beirut in particular was affected by the influx of Palestinians into Lebanon. The Palestinian presence in Beirut created two distinct urban morphologies. The first was that of the impoverished refugee camps (Sabra and Mar Elias in the sand dunes to the south, and Tel ez-Zaatar and Jisr el-Basha in the still-rural foothills around the city). In their social organization, attitudes toward the city, extended family solidarities, and political representation (usually by the *moukhtar*s of their villages), the camps had a distinctly rural atmosphere. Some of their traditions persist today, although the camps are now surrounded by new city neighborhoods. The second morphology was of the Palestinian urban bourgeoisie and upper class, who avoided the sordid camps and settled in established city neighborhoods. They quickly invested in land and businesses and were the driving force behind Beirut's successful new commercial and financial district, Hamra.

Hamra was the ideal site for the grounding of the new Lebanese economy. After World War II, Lebanese elites realized that the United States had supplanted old European allies such as France and created new global markets. At the same time, two major historical developments made Lebanon a regional economic center: the discovery of oil in Saudi Arabia and the Gulf states and the closure of Israeli ports to Arab ships. The oil-rich countries did not have the know-how, the personnel, or the banks to handle the vast sums of revenue generated by the precious resource. They turned to Beirut, with its history of entrepreneurism and its absence of strict banking laws, for help. The closure of Israeli ports to Arab traffic made Beirut the only modern, well-equipped Arab port in the eastern Mediterranean. All merchandise in transit to the inland states, which had not yet built their own ports, had to go through Beirut, which in turn extracted healthy revenues for its services.

Some of the profit from these new ventures was reinvested in Hamra, whose spaciousness and modern architectural character made the center of Beirut, with its now-quaint Mandate architecture, narrow streets, and stuffy family atmosphere, seem obsolete. The Beirut urban landscape became even more complex. The old city center settled into a slumber of neglect and decay, while Hamra, with its new buildings and Western air, became a unique attraction for Lebanese and foreigners alike. Hamra, whose main buildings are still standing, offered cafés, cinemas, shops, and offices, along with hotels that catered to foreigners doing business in Lebanon. It provided new jobs for both Lebanese and Palestinian refugees.

The modernization of Beirut (and of Tripoli, Sidon, and larger towns) occurred at a favorable moment in Lebanese history, when abundant capital and labor, linked to global economic interests, made Lebanon a major player in the world economy and guaranteed its protection by Western powers such as the United States. This was the case in 1958, when U.S. troops shored up the Lebanese government in order to ensure the unfettered activity of the oil companies in the region. Lebanon also benefited from the introduction of state socialism in many Middle Eastern countries, which suffered under a corresponding burden of state bureaucracy and the stifling of individual initiative. Unfettered Lebanon, in contrast, basked in the myth of the "Lebanese miracle."

The "Lebanese miracle," however, was no boon to the development of Lebanon's urban landscape. Economic prosperity justified the lack of state intervention in urban planning, even as to basic architectural and building codes. Belated plans drawn up during the Chehab period failed to address the issue of urban sprawl seriously. As a result, Lebanon's main towns and cities became chaotic cityscapes, a mixture of old and new, tall and low, business and residential, with little discernable hierarchy. In Beirut, the crowded Mandate suburbs were rebuilt to accommodate a never-ending influx of Lebanese from the interior (Furn el-Chebbak, Ain al-Rummaneh, and Chiyyah are typical examples of these suburbs). In Sidon and Tripoli, as in the larger towns, the same uncontrolled development produced a dense urban mass.

The new wave of development gave birth to Western-style upper-class residential communities on the heights above Beirut (such as Yarzeh, Rabieh, Naccache, Yanar, Bchemoun, Mechref, and Adonis) and new summer resorts in the mountains, along with an expansion of housing for middle-class Beirutis. Despite these islands of prosperity, the suburbs close to the city remained, as always, densely populated by lower- or middle-class white-collar workers, and on the periphery of the suburbs were slums or substandard housing that sheltered refugees and new immigrants from rural communities. The slums abutted the Palestinian refugee camps. Prosperous Beirut thus developed a spatial framework common to Third World cities, a framework that still exists today.

In this urban magma, previous social structures and allegiances and current social realities made a volatile mix. Urban Lebanese of the 1950s and 1960s retained their traditional rural ties because the Lebanese political system prevented the forging of new urban identities and elites. Residing in a city did not make you a citizen of the city: Lebanese still voted in the constituency of their parents, as defined by the 1932 census. Divided according to social status, and again by religion or by geographic origin, urban Lebanese constituted a politically amorphous mass, docile only as long as economic prosperity continued.

Throughout this period, wars and disorders in neighboring countries continued to benefit Lebanon. The 1956 Suez crisis and the closure of the Suez Canal made Beirut's port and airport undisputed regional relay points. The nationalization of businesses in Syria, Iraq, and Egypt brought fresh capital and well-educated immigrants to Lebanon. The extensions of its port and the opening of its new airport made Beirut newly important in the context of Western economic interests, especially after the 1967 war, when they provided the only access for land-locked Middle Eastern countries such as Jordan, Iraq, and Saudi Arabia.

Lebanon's cities, however, could not indefinitely absorb the workforce of the region. Increasingly, both Lebanese and foreign nationals emigrated to places such as the United States, Canada, Australia, Saudi Arabia, the Gulf states, and Africa in search of work opportunities. Money earned abroad made its way back to Lebanon, stimulating an unregulated building industry and an increasing urban disorder that would play a major factor in the Lebanese civil war.

The Urban Landscape and the Lebanese Civil War

There is a strong link between Lebanon's urban disorder and the outbreak of its civil war. The Palestinian and fundamentalist Muslim militancy that fed military conflicts such as Black September and the 1973 Arab-Israeli war was an urban or periurban phenomenon, bred in refugee camps and slums. Beirut was a center of such activity, providing a space for politically active Palestinian refugees, organized into disciplined military forces, to join together with Lebanese recently moved to the capital from other areas of the country.

The failure of Lebanon's liberal economy was physically expressed in Beirut's overcrowded, ever-expanding suburbs. While the "modern" parts of the city were being built (Hamra, the residential suburbs, Ras Beirut), and while some privileged sectors were prospering from Beirut's monopoly on regional travel, the rest of the economy was in decline. Agriculture was abandoned in favor of land speculation. Industry was never a national priority. Tourism and the service industry were left to small-scale family operations. The lack of jobs and continuing social and political marginalization drove the low-income population of the suburbs toward radical organizations that offered simple solutions to complex questions, using nationalism or religion as the main vector of their message.

Residents of the suburbs were tempted by the prosperous city centers, looking at them as the loci for money and stability. Control of the city centers meant control of wealth and power. The Lebanese civil war started in the Beirut suburbs, only spreading to the city center toward the end of 1975. Suburban militias plundered and destroyed the city center, and this takeover of the center by the periphery meant the start of a new phase in Lebanon's urban development.

In the first years of the war, Beirut was divided into two cities, undergoing the equivalent of ethnic purification along religious lines. The mostly Muslim survivors of the assaults against Tel ez-Zaatar, Karantina, and Jisr el-Basha camps flowed into what was now called West Beirut, while mostly Christian refugees from Damour, Moussaitbeh, Hamra, Ras Beirut, or Kantari crossed over to East Beirut. Incessant reciprocal shelling forced many of the city's inhabitants to move out of range of artillery, radically expanding the populations of Adonis, Ajaltoun, Reifoun, Jounieh or Dora, Aramoun, Choueifat, and Sidon. This first wave of urbanization caused by the war quickly transformed the coastal strip and lower slopes of the mountain (the villages of Mazraat Yachouh and Mansouriyyeh are good examples). The breakdown of the remaining municipal services, the control by the militias of the urban regulatory bodies, and the economic free-for-all further contributed to urban chaos.

A second wave of urbanization followed the first Israeli invasion of Lebanon in 1978. Within a few days, the main cities to the south of Beirut, as well as most of West Beirut, were overrun by refugees seeking shelter from the Israeli assault. Soon, refugees became illegal squatters on public and private property, largely in the southern suburbs, but also in closed or abandoned apartments in Ras Beirut and the pericentral sector of the city. Hamra, once the showcase of Lebanon's westernized economy and culture, now mirrored the rural habits of its new population. After the second Israeli invasion of Lebanon in 1982, the old bourgeois Achrafiyyeh neighborhood sheltered refugees from the Shouf alongside militiamen.

After 1984, the effects of the new urbanization were felt on the outskirts of the city. To the north, Jounieh was urbanized from Haret el-Sakhr to Adma and further inland above Tabarja. Ajaltoun and Feytroun nearly merged, and Faraya became a year-round residential center. New residential complexes were built on the beach for year-round use, and schools and universities were relocated to surprising locations. Branches of government ministries were opened in each militia-held territory, as were television and radio stations. Strategic roads were cut through the remaining open areas, while new ports and an airport were built toward Jebail.

To the south of the city, many militias vied for control of the coast. As soon as it secured territory, however, each militia encouraged the building of infrastructure that would make it less dependent on other areas. This happened in the Shouf, the Sidon area, and the Koura and Ehden-Bcharreh sectors.

The total breakdown of state authority, coupled with the total control of urban spaces by the militias, encouraged the uncontrolled urbanization of most of the western slopes of central Mount Lebanon. Economic liberalism was pushed to the extreme, with no controls on business or profit making. The militias were huge economic players, investing capital in import-export opportunities, collecting parallel taxes and protection money, and reinvesting in building projects, land, and infrastructure. They did not, however, provide any solutions to the deepening urban crisis. The militias merely continued the economic logic of prewar Lebanon: let the market economy reign, but without any social safety net or any real effort to make the system more productive.

The Urban Landscape in the Post–Civil War Era

After the end of the war, a new elite came to power, with a very different agenda than that of the militia and military leaders who controlled Lebanon during the civil war. This new group analyzed the urban crisis in clearcut terms: Beirut must regain its former status, both as the locus of national prosperity and as Lebanon's link to the new world economic order. The idea was simple: Beirut would again be the relay point between the financial, economic, and decision-making cities of the north (in the United States and Europe), the Gulf states, and the successful Asian states. Its strategic location, liberal economy, westernized culture, and white-collar labor force would make it an integral part of the new world economic order established after the failure of the Soviet Union. Capital from the oil-rich states would be managed by the Lebanese banks, stocks would be exchanged by Arabic-speaking brokers, and foreign investors would use the country as a fiscal haven. The success of Beirut would in turn herald economic prosperity for the rest of Lebanon.

For the first time since the start of the French mandate, the elite realized that urban planning, with controls and regulations, was necessary for the success of the new Beirut. The city center was to be rebuilt in accordance with a detailed plan that met international architectural and building standards. Implementing this plan required a clean slate. One investment company, Solidaire, was given a monopoly on rebuilding the city center, with the right to exercise eminent domain over all private property. In return, it issued bonds as compensation to property owners.

The plan mirrored current thinking on the role of space in the global economy: space has value only when it is organized according to the needs of potential investors, not according to its position in a city. This meant that the city center would no longer be the meeting point of all the country's population, containing the central bus station and the main *souks* (markets). For the sake of efficiency, the urban landscape would be radically changed, making the city center a place for white-collar workers. Economic productivity would be achieved at the price of diversity. The city center would become a safe, sanitized, politically neutral environment, so as not to endanger the trust of its international investors.

The elite that developed this reconstruction plan, however, still had to operate within the larger context of Lebanon's religious and political system. The confessional republic established in the 1920s survived the war, although the 1990 Ta'if Agreement made modifications in power sharing between the Christian and Muslim communities. In order to gain support for the reconstruction and consolidate a hold on the city center, the elite had to cede power to the periphery, giving control of other regions of Lebanon to religious leaders. These alliances ensured that the reconstruction would not be a forum for grassroots urban democracy or a resurrected Beirut Urban Authority. The CDR (Conseil du Développement et de la Reconstruction) was directly linked to the prime minister's office. Decisions relating to urban questions would be made under complete control of the political leaders.

The reconstruction project received unambiguous support from most parts of Lebanese and Beiruti society from 1992 to 1996. Any criticism was branded as sabotage, and no open debate on the project took place. The destruction of the old city center proceeded, creating a new urban landscape. Landowners, merchants, and bankers saw the reconstruction as an opportunity to recoup losses sustained during the war. Land could be sold at good prices (or shares obtained in an apparently prosperous and promising company, Solidaire), businesses and shops could reopen, and capital would once again be available. The lower classes saw the reconstruction as providing job opportunities in the building sites or in the service economy. Young Lebanese saw it as proof of a new era in their country's history, confirming the end of the old militia order and urban anarchy. Diaspora Lebanese welcomed the reconstruction as proof that the war had ended, that it was safe to come back to work and invest in Lebanon.

Elsewhere in Lebanon, other reconstruction projects were taking place with less fanfare. After more than ten years of interrupted work, the Linord project filled in the northern coast between Antelias and Dbayyeh and planned to link it with another infill between Dora and Antelias. This wholly private venture deeply marked the urban landscape and ecology of Lebanon. In Beirut's southern suburbs, a government project, Elisar, was redeveloping the areas around the Palestinian refugee camps, affecting Sabra-Shatila camps, Bir Hassan and Bourj-Barajneh, Moaʿawwad, and part of the Choueifat plain. An urban landscape of slums, illegal housing, and narrow streets was to be replaced by a model residential and light-industry city. A new network of roads was planned, including a toll highway that would link Beirut to other cities and a widening of the Beirut-Damascus highway to link the city center, port, and new airport.

This flurry of development gave observers grounds for optimism. Jobs had been created (albeit for the foreign work force), the national economy had benefited, and there had been a building boom (although the thousands of luxury apartments produced remained empty). The problem of squatters had been solved to the general satisfaction of all concerned, from the displaced persons to the politicians who protected them, and the city's infrastructure had been put into semi–working order.

The political system, however, seemed more conservative than ever. There was little room for the development of new political parties or of a new political consciousness among the urban citizens of the country, who still voted in their ancestors' place of origin. The concrete aspects of Lebanon's inclusion in the new global economy had been planned, but the social aspects had been ignored.

Lebanon's Reconstruction and the New Global Economy

Beirut is at a turning point, with the heritage of the past hundred years still evident and the future urban landscape still taking shape. The Solidaire project is planned to end in the early 2020s, and the northern coast infill will not be completed until the 2010s. The new road infrastructure and the extensions of the port and airport will not be totally operational before 2010. Reconstruction projects in other Lebanese cities are on the same timetable.

The economic benefits of the reconstruction for Lebanon, however, do not seem as great as in the early to mid-1990s. The recent global economic crisis, together with the collapse of Asian markets, the destabilization of the major currencies, and the possibility of recession, poses important questions as to the value of the new Beirut as a regional financial hub. The Lebanese workforce is expensive and not particularly knowledgeable in sophisticated production techniques. It is cheaper to produce goods elsewhere. The local market (three million inhabitants) is small, the technology used is simple, and the added value very minimal. The use of foreign labor is no solution to the problem, as the resulting export of capital affects the national currency and increases the prices of goods. The heavy, inefficient, and corrupt state bureaucracy further stifles the mediocre profit-earning capacity of local industry and services. Even Lebanon's much-vaunted banks make more profit abroad, investing in stocks and shares or speculating on exchange rates, than they do in Lebanon. The spread of the use of the Internet for business has reduced the value of Lebanon's physical location. Space, its value and distribution, is no longer at the heart of the global economy.

Syria, Jordan, Saudi Arabia, and the Gulf states have all built state-of-the-art ports or container terminals, limiting Beirut's traditional role as the center of Middle East transit. Beirut International Airport has lost its position as a forced technical stop for aircraft on the Europe-Asia route. Planes now fly nonstop to destinations in Southeast Asia, or stop off in the Gulf states. Even Lebanon's network of roads is outside the region's overland transit routes. Trucks from Turkey now pass through Syria to Saudi or Jordanian markets.

The failures of the Middle East peace process and the continuing violence in southern Lebanon after the Israeli withdrawal also affect the prospects for a reconstructed Beirut as a financial center of the new global economy. Israeli banks, with their access to international financial networks and their familiarity with current international financial practices, are serious competitors with Lebanese banks for business even among Arab countries, Arab solidarity notwithstanding.

Internal criticism of the reconstruction has also become more vocal, sparked by the destruction of the historic, architecturally rich district of Wadi Abou-Jmil. When protests did not save the district from being flattened, it seemed that the alliance between the country's power structure and Solidaire was confining Lebanese society. At a moment when democratic expectations were being expressed all over the world, especially in

Eastern Europe, the limits imposed on debate over the reconstruction chilled enthusiasm for the project. Beirutis began to realize that the project would not benefit all of the urban population, only a privileged few who would be able to afford luxury residences or new offices. Former landowners felt cheated at having been forced to cede their property at Solidaire-imposed prices, then seeing Solidaire resell the property at wildly inflated rates. The reconstruction of Beirut began to appear as an island of prosperity for the inner circle of the country's ruling class, with the rest of the population left to manage on its own.

Lebanon suddenly realized that the rest of the world had not waited for the Lebanese civil war to end. The global economy now worked according to a different set of rules, and space was no longer an important part of the equation. Beirut's traditional advantages were no longer relevant, particularly in light of its continuing political and social problems, small size, technology gap, and expensive land and labor. Lebanon was no longer a serious competitor in the global marketplace.

The Future of Lebanon's Urban Landscape

Lebanon's urban landscape is again being transformed. As Solidaire has destroyed Beirut's Ottoman-era city center in preparation for reconstruction, historic buildings in the pericentral districts are becoming more valued. The latest craze is to rehabilitate old buildings and either live in them or transform them into chic restaurants or clubs. Remaining historic neighborhoods, as well as individual buildings, are prized for aesthetic, cultural, and social reasons.

The Lebanese urban landscape, however, is increasingly grim. Beirut is rapidly becoming a series of "urban canyons" choked by traffic. Upperclass neighborhoods exert some control on the quality of their environment, but elsewhere the population has to cope with pollution, noise, and lack of road maintenance. In many places in Lebanon, the natural environment has been destroyed, rock quarries disfigure the mountains and the valleys, forests have been burned or leveled, water and air pollution is endemic, and the sea is just a refuse dump.

One Lebanese in two now lives in Greater Beirut, and more than two out of three Lebanese live in cities or large towns. Continuing urban migration is likely to result in an uninterrupted amorphous mass of urbanization extending from Jebail to Sidon, with today's tourist towns expanding into full-time residential areas. Tripoli will overflow into the Koura along the main roads to Amioun or Zghorta, and Sidon will fill in the space from the Awali to Zahrani, annexing the villages in the foothills. Tyre will fill the sand dunes to the south and any available space on the coast. Similar growth will be seen in the Baalbek and Zahle-Chaura areas.

The current division of the cities into upper-class, middle-class, lower-class, and slum areas will continue. The Palestinian camps will not disappear, unless another solution is found for their inhabitants. The nomad camps around the cities will also exist as long as a low-wage workforce is required to build the urban extensions and infrastructure. The upper-class residential centers will maintain their appeal because of their exclusive character; due to lack of space, very few new ones will be created. The inner cores of villages and towns will slowly be replaced by commercial centers, shopping malls, and residential buildings, thus destroying the remaining remnants of the old architectural and social order.

Around Beirut itself, the commercial and business district that currently spreads between Mkalles and Dbayyeh (the "Beirut Blue Banana") will be consolidated, offering services and products to the local market. In Tripoli, the old *souk*s will decline further, or be rehabilitated (the gold *souk* is an example); real commercial activity will take place in the Azmi and Al-Mitain streets, and the city's center will slowly decline. The old center of Sidon, encircled by rapid-transit boulevards, will struggle to maintain some of its character, but land speculation will slowly encroach on the old *souk*s, which will be either destroyed or transformed into the ersatz *souk*s of Jebail.

This harsh analysis is based on the assumptions that Lebanon's liberal economic system and confessional political system will not change and that Lebanon will not be able to recapture the place that it occupied in the global market in the years following World War II. The successes of the 1950s and 1960s were a consequence of favorable historical circumstances, not of national will and planning. Beirut no longer has any particular place in the hierarchy of world cities, and the global economy has no real need of Beirut.

A totally free market economy like Lebanon's is not conducive to large-scale investment, as the absence of state controls limits the building of the infrastructure necessary for profit making. The lack of a social safety net increases political and social unrest, with the only solution being a repressive regime backed by military force. Such countries are rife with violence, as conflicts in Asia, Africa, and Central and South America have demonstrated. Investors are increasingly wary of countries that are unable to offer social stability without repressive violence. In Lebanon, privatization is the new catch phrase, and the state is further decreasing its minimal social services.

Lebanese are deeply disenchanted with politics. The revolutionary slogans of the 1970s and 1980s, the religious slogans of the later years of the civil war, and the nationalist slogans of the 1990s have disappeared. *Albalad macheh* is now the object of cynical jokes. In the absence of democratic planning structures such as a Greater Beirut Authority, social fragmentation and political feebleness will continue to characterize the Lebanese urban landscape. The power structure will become increasingly repressive. Social tension will be a way of life, with a privileged few profiting from the uncontrolled system, while the others struggle to survive, fighting for jobs that will go to cheaper foreign labor or to other countries. Emigration from Lebanon will persist, and its cities will slowly decline. Indonesia, the Congo, and Algeria are demoralizing examples of what Lebanon may become.

Conclusion

The Lebanese urban landscape has developed more as a consequence of outside historical influences than of long-term urban planning, a fact that does not bode well for Lebanon's future. The gracious modern Beirut of the Ottoman era was altered under French military rule following World War I. From the 1920s through the 1940s, Lebanon's cities grew unchecked due to massive emigration from rural areas, overseen by religious elites who used the cities to support their traditional rural constituencies. The influx of Palestinian refugees into Lebanon in 1947–48 added permanent refugee camps and fomenting political unrest to Lebanon's urban sprawl but also spurred the growth of Beirut's new financial and commercial center, Hamra.

The prosperity of the 1950s and 1960s was due to Lebanon's position as a cosmopolitan relay point between the oil-producing Middle Eastern countries and the West, at a time when neighboring countries were viewed as unstable and hostile to Western interests. The Lebanese civil war of the 1970s and 1980s, inflamed by regional conflicts, divided Beirut into sectors controlled by competing militias with short-term interests and removed Lebanon from the global marketplace at a time of great technological change. The redevelopment schemes of the 1990s were hampered by the limitations of Lebanon's confessional political system, as well as by a global economy that had bypassed Lebanon and made its location, traditionally an asset, irrelevant.

The Lebanese confessional political system, suited to prosperity, cannot cope with economic fragility or a global economy whose rules and scale of operation far exceed Lebanese know-how. A dogma of "no state interference" continues to hobble Lebanon's development in an era in which strong governmental services ensure political and economic stability and attract global investment. Because there has been no real improvement in Lebanon's political system, Lebanon's reconstruction is doomed to failure.

10

The Ecological Crisis in Lebanon

Fouad Hamdan

Lebanon is experiencing an ecological crisis that is the result of decades of uncontrolled and unregulated development and nearly sixteen years of civil war (1975–90). The improper disposal of household, industrial, and hospital waste and industrial pollution have compromised the quality of Lebanon's air and water. Over 50 percent of Lebanon's water sources are contaminated, by World Health Organization standards, and smog has become a daily reality in its overdeveloped cities and industrial areas.

The biodiversity of the Lebanese environment has been compromised by the destruction of its forests through urban development and uncontrolled fires, illegal logging, and unregulated stone quarries. The percentage of the country covered by forests has shrunk from 20 percent in 1975 to 5 percent in the late 1990s. Illegal hunting and the use of chemicals in agriculture have further aggravated these problems. The redevelopment of Beirut and other Lebanese cities in the wake of the civil war will bring more waste and pollution to Lebanon.

This chapter details the extent of the pollution of Lebanon and the efforts of environmental organizations, using the example of Greenpeace, to influence government, private industry, and individual citizens to stop practices that contribute to the problem. It also outlines the steps necessary to make twenty-first-century Lebanon cleaner and more productive.

The Waste Disposal Crisis

Lebanon is in the process of drowning in its own waste. There are dozens of waste dumps all along the Lebanese coastline, in the mountains, and in the Beqaa Valley. More than 4,000 tons of household waste are generated every day in Lebanon, much of which ends up in open landfills or in the sea. In Greater Beirut, according to 1998 official data, 1,700 tons of waste per day is separated in two plants in Karantina and Amrushieh. Fifty percent of this waste is composted for agricultural purposes, and 10 percent is recycled. The rest is dumped into a "sanitary landfill" in the Naameh Valley south of Beirut. Lebanese authorities plan to build similar so-called sanitary landfills all over the country, including in Zahle, Baalbek, and the south. Unfortunately, the World Bank and other international institutions want to finance these projects.

Environmental groups are concerned about an unknown amount of hazardous hospital waste and industrial toxic waste being dumped in Naameh. The British company Fairhurst International, which helped build the Naameh landfill, estimated that the lining of the landfill, designed to isolate waste from the environment, would not last more than ten years. This is a highly dangerous situation. Toxic substances in landfills create leachate, a toxic fluid that leaks into groundwater reservoirs and poisons them. Sanitary landfills that contain toxic and hazardous waste are ecological time bombs. Only nonrecyclable, noncompostable, and nontoxic wastes should be placed in landfills, especially in a country like Lebanon, whose geological composition is mainly sand and fractured rocks like limestone.

Outside the Greater Beirut area, wastes are dumped or treated through open-air incineration, the most dangerous way to dispose of toxic waste. The most infamous dump sites are the coastal dumps in Tripoli, Sidon, and Tyre, as well as the inland dumps of Balamad, Baalbeck, Zahle, Uyun al-Siman, and Sibline. A 1998 Lebanese environmental scandal involved the illegal transfer of a hazardous waste dump. Two Spanish construction companies and a Lebanese company had been paid $102 million dollars by the Lebanese Council of Development and Reconstruction (CDR) to complete an on-site rehabilitation of the dump at the Beirut port, which had been closed in 1991 to make room for the expansion of the port. This dump contained hazardous hospital and industrial waste from the period of the Lebanese civil war, toxic ash from the nearby Karantina incinerator, and toxic waste imported to Lebanon from Italy in 1987. Instead of accomplishing the job as promised, the firms brought the waste to the Monteverde region in the mountains outside Beirut.

Greenpeace discovered the illegal activity, and the waste was returned to the Beirut port for on-site treatment, but it had already contaminated the Monteverde dump site. More than 20,000 tons of waste and 10,000 tons of contaminated soil had to be removed, and a thousand trucks were needed to carry out the operation. There are fears that leaking toxic substances may have poisoned the Beirut River and the Dayshunieh well underneath the Monteverde dump site. About 600,000 people in Beirut receive drinking water from Dayshunieh.

Sample test results carried out by Greenpeace's scientific laboratory in Exeter University in England showed that leachate and sediments from the dump contained high levels of toxic heavy metals like chromium, nickel, cadmium, mercury, and lead. Some metals were found at levels ten times greater than one would expect in uncontaminated sediments. These heavy metals are known to be toxic to the aquatic environment even at very low concentrations. Cadmium damages the kidneys and bones and may cause cancer. Lead severely damages the brain, especially in children. Mercury affects the kidneys and the brain, while nickel and chromium have negative effects on the kidney and liver.

A report published by Greenpeace, "Waste Management Alternatives in the Mediterranean: A Case Study for the Spanish Island of Mallorca," gives detailed steps that should be applied to solving Lebanon's waste crisis. The report opposes waste incineration and dumping toxic and hazardous wastes in any sort of landfill.[1] Its alternative plan involves waste reduction, selective waste collection, waste classification, recycling, and composting and includes cost estimates for implementing the new procedures. It also outlines public awareness campaigns that encourage citizens to consume local products, buy from small shops or markets, eliminate toxic products like batteries and solvents, avoid products that make excessive use of packaging materials, and refuse throwaway products such as plastic bags, one-way plastic bottles (especially those that contain toxic polyvinyl chloride, or PVC), and aluminum cans in favor of glass and recyclable materials.

In the meantime, several Lebanese villages have gone their own way and implemented environmental campaigns. In the town of Bsharre (Kesrowan), the local Association for the Protection of the Environment is cooperating with the municipality to separate waste at its source and recycle as much waste as possible. Batteries are stored in containers. Eighty percent of the town's 10,000 residents took part in the 1998 project, which was funded by the United Nations Development Program (UNDP)/ LIFE program. Local groups in the southern villages of Arab Salim and Maghdushe are successfully implementing similar projects.

The Selaata Incinerator and Hazardous Hospital Waste

The Lebanese Ministry of Environment and the CDR had planned to build a hospital waste incinerator in Selaata in northern Lebanon. A study commissioned by the CDR and financed by a World Bank loan listed the expensive and polluting facility as an environmentally friendly and relatively inexpensive solution to the problem of hospital waste. Government authorities have refused to publish the study.[2]

Greenpeace believes it is a myth that incineration definitively eliminates hazardous waste. The "cleaner" the smoke and fly ash from incineration, the more toxic the residual ash in the kiln. This toxic ash, when dumped in a landfill, will contaminate groundwater reservoirs and soils. Lebanese medical facilities currently produce approximately forty-six tons of waste daily, about nine tons of which are hazardous.[3] The first logical step in managing this waste involves separating infectious from noninfectious waste. Infectious waste can be sterilized through microwaving or steaming and can then be shredded and recycled. Body parts and animals used in medical testing constitute no more than one percent of the total hospital waste pool; careful cremation or burial are environmentally sound techniques of disposing of them. Radioactive waste should be sealed in special isolating containers and stored above ground to avoid leakage.

For the remaining waste, hospitals should implement waste separation systems, substituting reusable and durable products for disposable products, and introducing recycling programs for plastics, paper, and metal. PVC, which is the most widely used plastic in the health care field, must be phased out in all products. Alternatives to PVC exist for use in medical equipment.[4]

Environmental groups have made appeals to CDR and the Ministry of the Environment to stop any incinerator projects and seek safe, economical alternatives to the incineration of hospital waste. Neither institution has responded, fueling fears that incinerators will be built despite the fact that they will encourage excessive waste generation and the diversion of public and private capital from constructive waste prevention and recycling activities.

The Problem of Industrial Waste

Industrial waste in Lebanon is increasing along with Lebanese industry, without any environmental controls as to its treatment or disposal. A 1995 report by the Mediterranean Environmental Technical Assistance Program (METAP) estimated the total solid waste from Lebanese industry to be about 326,000 tons per year. An unknown amount is toxic. Given the concentration of industry in Mount Lebanon, it follows that most industrial waste is generated there. Assuming an annual growth in industrial output of 8 percent, the METAP report projected that by 2010 Lebanese industrial waste could be over 1 million tons per year.[5] Official unpublished reports by Greenpeace estimate that industrial solid waste in Lebanon is expected to increase from 1,051 tons/day (383,615 tons/year) in 1994 to 4,090 tons/day (1.49 million tons/year) in the year 2020. Solid toxic waste is projected to increase from 51 tons/day (18,615 tons/year) to 177 tons/day (64,605 tons/year) in the same period. In addition to solid waste, industrial wastewater is expected to increase all over Lebanon from 61,120 cubic meters/day in 1994 to 191,625 cubic meters/day in 2020.

Most industrial wastewater is discharged into the Mediterranean Sea or inland rivers and streams without treatment, sometimes through pipes owned by the company, or through ordinary sewage pipes. Contaminated groundwater is the result. Some industries dispose of their wastewater through deep bore holes, risking contamination of underground waters and springs in other locations. Solid industrial waste is dumped in the sanitary landfill at Naameh, at other dump sites, or in the wild. These wastes, some of which are toxic, are generally mixed with municipal refuse without any safety measures.

Cement production, cement pipes with asbestos, and chemical industries in Chekka and Selaata are a major source of marine, soil, and air pollution in the Kura, North Lebanon. Sample tests carried out by the Greenpeace research laboratory at Exeter University showed that groundwater in Chekka is polluted by a wide range of toxic chemicals, while emissions from the cement factories pollute the air and the Mediterranean Sea.[6] A petrocoke sample from the Cimenterie Nationale (CN) showed a wide range of polycyclic aromatic hydrocarbons (PAH) and dibenzothiofurans. PAHs cause cancer. CN and the Société du Ciment Libanais (SCL) discharge their toxic effluents directly onto beaches or near beaches where people swim.[7]

Lebanese authorities are not only allowing but promoting the use of the deadly fiber asbestos in the production of cement pipes and roof tiles. This is in stark contrast to other countries, where increasing public concern, objections by workers, government regulations, and mounting liabilities have resulted in a precipitous decline in asbestos use. In the United States, asbestos use peaked at around 780,000 metric tons in 1974 and declined steadily to around 21,000 metric tons in 1997. World asbestos production (and consumption) declined from an estimated 4.2 to 4.8 million metric tons in 1986 to 2.07 million metric tons in 1997. The U.S. Environmental Protection Agency (EPA), the World Health Organization, and the British Health and Safety Commission (HSC) have all advised against using asbestos, suggesting that there is evidence of a strong causal relationship between asbestos exposure and cancers in the esophagus, larynx, oral cavity, stomach, colon, and kidneys.[8]

In Lebanon, Greenpeace has campaigned for a ban on the use of asbestos in all applications, including sewage pipes, roof panels, and braking pads. A major stumbling block in banning asbestos in Lebanon is an agreement signed between the Ministry of Environment and the asbestos producer Eternit in March 1997, which allows the company to use asbestos forever. The protocol gives the illusion that asbestos can be dealt with in a safe way, and authorities in Lebanon plan to use asbestos cement pipes in many areas as part of the country's reconstruction program.

The CDR and the Ministry for Water and Electricity Resources completed the installation of asbestos cement pipes for drinking water in the Tripoli district of Damm wa Farez, near al-Salam Hospital, in March 1998. The installation of sewage systems with asbestos cement pipes began in the northern town of Miniah in Akkar in June 1998. The CDR and the Ministry of Environment have refused to inform the public about the kind of pipe that will be used in new drinking water systems in the southern towns of Nabatieh and Tyre.

Despite these setbacks, the campaign against asbestos use in Lebanon has had some successes. In June 1998, the CDR and the Ministry of Hydraulics and Electricity chose to use asbestos-free pipes (iron pipes, GRP or fiberglass pipes, and polyethylene plastic pipes) on the Kesrowan coast and in the town of Batrun. The Kesrowan project was financed by the Overseas Economic Cooperation Fund (OECF) of Japan, which refused to fund any project that included asbestos pipes. This raises the question of a double standard in politics. Why did CDR insist on using asbestos cement pipes in sewage projects in al-Miniah in Akkar, in Jiyyeh, south of Beirut, and in the Damm wa Farez district in Tripoli, when it has opted for safer alternatives in other areas?

Lebanon must introduce laws requiring industries to shift toward investing in clean production technologies. This can be done with the help of such incentives as tax reduction, customs tax reduction for imported raw materials, and soft loans. For example, producers of PVC plastics should switch to acceptable plastics like polyethylene (PET) or polypropylene (PP). Paints should be free of toxic solvents, and tanneries should phase out the use of the toxic heavy metal chromium.

In all industrial sectors, management should implement "sustainable development," defined as progress that meets the needs of the present without undermining the well-being of future generations. The essential elements of sustainable development are to avoid emissions of pollutants into the air, soil, and water and to control the use of raw materials and energy. The aim is zero toxic-waste production. Sustainable development means that industry must consider the environmental effects of its operations during all stages of production: manufacture, consumption, and disposal.

Industry must make environmental protection a priority out of concern for future generations, not just because of legal regulations or pressure from environmental groups. If industry does not change its methods, sooner or later the capacity of the Lebanese ecosystem to absorb pollutants will break down completely.

The Fight against Imported Toxic Waste

Toxic waste imported from Italy in 1987 was noted among the waste at the Beirut port dump that was moved illegally to Monteverde in 1998, where it contaminated soil and water. The Beirut port scandal, however, is just one example of problems caused for Lebanon by illegally imported toxic waste. The Italian toxic waste came to Lebanon during the chaos of the civil war, in a deal hammered out with a Lebanese firm and supervised by members of the now-disbanded militia, the Lebanese Forces.[9]

An Italian company shipped 2,411 tons of the waste in 15,800 barrels and 20 containers in 1987. When the deal became known in 1988, public outrage in Lebanon forced the Italian government to promise to return the toxic material to Italy. But only 5,500 barrels were returned, loaded in 9,500 new barrels that left in four ships at Beirut Port in 1988–89. The contents of more than 10,000 barrels and the twenty containers remained in Lebanon. Some of the remaining waste was used as fertilizer, pesticide, or raw material to produce paints or foam mattresses. Many barrels were burned in the open air. Others were dumped in the Kesrowan Mountains east of Beirut, endangering groundwater reservoirs. In some cases, barrels were emptied and sold for storage of gasoline, water, or food.

The shipment from Italy contained a deadly cocktail of toxic materials. Among them were the explosive substance nitrocellulose, outdated adhesives, organo-phosphoric pesticides, solvents, expired medications, oil residues, and substances contaminated with highly toxic heavy metals such as lead, mercury, and cadmium, as well as arsenic, chlorinated substances, and PCBs.

In November 1994, samples were taken from barrels at the Beirut port that had been brought there from the Kesrowan Mountains. Greenpeace test results showed that solid waste contained heavy metals, hydrocarbons from oil residues, and chlorinated substances like HCBD, a highly toxic chemical that causes neurological and kidney damage and is a suspected carcinogen.

After Greenpeace revealed that most of the Italian waste had remained in Lebanon, months of confrontation between Lebanese authorities and the Greenpeace representative followed. Government ministers tried to cover up the issue, and there were open threats and two lengthy interrogations of the local Greenpeace campaigner by the state prosecutor. Greenpeace, however, managed to convince the authorities to reopen the case. As a result, seventy-seven tons of contaminated land and toxic waste were returned to Europe in April 1996. Greenpeace is continuing to pursue the issue until all of the waste that can be found is returned to Italy.

Published documents show that there are at least five sites in Lebanon contaminated by the toxic waste from Italy: Shnanir (near Jounieh), Zelahmaya, Halat, Uyun al-Siman, and Tripoli. The Shnanir quarry was used as a dump and burn site for most of the waste. The Lebanese environment minister had promised since 1996 that this waste site would be decontaminated, but nothing was done. In January 1998, the quarry was reopened, with the potential to spread tons of contaminated soil all over Lebanon. Greenpeace asked two of the three owners of the Shnanir quarry not to touch the contaminated areas of the quarry, and they pledged to keep their workers away from them.

Italy is not the only country to have exported toxic waste to Lebanon. Thirty-six containers of contaminated plastic waste were illegally imported to Lebanon from Germany in August 1996. Greenpeace made this illegal trade public and provided the authorities with official documentation. Thanks to the efforts of the Greenpeace Mediterranean office and Greenpeace Germany, all thirty-six containers were returned to Germany in two batches in May and June 1997.[10] Two containers of Belgian plastic waste were returned to the sender. The Belgian company that illegally exported them to Lebanon in 1996 took them back.

In December 1996, the Lebanese Ministry of Environment adopted a regulation banning the import of all hazardous waste into Lebanon, even under the guise of recycling. Greenpeace, which helped draft the strict regulation, regards it as another success in the ongoing struggle against the pollution of Lebanon.

Regional Antipollution Accords

Greenpeace's work in Lebanon is part of a regional campaign in the Mediterranean to pressure governments to ratify all protocols and amendments related to the 1976 Barcelona Convention. These amendments ban industrial and other toxic discharges along the coast and in rivers, waste dumping at sea, toxic- and nuclear-waste trade, and oil pollution. They also protect the biodiversity of the Mediterranean basin. Fish stocks in the basin are threatened with extinction because of illegal drift netting. Oil exploration and toxic pollution from industry and agriculture poison marine life and the atmosphere. In addition, tourism and uncontrolled coastal development are destroying ecosystems and the habitats of species.

Land-based sources account for 85 percent of the pollution in the Mediterranean. Most of the toxic pollution originates from Spain, France, and Italy, although developing countries like Lebanon and Egypt are contributing more and more to the problem. For the amendments to enter into force, three-fourths of the Mediterranean states have to submit written acceptance to the Convention Secretariat in Barcelona. In 1998, the only states that have done so are Monaco and Tunisia.

Greenpeace's Philosophy and Role in Lebanon

Since its inception in 1971, Greenpeace has operated on the principle of peaceful protest against environmental degradation and injustice. It follows the Christian Quaker tradition of "bearing witness," the nonviolent civil disobedience of the American civil rights movement, and the nonviolent direct action of the Indian leader Mahatma Gandhi. Bearing witness means sailing or walking to the scene of the environmental crime. Documentation is done with photos and videos, and attempts are made to prevent pollution with nonviolent actions. The images are then used to influence public opinion. The scene can be in the middle of the sea, where Greenpeace samples industrial outflows or prevents nuclear testing and toxic-waste dumping. It can be inland, where Greenpeace samples toxic-waste dumps, the premises of a polluting company, or the toxic ash of a waste incinerator.

Many Lebanese officials, ministers, and industrialists have criticized Greenpeace's actions as a media show. The truth is that no industrialists would be willing to talk to Greenpeace in Lebanon or elsewhere were they not certain that Greenpeace is in a position to damage their polluting businesses and images. Greenpeace is effective not only because it documents environmental abuses but also because it develops links with local activists, community groups, government officials, and the media. Greenpeace's allies in Lebanon provide important information on environmental scandals and take an active role in campaigns for antipollution laws and regulations.

Greenpeace cooperated with the Popular Committee in Hay al-Sellom in the southern suburbs of Beirut against the polluting Amrushieh waste incinerator, as well as with seventeen local groups taking soil samples along the Lebanese coast from Tyre to Akkar in October 1997. In May 1997, students in Monteverde informed Greenpeace that trucks were dumping waste near their town in the Metn.

Greenpeace's contact with people, directly or indirectly via the media, has a democratic influence in a society where public debates involving business people and politicians from influential families are a rarity. Although Greenpeace was advised to give up its Western way of campaigning in Lebanon by those who argued that a Middle Eastern society would not accept naming and pressuring ecological culprits, the Greenpeace style, with a Middle Eastern touch, proved to be successful.

Greenpeace's openness about its work and finances is another part of its success in Lebanon, where corruption has sullied political life. A private financial company regularly audits the Greenpeace Mediterranean outpost in Lebanon, and the financial statement is made public so that everyone can know how Greenpeace spends money received from donors. These nonviolent and democratic tools are models for social transformation in Lebanon, as well as essential to safeguarding the Lebanese environment and the health of its citizens.

An Environmental Plan for Lebanon in the Twenty-first Century

In the twenty-first century, Lebanese activists will continue to struggle to get the Lebanese government to implement nationwide environmental policies, in the face of increasing pollution from all sources. A safe environment is necessary not only for public health but for the health of the Lebanese economy as well. Squandering the natural resources and beauty of Lebanon affects its agriculture and tourism, among other industries.

According to a 1996 report issued by the World Bank, the estimated annual cost of environmental and natural resource degradation in Lebanon is over $315 million in U.S. dollars. The cost breaks down as follows: safe water, sanitation, and hygiene, $130 million; air pollution and overcrowding, $100 million; degradation of farming terraces, $55 million; and soil erosion with degraded rangeland, $30 million. Since this report was based on 1992 figures, it can be assumed that these costs have increased.

After the civil war, the Lebanese government focused on rebuilding Lebanon's infrastructure. Funds have been spent almost entirely on repairing the electricity, road network, telecommunication, and water systems and restaffing an overinflated, corrupt, and inefficient public sector. Protecting the environment is not a priority. The Ministry of Environment, established after the war, is small and badly equipped, without an effective professional staff. Since 1996, however, the Ministry of Environment has taken a role in issues such as the banning of toxic-waste imports. It has helped to establish national reserves in parts of Lebanon and has been increasingly outspoken on environmental issues. These small projects must grow into large government and industry initiatives.

Lebanese authorities and businesses can invest in propaganda claiming that Lebanon has regained its prewar beauty. They can use Internet websites and television shows to spread the image that Lebanon is again the "Switzerland of the Orient" and Beirut the "Paris of the Orient." Lebanese expatriates and Gulf Arabs will want to believe this, but one trip back will rip the mask from Lebanon's polluted and ravaged face. In order to make "Green Lebanon" truly rise from the ashes of war, the government, the Lebanese Industry Association (LIA), and others in the private sector must agree to channel funds and human resources to end and repair environmental damage.

In developing an effective environmental policy, Lebanese authorities can count on the support of nongovernmental organizations (NGOs) such as Greenpeace. Before this can happen, however, the Ministry of Environment and CDR must stop interfering in the internal affairs of NGOs and start providing them with government reports and other vital information on environmental issues. They also must stop trying to neutralize local NGOs through the corrupt distribution of financial aid and lucrative, UN-funded jobs. International organizations such as the World Bank and UNDP, as well as many Western nations, would increase their financial support to save Lebanon's environment if the government were willing to involve NGOs in the decision-making process and to end large-scale corruption in public projects.

In 1998, Lebanon jumped from 4 to 10 on the corruption scale of the International Country Risk Guide, putting it on a par with Colombia and ahead of Indonesia (8), Morocco (5.8), and Jordan (4). World Bank economist Daniel Kaufmann stated that corruption in Lebanon was rising faster than anywhere else in the world. The World Bank has approved

$667 million in U.S. dollars for development projects in Lebanon, but only 28 per cent of that money was actually spent by June 1998.[11] About $55 million earmarked for the waste-management sector is still waiting to be spent, pending development of sound environmental practices.

Lebanon is not dealing with unmanageable problems. Arguments for clean industrial practices and effective waste management are not utopian, but realistic. The Lebanese industrial sector is relatively small, and often a few small factories are responsible for polluting large areas of the coastline and river systems. In the absence of primary manufacturing industries such as smelting, chlorine manufacture, and pulp bleaching, Lebanon's industrial waste can be managed appropriately and effectively. Government and industry must start the process by taking the following steps:

- Expand the powers and increase the budget of the Ministry of Environment so that it can play an active role in cooperation with other institutions, such as the CDR and the ministries of industry, tourism, and education. Reshape this ministry into a Ministry of Environment and Technology. This new body would formulate environmental plans and coordinate and supervise their implementation. It must have a right of veto over private development.
- Establish an overall waste-management program focusing on waste prevention, separation at source, reuse, recycling, and composting. New laws and tax incentives should encourage industry to invest in clean production methods.
- Enforce the use of catalytic filters and lead-free gasoline in automobiles. Encourage Lebanese to purchase small and energy-efficient cars, and structure import taxes to favor small cars, not large ones that use excessive fuel. Expand and modernize public transport to make it attractive to people from all walks of life.
- Phase out the use of fossil fuels in power plants. Introduce energy-saving programs and shift to renewable energies like solar, wind, and biomass.
- Restrict quarries to areas where no ecological damage could occur, and regulate their operations according to stiff laws.
- Start to implement a long-term environmental strategy. The United Nations and the World Bank have set forth sustainable-development strategies in papers that can serve as guides for Lebanon.

The time has come for Lebanese authorities to use their historic opportunities to rebuild Lebanon on a sound environmental basis. They must acknowledge environmental problems, set sound environmental strategies, and work with NGOs and Lebanese citizens to ensure the country's health and prosperity in the new century.

Notes

1. Greenpeace report, "Waste Management Alternatives in the Mediterranean: A Case Study for the Spanish Island of Mallorca" (English) and a summary (in Arabic and English), 1997.

2. Greenpeace briefing paper, "The Hospital Waste Crisis in Lebanon," August 1998.

3. Information given at a presentation by Dr. Rita Karam, Medical Waste Management Workshop, Beirut, October 1997.

4. "The Hospital Waste Crisis in Lebanon."

5. Report by the Mediterranean Environmental Technical Assistance Program (METAP), "Lebanon: Assessment of the State of the Environment," 1995.

6. Greenpeace report, "Heavy Metal and Organic Screen Analysis of Environmental and Waste Samples Associated with Industrial Activities in Lebanon" (Exeter: Greenpeace International Laboratory, University of Exeter, July 1998).

7. Greenpeace report, "Organic Screen Analyses of Waste and Environmental Samples Associated with the Cement and Chemical Industry in Lebanon" (Exeter: Greenpeace International Laboratory, University of Exeter, May 1995).

8. "EPA Background Information for Promulgated Asbestos, NESHAP Revisions" (Washington, D.C.: Environmental Protection Agency, Emissions Standards Division, Office of Air and Radiation, Office of Air Quality Planning and Standards, October 1990).

9. Greenpeace report, "Toxic Attack against Lebanon, Case One: Toxic Waste from Italy," May 1995.

10. Greenpeace report, "Toxic Attack Against Lebanon, Case Three: Plastic Waste from Germany," October 1996.

11. *Daily Star* (Beirut), 8 September 1998.

11

The Lebanese Economy in the Twenty-first Century

Wassim N. Shahin

Predicting the long-term behavior of a country's economy is difficult because of the speed at which systems and performances change in today's global environment. Political considerations also affect economic behavior, and it remains an open question whether the Lebanese economy, whatever its individual performance, can achieve a soft landing on the bumpy regional runway of the Middle East.

This chapter offers an analysis of Lebanon's current economic performance that eschews political considerations. Section 1 compares the actual performance of the Lebanese economy to predictions made by the government after Lebanon's civil war ended and the massive reconstruction of the country's infrastructure began. Section 2 outlines the mechanics behind Lebanon's current economic situation. Section 3 recommends a macroeconomic plan for Lebanon to achieve growth and stability in the new century. Section 4 is a proposal for an Arab Economic and Monetary Union (AEMU) based on that of the European Community (EC), taking into consideration both the benefits of and obstacles to such a plan.

Lebanon's Economy in the Post–Civil War Era: Anticipated and Actual Performance

When the first Hariri government came to power at the end of 1992, many observers believed that Lebanon had begun its return to economic development, growth, and stability. The reconstruction plan for Beirut and the suburbs, along with the peace dividend from domestic (and potentially regional) detente, were expected to attract a major flow of capital into long-term investments. In order to encourage foreign direct investments and motivate domestic business, the government reformed its tax laws, making Lebanon a tax haven for domestic and foreign enterprises. By the end of 1992, Lebanese currency had improved its standing against the U.S. dollar, from $1 = 2,420 LL (Lebanese lira) to $1 = 1,838 LL. This trend continued into 1993 ($1 = 1,713.18 LL) and mid-1994 ($1 = 1,670 LL).

In the second half of 1994, Lebanese government officials and economic advisors developed a optimistic plan to project the major macroeconomic variables in the Lebanese economy from 1995 to 2007. This plan, unofficially known as Horizon 2000 (see table 11.1) predicted a continuous growth rate for real gross domestic product (GDP). Growth was projected at 9 percent per year until 1998, 8 percent for 1999–2002, 7 percent for 2003–2005, and 6 percent for 2006–2007. This ambitious growth rate was to be accompanied by an inflation rate of 4 percent annually from 1998 to 2007. The standing of the Lebanese lira against the U.S. dollar was expected to remain stable, while interest rates were to reach single digits by 1999.

The ratio of internal debt to GDP was projected in the area of 50 percent, with the ratio of total debt to GDP reaching 90 percent by the end of the century. The government expected a high ratio of external debt to GDP because it planned to market its debt abroad and in foreign currency, at lower interest rates. Total interest payments on debt were to reach two trillion LL by the end of the century, a figure that represented 28 percent of Lebanon's current expenditures and 27 percent of its current revenue.

A comparison between actual indicators and Horizon 2000 plan assumptions (see table 11.2) shows that the plan's predictions were far from accurate. The most erroneous predictions were for the growth rate in real GDP, debt and deficit figures, and interest payments on debt, especially as percent of revenue and expenditure. The growth rate in GDP was 4 percent in 1996 and 1997 instead of the expected 9 percent. The ratio of internal debt to GDP reached 88.81 percent in 1997, instead of the expected 54.7 percent, while the ratio of external debt to GDP was half its projected amount. Total debt to GDP exceeded its projected amount by 100 percent in 1996 and 1997. The total deficit reached 5.203 trillion LL in 1997, much higher than the projected deficit of 3.63 trillion LL.

Even more worrisome were the total interest payments on debt, which in 1997 were 3.384 trillion LL, more than double the projected figure of 1.545 trillion LL. The real danger was reflected in the ratio of total interest payments on debt to current expenditures (44.5) and to total revenue (90.97). Horizon 2000 estimated the ratio of interest on debt to total revenue in 1997 at only 34.2. What made this figure alarming is that the

Table 11.1. Lebanon's Horizon 2000 plan: Underlying assumptions

	1994	1995	1996	1997	1998	1999	2000	2001	2002	2003	2004	2005	2006	2007
Real growth in GDP (%)	—	9.00	9.00	9.00	9.00	8.00	8.00	8.00	8.00	7.00	7.00	7.00	6.00	6.00
Growth in CPI (%)	—	6.00	5.00	4.50	4.00	4.00	4.00	4.00	4.00	4.00	4.00	4.00	4.00	4.00
LL/$ rate	1,685	1,660	1,660	1,660	1,660	1,660	1,660	1,660	1,660	1,660	1,660	1,660	1,660	1,660
Domestic interest rate (%)	—	15.3	13.50	11.50	10.50	9.00	9.00	9.00	9.00	9.00	8.00	8.00	8.00	8.00
Government expenses/GDP (%)	—	41.6	38.90	37.20	35.20	33.70	32.20	31.20	29.50	28.50	26.70	25.20	23.90	22.90
Government revenues/GDP (%)	—	18.80	19.60	20.60	21.60	23.00	24.10	25.20	25.60	26.10	26.30	26.50	26.80	27.00
Internal debt/GDP (%)	—	52.30	52.60	54.70	52.70	50.20	47.00	43.90	41.40	39.90	38.70	36.40	33.00	28.70
External debt/GDP (%)	—	19.10	28.00	32.00	37.20	40.70	42.20	41.50	38.50	34.40	28.50	22.60	17.60	13.20
Total debt/GDP (%)	—	71.40	80.70	86.70	89.90	91.00	89.20	85.40	79.90	74.30	67.20	59.00	50.70	41.90
Government current expenditures (current prices, bill LL)	—	4,296	4,708	5,267	5,929	6,461	7,199	7,963	8,761	9,534	10,164	10,974	11,701	12,415
Government current revenues (current prices, bill LL)	—	3,151	3,773	4,517	5,379	6,404	7,533	8,878	10,083	11,455	12,854	14,432	16,045	17,839
Government capital expenditures (current prices, bill LL)	—	2,695	2,797	2,909	2,838	2,952	2,868	2,983	2,883	2,999	2,882	2,752	2,607	2,711
Total deficit (current prices, bill LL)	—	-3,481	-3,732	-3,660	-3,388	-3,010	-2,534	-2,068	-1,561	-1,078	-193	706	1,737	2,713
Total debt (current prices, bill LL)	—	11,987	15,553	19,046	22,368	25,377	27,911	29,979	31,540	32,618	32,811	32,105	30,368	27,654
Gross internal debt (current prices, bill LL)	8,484	8,778	10,150	12,024	13,121	14,011	14,717	15,415	16,341	17,503	18,894	19,786	19,803	18,952
Gross external debt (current prices, bill LL)	—	3,209	5,403	7,023	9,247	11,366	13,194	14,564	15,199	15,115	13,917	12,319	10,565	8,703
Total interest payments (current prices, bill LL)	—	1,396	1,410	1,545	1,754	1,828	2,057	2,248	2,407	2,535	2,458	2,486	2,445	2,324
Interest payments/current expenditures (%)	—	32.50	29.95	29.33	29.58	28.29	28.57	28.23	27.47	26.59	24.18	22.65	20.90	18.72
Payment interests/current revenue (%)	—	44.30	37.30	34.20	32.60	28.50	27.30	25.30	23.87	22.13	19.10	17.22	15.20	13.02

Source: Government of Lebanon Ministry of Finance.

Table 11.2. A comparison between Lebanon's actual indicators and Horizon 2000 plan assumptions

	1994	1994a	1995	1995a	1996	1996a	1997	1997a
Real growth in GDP (%)	—	8.00	9.00	6.50	9.00	4.00	9.00	4.00
Growth in CPI (%)	—	11.80	6.00	11.30	5.00	8.87	4.50	7.75
LL/$ rate	1,685	1,647	1,660	1,596	1,660	1,552	1,660	1,527
Domestic interest rate[b] (%)	—	13.05	15.30	15.40	13.50	13.80	11.50	12.68
Government expenses/GDP (%)	—	34.71	41.60	33.15	38.90	36.24	37.20	41.12
Government revenues/GDP (%)	—	14.94	18.80	17.17	19.60	17.72	20.60	17.19
Internal debt/GDP (%)	—	62.35	52.30	67.92	52.60	86.42	54.70	88.81
External debt/GDP (%)	—	8.48	19.10	11.79	28.00	14.25	32.00	16.68
Total debt/GDP (%)	—	70.83	71.40	79.71	80.70	100.67	86.70	105.35
Government current expenditures (current prices, bill LL)	—	3,954	4,296	4,640	4,708	6,002	5,267	7,605
Government current revenues (current prices, bill LL)	—	2,240	3,151	3,033	3,773	3,532	4,517	3,830
Government capital expenditures (current prices, bill LL)	—	1,250	2,695	1,216	2,797	1,223	2,909	1,557
Total deficit (current prices, bill LL)	—	-2,912	-3,481	-2,706	-3,732	-3,756	-3,630	-5,204
Total debt (current prices, bill LL)	—	10,619	11,987	14,079	15,553	20,070	19,046	23,470
Gross internal debt (current prices, bill LL)	8,484	9,348	8,778	11,997	10,150	17,229	12,024	19,787
Gross external debt (current prices, bill LL)	—	1,271	3,209	2,082	5,403	2,841	7,023	3,717
Total interest payments (current prices, bill LL)	—	1,488	1,396	1,875	1,410	2,653	1,545	3,384
Interest payments/current expenditures (%)	—	37.63	32.50	40.41	29.95	44.20	29.33	44.50

a. These four columns represent actual indicator.
b. Domestic interest rate is taken as nominal rate on 3-month treasury bills, end of period.
Source: Government of Lebanon Ministry of Finance, World Bank, Consultation and Research Institute, Association of Banks in Lebanon (ABL) Estimation.

government spent over 90 percent of every lira raised in revenue (which includes taxes, fees, and fines) to service government debt.

Every other major macroeconomic indicator pointed to a troubled economy, as shown in table 11.3. The debt-to-export ratio increased from 1,250 in 1994 to 2,262 in 1997. The external debt-to-export ratio also worsened, from 147 in 1994 to 366 in 1997, along with the ratio of interest payments on debt to exports, from 172 in 1994 to 341 in 1997.

The ratio of private loans to public loans was more or less constant starting in 1994 at 112 and ending 1997 at 116. In the same period private-sector construction permits showed a major decline. Although the net foreign-currency reserves of Lebanon's Central Bank (defined as gross revenues minus bank deposits) increased in 1995 and 1996, they dropped drastically in 1997, after major interventions in the foreign-exchange market to support the national currency. This means that the current ratio of money supply to net foreign-exchange reserves held by the Central Bank increased, from 2.33 in 1994 to 5.43 in 1997. The ability of the Central Bank to defend the local currency weakened, since net foreign-exchange reserves represented only 20 percent of the local-currency liquid assets in the hands of the nonbanking public, as opposed to 45 percent in 1994. (The money supply, M_2, includes domestic currency in circulation and all bank deposits in domestic currency, plus treasury bills held by the public.) Whereas the total money supply, M_3 (defined to include M_2 plus all foreign-currency deposits), experienced a high rate of growth, this growth was not transmitted to the real sector, because the M_3 velocity of circulation declined by 11 percent in 1996 and 7 percent in 1997.

The Mechanics behind Lebanon's Economic Situation

This section analyzes the mechanics behind Lebanon's economic situation at the end of 1997, using a model of causality that links government instruments to factors that affected the stated policy goals of output and employment growth. In 1993, at the start of the detente period, the government issued treasury bills (T-bills) at high interest rates. (As table 11.4 shows, these interest rates were around 22 percent for T-bills that matured in a year, and 26 percent for T-bills that matured in two years.) The high interest rates were intended to encourage the marketing of government debt in local currency and to prevent the Lebanese lira from depreciating. This strategy took effect at a time when the Lebanese public was beginning to have more confidence in the economy and Lebanese currency had started gaining in value. Expectations were that the government would

Table 11.3. Other major economic indicators in Lebanon

	1994	1995	1996	1997
Deficit/GDP (%)	19.4	15.3	18.8	23.3
Interest debt payments/GDP (%)	9.92	10.61	13.30	15.10
Debt/exports (%)	1,250	1,312	1,751	2,262
External debt/exports (%)	147	198	255	366
Interest debt payments/exports (%)	172	173	230	341
BDL foreign-currency reserves (gross)[a]	3,840	4,487	5,886	5,932
BDL foreign-currency reserves (net)[a]	2,732	3,030	4,079	2,463
M_2 + TBs held by public/BDL net FX reserves	2.33	2.69	2.92	5.43
Bank claims private/public (%)	112	129	105	116
Construction permits[b] (in square meters)	8,567,953	6,325,999	3,337,619	2,122,40
Rate of growth of M_3 (%)	—	16.4	27.7	19.3

a. In million U.S.$.
b. Measured by first quarter per year and fourth quarter for 1994.
Source: Figures computed by author based on data from Association of Banks in Lebanon and *Quarterly Bulletin*, Banque du Liban.

gradually lower interest rates as public confidence in the economy grew. By the end of 1994, this prediction was justified, and interest rates fell to less than 15 percent.

In the third quarter of 1995, however, the government jacked up interest rates to support the Lebanese currency, spurred by the fear that the coming presidential election would cause political instability. T-bill rates escalated to levels unprecedented in the history of the two Hariri governments. The interest rate on twelve-month T-bills reached 37.85 percent; on three-month T-bills, 25.3 percent; on six-month T-bills, 27.9 percent, and on twenty-four-month T-bills, 29 percent. High interest rates caused major increases in the interest payments on debt, from 1.875 trillion LL in 1995 to 2.653 trillion LL in 1996 to 3.384 trillion LL in 1997. The result was a major increase in the ratios of debt service to revenue and debt service to expenditure.

High interest rates also meant high lending rates for private-sector loans made in Lebanese currency. As table 11.4 shows, the lending rate remained above 20 percent from 1993 through 1996 (29 percent in 1993, 22 percent in 1994, 29 percent in 1995, and 25 percent throughout 1996). These rates were extremely high, given that during the same period the value of Lebanese currency was increasing and the much lower inflation rate was dropping (11.8 percent in 1994, 11.5 percent in 1995, and 8.87 percent in 1996). Banks had no choice but to charge high rates for loans, however, as they were paying such high returns on T-bills and were required to hold a significant percentage of their stock of Lebanese currency in T-bills (60 percent up to 1994 and 40 percent between 1994 and the first quarter of 1997).

Many banks held far more than the required percentage of Lebanese currency in T-bills, paying deposit rates up to two percentage points below the T-bill rates and investing the proceeds in T-bills. This policy, combined with high loan rates, stifled private-sector investment (see table 11.3) in a period of economic recovery. The ratio of private to public loans remained stagnant, and the number of private construction permits declined because many Lebanese were unable to finance housing loans at the inflated rates. The housing sector became characterized by excess supply, with many newly built units standing empty.

High interest rates on T-bills encouraged short-term investments rather than the long-term investments in fixed capital needed for economic growth. Short-term financial investments do not filter into GDP growth unless they become permanent funds loaned to the government and spent in productive ways, or unless they become permanent bank deposits channeled to private-sector loans. It is long-term investments in fixed capital that foster growth in production and employment.

Lebanon's debt and deficit figures also escalated as a result of a decrease in government revenues. In order to create a tax haven that would attract capital, motivate business, and encourage compliance, the government embarked on a tax reform policy that became effective in 1994. This policy reduced the top personal income tax rate from 32 percent to 10 percent. Financial companies were charged a flat rate of 10 percent on their profit, with a special discounted rate of 5 percent applying to those involved in building and selling residential buildings. Commercial and industrial companies were subjected to a 3–10 percent progressive tax on profits.

These tax rates are low compared to those of other countries that implemented tax reforms in the same period (see table 11.6, p. 199). A 1998 study by Dah, Dibeh, and Shahin found that moving to a progressive tax system, similar to that implemented by some of the countries represented in table 11.6, is not only more equitable but generates more revenue as well.[1] Low tax rates, coupled with the inability of the government to levy additional indirect taxes at a time when wages are being held down

Table 11.4. Weighted average yield on treasury bills and lending rates, Lebanon, 1992–1997 (in percentage)

| | Treasury bill rates | | | | |
	3 months	6 months	12 months	24 months	Lending rates
1992(1)	23.84	25.34	29.01	30.50	44.20
1992(2)	23.84	24.34	29.01	30.50	45.81
1992(3)	34.18	35.28	34.20	33.59	51.13
1992(4)	13.00	15.00	20.99	26.00	27.45
1993(1)	21.01	22.01	22.01	26.00	27.04
1993(2)	18.48	20.08	22.01	26.00	28.74
1993(3)	18.06	19.85	21.00	24.99	29.25
1993(4)	17.22	19.65	21.07	23.99	29.29
1994(1)	16.33	18.04	19.92	20.34	27.35
1994(2)	15.30	17.47	19.31	20.07	23.09
1994(3)	14.47	17.21	19.04	18.53	22.01
1994(4)	13.49	14.83	14.73	15.84	21.28
1995(1)	16.55	18.00	19.66	18.81	21.32
1995(2)	19.94	21.70	26.45	24.06	22.76
1995(3)	25.30	27.91	37.85	29.05	27.63
1995(4)	16.01	17.21	18.26	23.39	28.99
1996(1)	15.81	17.16	18.15	23.25	25.95
1996(2)	15.56	16.99	17.96	23.08	24.99
1996(3)	14.61	16.92	17.80	22.83	24.43
1996(4)	14.29	16.15	17.02	20.54	24.68
1997(1)	13.75	14.49	15.20	16.73	20.47
1997(2)	13.40	14.21	15.20	16.73	19.86
1997(3)	13.09	13.97	15.20	16.73	19.36

Sources: Government of Lebanon Ministry of Finance, *1998 Budget Report*, 12; Banque du Liban, *Quarterly Bulletin*.

to reduce expenditures, result in inadequate government revenue. In turn, they inhibit the growth of GDP and increase deficit and debt, particularly when they are coupled with high government expenditure and waste, as in Lebanon. The growth of Lebanon's GDP was also stalled by allocating financial resources to projects that did not result in increased business productivity, as well as by the practice of legal and illegal transfer payments.

Political instability was a major factor in the disappointing performance of the Lebanese economy. This instability was both regional and domestic, encompassing the continuing Arab-Israeli conflict, the 1996 Israeli attack on Lebanon that destroyed infrastructure, and the turmoil surrounding Lebanese elections (the presidential elections of 1995, as

Table 11.5. Business polls in Lebanon: Industry and commerce

	1995	1996	1997				1998
	Quarter 4	Quarter 4	Quarter 1	Quarter 2	Quarter 3	Quarter 4	Quarter 1
Industry							
Evolution of opinion polls in relation to the previous quarter							
Production	14	-17	-23	-23	-10	-8	-25
Demand (total)	-1	-31	-37	-35	-19	-16	-31
Demand (foreign)	-8	-18	-16	-14	-10	-9	-18
Number of employees	4	-10	-15	-13	-11	-10	-19
Volume of investments	41	6	-1	-6	1	1	-17
Commerce							
Evolution of opinion polls in relation to the previous quarter							
Volume of sales	4	-17	-22	-22	1	-3	-29
Number of employees	19	8	8	4	3	-3	-3

The opinion poll reflects the difference between the proportion of enterprises estimating that there is progress and those estimating a deterioration.
Source: Banque du Liban, *Quarterly Bulletin*, 1st quarter 1998.

mentioned, motivated hikes in T-bill rates, and the municipal elections of 1997 were postponed). A lower-than-expected peace dividend as a result of these conflicts was mirrored by lower-than-expected long-term capital flows in fixed investments and a decline in regional demand for industrial products, an indicator of low confidence in business.

Table 11.5 shows the results of opinion polls of Lebanese industry and commerce from the fourth quarter of 1995 to the first quarter of 1998. The polls demonstrate that during this period, the confidence of business people in Lebanon's economic progress declined steeply. Political instability, the inefficient allocation of government resources, the inability of the government to develop and implement a plan for salary increases, the weak inflow of long-term fixed investments, high interest rates, and poor macroeconomic figures all contributed to this decline.

There are a few encouraging features in Lebanon's economic landscape. Monetary policy has promoted stability in prices and exchange rates. The Central Bank has been able to maintain the necessary amount of liquidity, subject to a declining M_3 velocity. The inflation rate is under control, reaching single-digit figures in the late 1990s.

A Macroeconomic Plan for Lebanon's Twenty-first Century

This section outlines a macroeconomic plan designed to put twenty-first-century Lebanon on the path of growth, equity, and stability. It includes specific recommendations on fiscal policy, monetary and financial markets policy, and the development of new technology.

Fiscal Policy

Lebanon's high level of debt and deficit may result in future economic instability. To avoid falling into more debt traps, Lebanon should make major structural reforms in its tax system, as well as improve its tax administration personnel and methods. Special emphasis should be placed on reducing the enormous waste in government expenditure. The need for continued expenditure to repair and rebuild Lebanon's infrastructure will make it difficult to achieve a balanced budget, but steps can be taken to move Lebanon in that direction. The six policy points necessary for Lebanon's fiscal health in the new century are outlined below.

Achieving an Acceptable Level of Deficit. Lebanon can reduce its ratio of debt (D) to gross domestic product (GDP) to acceptable levels without losing its ability to finance reconstruction projects. Given a growth rate of GDP of 4 percent for 1996 and 1997 and a debt figure of 23.47 billion LL for 1997, the allowable deficit that would keep the ratio constant is 0.93 billion LL, compared to the actual deficit of 5.2 billion LL. The Lebanese government should bring its deficit down to less than 1 billion LL and gradually move in the direction of a balanced budget.

The equation is as follows: Starting from a position of equality between the rate of growth in debt (XD/D) and the rate of growth in GDP (XGDP/GDP), where X = change, the change in debt XD that keeps the ratio constant is equal to (XGDP/GDP).D. Since XD is equal to the annual deficit, this figure stands for the maximum allowed deficit that keeps the ratio constant.

Issuing Debt to Finance Debt Service. If the real output growth of the Lebanese economy equals or exceeds real interest rates, the government can issue debt to finance debt service without a negative impact on the ratio of debt to GDP. In 1997, given a nominal interest rate on twelve-month T-bills of 15.20 percent and an inflation rate of 7.75 percent, the real interest rate was 7.45 percent, while the GDP growth rate was 4 percent. These two figures should be equalized before additional debt is issued.

Reducing Debt Service. Lebanon can reduce the money it spends on debt service either by reducing the debt or by reducing the interest rates at which the government borrows on debt. (Recommendations for debt reduction will be addressed in the section on tax and expenditure reforms.) Reducing the rate of borrowing on debt will require either a change in monetary policy or a reallocation of debt from high-interest-rate to low-interest-rate instruments.

The Lebanese government has been floating Euro Bonds in U.S. currency at a risk premium of 280 basis points above U.S. T-bill rates, and 6 to 7 percentage points below Lebanese borrowing rates. There is a tight market demand for these securities, which increases the amount of interest Lebanon must pay to foreign governments and decreases domestic wealth. The government should reallocate debt-to-dollar-indexed government bonds, whose advantages are discussed in Shahin and Dah.[2] Use of dollar-indexed bonds would keep interest payments in the country, provide investors with security against exchange rate risk, and minimize interest payments on internal debt.

Reforming the Tax System. The study by Dah, Dibeh, and Shahin on the income distributional impact of the Lebanese tax system found both direct and indirect taxes to be regressive. To generate additional revenue and provide a more equitable tax system, the study recommends raising Lebanon's marginal personal income tax rates to 20 percent and its mar-

Table 11.6. Pre- and post-reform marginal income tax rates in OECD member countries, 1990

Country	Top tax rate after reform (Percent) (Personal income)	Reduction from reform (Percentage points)	Top tax rate after reform (Percent) (Profit)	Reduction from reform (Percentage points)
Australia	47	10	39	10
Austria	50	12	30	n.a
Belgium	55	17	41	2
Canada	29	5	25	21
Denmark	40	5	40	10
Finland	43	8	33	0
France	57	8	37	13
Germany	53	3	50	6
Greece	50	13	46	n.a
Iceland	33	5	50	n.a
Ireland	53	5	43	7
Italy	50	12	36	10
Japan	50	20	37.5	5.5
Luxembourg	56	1	34	2
Netherlands	60	12	35	7
New Zealand	33	24	28	20
Norway	20	20	27.8	0
Portugal	-	-	36.5	1.5
Spain	56	10	35	0
Sweden	20	30	40	12
Switzerland	13	0	3.6–9.8	0
Turkey	50	0	46	0
United Kingdom	40	20	35	15

Source: Yolanda Kodrzycki, "Tax Reform in Newly Emerging Market Economies," *New England Economic Review* (November/December 1993): 7.

ginal profit tax rates to 25 percent. Table 11.6 shows the income tax rates for other countries that have recently conducted major tax reforms. For most of these countries, the top marginal income tax rate remains around 50 percent and the top marginal profit tax rate over 40 percent. Even with the recommended hike in tax rates, Lebanon will still enjoy a tax advantage over these countries.

Other tax reform measures include halting the increase in indirect taxes and fees and providing revenue through a progressive value-added tax system, a capital gains tax, and taxes on interest income from bank deposits and government bonds. Lebanon should not, however, levy Tobin-type financial transaction taxes that may hinder the development of secondary financial markets.

Abolishing Waste and Prioritizing Expenditures. The Lebanese government needs to develop a plan to combat waste in spending. Expenditures that do not contribute directly to the formation of capital should be avoided. Improvements in government efficiency and the reallocation of funds and priorities will spur both capital formation and productivity.

Reforming Tax System Administration. A more efficient tax system administration would improve taxpayer compliance, reduce cases of tax fraud and evasion, and shorten time lags in the receipt of tax payments. It would also increase tax revenue. The Lebanese government should commit itself to policies that improve tax administration personnel and methods and tax collection techniques.

Monetary and Financial Markets Policy

Lebanon's monetary and financial markets policy should have as its goal a low and stable rate of inflation. Although the Lebanese government has been successful in keeping inflation down, its challenge is to establish price stability in the face of continual fluctuations in supply and demand.

It is difficult to target monetary aggregates or assign predetermined growth rates for money in a country as "dollarized" as Lebanon. This is the result of several factors, including the decline and erratic behavior of M_3 velocity, the impossibility of computing the amount of U.S. dollars in circulation in Lebanon's open market, the common practice of moving Lebanese bank deposits to other countries in times of political instability, and the fact that the Central Bank has tied price stability to exchange rate stability and the vagaries of foreign-exchange markets. Therefore, the government should adopt a policy of discipline, projecting money supply growth using short-term interest rates.

At the same time, the government must allow interest rates to move gradually toward market equilibrium levels. In the long run, this will ensure exchange rate stability and reverse dollarization. A study conducted by Shahin and Freiha (1998) showed that Lebanese investment portfolios remain dollar-heavy because the public is skeptical about the validity of current interest rates.[3] Forced interest rate stabilization by the government may be contributing to this situation.

Lebanese financial markets are still characterized by lack of depth, breadth, and resiliency. There are too few orders for financial securities, and most orders come from a narrow investment pool that does not include the middle-class public. New orders do not pour promptly into the market in volume to take advantages of fluctuations in prices, due to rigid primary markets and sluggish secondary markets. Lebanon should speed the development of secondary markets for various financial instruments and liberalize the financial sector to broaden and increase the ownership of securities.

Lebanon can no longer rely on the financial strategies that brought it success in the 1950s and 1960s. At the time, the Lebanese banking industry prospered due to secrecy laws, the lack of financial development in neighboring Arab countries, and the relative political stability of Lebanon. The Middle East is now very different, and many neighboring countries have stock markets, bond markets, and booming banks. In order to regain its competitive edge, Lebanon must increase and modernize its electronic banking facilities, create new financial instruments such as derivative securities, and offer incentives for Lebanese businesses to become publicly held corporations that issue stock to investors.

Development of New Technology

In order for its GDP to grow, Lebanon must develop new technologies. A country as small as Lebanon will not make major technological breakthroughs, but it can greatly improve existing processes and techniques. Automation is the key to increased efficiency and productivity in all sectors. The financial-service industry would benefit greatly from improved automation, as the current system of partial automation is frustrating for both consumers and institutions. Better management of labor and material is also crucial to Lebanon's economy, especially in the industrial sector. Quality control should be a priority. Research and development should be encouraged because of its potential social benefits, and the government should offer tax exemptions for research and development expenditures.

An Arab Economic and Monetary Union (AEMU) and Lebanon

Although this chapter does not predict the development of an Arab Economic and Monetary Union (AEMU) similar to that of the European Community (EC), it sets up conditions for the development of such a union based on the European model. It also uses a theoretical model to demonstrate the difficulties that would face the hypothetical AEMU.

An economic and monetary union implies that the member countries pursue agreed-upon macroeconomic policy changes, through mechanisms designed to achieve collective goals. The implementation of policies leading to economic integration has three stages.[4]

In stage one, member nations must agree on the type of changes to undertake. Given that the Arab countries have different economic systems and different macroeconomic and financial policies, union would require major structural changes. Economic reforms to bring about free enterprise systems in all Arab countries would be essential. This would entail reducing the role of government in economic activity, privatizing public enterprises, abolishing restrictions on trade and markets, creating a single Arab internal market, allowing unconditional movement of capital across member countries, developing efficient financial markets and institutions, agreeing on exchange rates, and linking all national currencies to the new system.

In stage two, member nations would develop an Arab monetary institute to administer the monetary system and prepare the ground for an Arab central bank. This institute would be in charge of coordinating national monetary policies by creating relevant instruments and procedures. During this stage, member nations would negotiate the distribution of the gains from the union by agreeing on economic indicators.

In stage three, member nations would develop agreements to ensure compliance by all member states on economic policy. To help them coordinate policy, they would have to develop convergence criteria similar to those adopted by the European Community.[5]

There are five broad criteria for convergence, designed to ensure economic stability in all member states.

- For at least two consecutive years, each country's exchange rates against currencies of other member countries must remain within boundaries defined by a common exchange rate mechanism.
- A country's inflation rate must not exceed the average of the countries with the three lowest inflation rates by more than 1.5 percentage points.
- The long-term interest rate of any member state must not exceed the average interest rates of the three member countries with the best inflation performance by more than two percentage points.
- Member states must keep the ratio of budget deficit to GDP at no more than 3 percent.
- Member states must keep the ratio of total public debt to GDP at a maximum of 60 percent.

The remainder of this section will assume that the Arab nations have achieved stage one and will discuss their readiness to create an AEMU by analyzing convergence criteria, based on data from Arab countries. There-

Table 11.7. Convergence criteria for a possible Arab Economic and Monetary Union (AEMU)

	Deficit/GDP	Debt/GDP	Growth in liquidity	Inflation rate	Exchange rate
Lebanon	-18.80	79.71	27.78	8.87	11.10
Jordan	1.47	119.60	0.30	6.50	0.82
UAE	-4.31	-	6.86	3.30	0
Bahrain	-2.73	-	2.89	1.20	0
Tunisia	-2.02	55.85	4.97	5.00	1.03
Algeria	3.02	127.05	11.81	15.10	24.27
Saudi Arabia	-3.73	-	7.69	1.00	0
Sudan	-2.02	287.5	65.18	85.00	139.65
Syria	-4.74	131.13	9.10	8.00	0
Oman	-3.31	22.58	8.06	2.00	0
Qatar	-10.10	-	5.56	3.00	0
Kuwait	-7.04	-	-0.60	0.90	0.70
Libya	0.25	-	2.68	7.00	4.98
Egypt	-1.31	56.43	12.24	7.20	0.86
Morocco	-4.57	67.25	6.49	3.00	0.02
Yemen	-2.72	138.25	10.61	29.00	38.32

Figures are for 1996 except for Debt/GDP, which are for 1995.
Sources: IMF, Arab Economic Report, 1997 International Financial Statistics 1997, Global Development Finance, 1997.

after, a theoretical model will be used to discuss the obstacles to an AEMU, even given the readiness of Arab countries to enter into such a union.

Convergence Criteria for an Arab Economic and Monetary Union

Assuming that the institutional reforms required for the completion of stage one are achieved, the most important question is the ability of Lebanon and other Arab nations to meet the convergence criteria for the AEMU. Table 11.7 analyzes the degree of readiness of each Arab nation based on figures published in 1997 on deficit/GDP ratio, debt/GDP ratio, growth in liquidity, inflation rate, and exchange rate.

Exchange rates are extremely dissimilar, as exchange rate policies are pegged to different currencies and indicators by each country. The average change in exchange rates between 1991 and 1996 also varies greatly, registering little or no change in most Arab countries (Lebanon, Algeria, Sudan, and Yemen are the exceptions).

The differences in the figures on growth in liquidity also indicate major differences in financial-policy objectives. (No data on interest rates are provided because many countries do not have enough instruments with market-determined rates. Some countries report only the discount rate, others the money market rate, some the treasury bill rate, and a few the loan rate.) Inflation rates are mostly in the single digits, reflecting price control measures across various Arab nations. The average inflation rate for the lowest three countries is about 1 percent. Using the convergence criteria, however, means that only countries with rates of less than 2.5 percent (four countries) could join the union.

Deficit-to-GDP ratios are under 5 percent for most countries, and around 3 percent or less for nine countries. In contrast, debt-to-GDP ratios, when available, are wildly erratic, with very few countries meeting the convergence criteria.

This analysis reveals that most Arab nations must develop foreign-exchange and interest rate policies before they can establish convergence criteria. This can be achieved only through major economic reforms, deregulation, the introduction of financial markets and instruments, and the pursuit of free market economies. Lebanon is one of the few Arab countries succeeding in this endeavor. The objectives and goals of Lebanon may differ from other potential AEMU members with respect to macroeconomic and financial policies. Given the structural divergence in economic systems and in exchange rate and interest rate policies and arrangements, it appears that the costs of union may outweigh the benefits.[6]

Conclusion

Predicting the path of any economy over the course of the new century requires careful attention to its current performance, potential, and the willingness of its policymakers to pursue macroeconomic reforms and stabilization plans that will lead to growth and security. Lebanon's future depends on its willingness to consider and adopt the recommendations made in this chapter.

At the same time, analysis shows that it is not to Lebanon's advantage to join an Arab economic and monetary union. Lebanon must establish independent objectives and policies. It can cooperate with its Arab and Mediterranean neighbors by sharing information about global issues, regional shocks and disturbances, and economic policy in a manner consistent with long-term Lebanese interests.

Notes

1. Abdullah Dah, Ghassan Diben, and Wassim Shahin, "The Distributional Impacts of Taxation in Lebanon" (Oxford: Lebanese Center for Policy Studies, 1998, mimeographed).

2. Wassim Shahin and Abdullah Dah, "Managing Public Debt with Foreign Currency Linked Bonds: A Lebanese Application" (working paper, 1998).

3. Wassim Shahin and Fadi Freiha, "Hysteresis in Currency Substitution: The Middle East and North-Africa" (working paper, 1998).

4. A discussion of the three stages of international policy coordination is found in Jeffery Frankel, "Obstacles to International Macroeconomic Policy Coordination," *Princeton Studies in International Finance*, no. 64 (December 1988): 2–5.

5. The stages of implementation and the rules of the convergence criteria are discussed in Michele Fratianni, Jurgen Von Hagen, and Christopher Waller Christopher, "The Maastricht Way to EMU," in *Essays in International Finance* (Princeton, N.J.), no. 187 June 1992).

6. See the appendix, p. 223, "A Mathematical Model Explaining the Obstacles to AEMU." The models used in both studies slightly differ but could be extended to many countries, targets, and instruments. The results reached are very similar. See Frankel, "Obstacles," and Owen Humpage, "A Hitchhiker's Guide to International Macroeconomic Policy Coordination," *Economic Review* (Federal Reserve Bank of Cleveland), quarter 1, 1990, 2–14.

Epilogue

Kail C. Ellis

In the late 1980s, the term *Lebanonization* entered the political lexicon to describe political, social, and economic situations whose resolution seemed intractable. At the same time, the name *Beirut* became popular shorthand for chaos and destruction, much like Berlin after World War II. More recently, bloody conflicts in the former Yugoslavia, Rwanda, and East Timor, and in cities such as Sarajevo and Srebrenica, have expanded the political and popular vocabulary of destruction far beyond *Lebanonization* and *Beirut*. As Lebanon continues to recover from its fifteen-year civil war (1975–90), it has emerged as a nation in the midst of a cautious revival.

The authors in this volume evaluate Lebanon's prospects for the twenty-first century. Given its regional position—sandwiched between two powerful neighbors, Syria and Israel—and the strained political, economic, and social resources at its disposal, Lebanon faces enormous obstacles in its quest for prosperity and stability. Prominent among these are the divisive internal controversy over the withdrawal of Syrian troops and the deteriorating Middle East peace process. Integral to the resolution of both issues is the regularization of the status of the 400,000 Palestinian refugees who reside in Lebanon. As long as Lebanon's Palestinians remain in desperate circumstances, crowded into refugee camps and barred from full participation in Lebanese society, their presence will continue to undermine Lebanon's political stability and security.

Lebanon must deal with the shifting political alliances among its eighteen religious communities, whose most powerful and prominent factions are the Maronite Christian, Shi'a, and Druze communities, whose complicated mutual histories encompass periods of harmony as well as periods of hostility. Sectarian relationships have also been affected by the displacement (and ongoing resettlement) of thousands of internal refugees from the Lebanese civil war. Another legacy of this war is Lebanon's "brain drain." The nation continues to struggle to slow the emigration of its educated young people and to lure back expatriates who have the means to invest in the country's economic development. This epilogue is devoted to an analysis of these salient issues.

Lebanon's Internal Refugees

According to a study by Boutros Labaki, the forced displacement of Lebanese citizens from their homes and villages during the civil war affected 25 percent of the population (827,000 people). Muslims accounted for approximately 20 percent (157,500) of this total, while 80 percent (670,000) were Christians.[1] This displacement resulted in huge losses of property, places of employment, educational institutions, and public infrastructure and seriously damaged the Lebanese model of Muslim-Christian coexistence. Villages that were once comprised of mixed sects, primarily Maronites, Orthodox, and Druze (other religious sects for the most part did not intermingle), suddenly became homogenous, further distancing the religious communities from one another.

At the end of the civil war, refugees began to return to their places of origin. The process became acrimonious, however, when Christian claims on property in the Shouf mountains sparked conflict with the Druzes. The Druzes feared that the return of Christians to the Shouf would undermine their dominant position in the area, while Maronite families angrily alleged that monies from the Lebanese government's National Fund for the Displaced were going primarily to Druze families who were illegally occupying Maronite homes. The situation was further complicated by the fact that some refugees refused to return to their places of origin because of concerns for personal safety, while others had successfully integrated into new Lebanese communities or had emigrated to other countries.[2]

The pragmatic Druze leader, Walid Jumblat, moved to resolve the stalemate when he realized that Palestinian refugees or the Shi'a population would spill over into the underpopulated Shouf. Deciding that Druze interests would be better served by improved relations with his traditional neighbors, Jumblat began to cooperate with the government in bringing displaced Christians from the Shouf back to their homes.[3] Consequently, the resettlement of Christians begun in 1991 in the regions of Saida and Jazzine was gradually extended to the Shouf as well as to Aley, Baabda and the Metn, Baalbek, and Akkar.[4]

Jumblat's overtures to the Christians were viewed with suspicion by the leaders (both religious and lay people) of other religious communities, because they heralded the reemergence of the old Druze-Maronite alliance that under the rule of the Ottoman Empire had established Mount Lebanon as a political entity. The renewed alliance posed a challenge to the political base of other religious groups and that of their patron, Syria. It also strengthened the position of organizations calling for the withdrawal of Syrian troops from Lebanon and for the reassessment of Lebanon's relationship with Syria.

The Druze-Maronite rapprochement officially began at the "Beiteddine Conference" in July 1998.[5] By the time Jumblat invited the Maronite patriarch, Nasrallah Butros Sfeir, to visit the Shouf in first part of August 2001 (the region had seen some of the bloodiest sectarian conflict during the civil war), its momentum had increased. By the end of August, however, Lebanon was in the midst of a constitutional crisis sparked by the arrest of some 200 supporters of the banned Lebanese Forces and the Free Patriotic Movement, who had called publicly for the withdrawal of Syrian troops, and by the harsh treatment of these detainees at the hands of plainclothes police loyal to the pro-Syrian government. Opposition forces, both Christians and Druze, clamored for the establishment of an independent Lebanese judiciary and for the repeal of laws that restricted freedom of speech and political activity. They asserted that without such measures, both Lebanese democracy and Lebanese economic prosperity were in jeopardy.

Emigration and the Brain Drain

Lebanon's communal balance and economic well-being have been gravely affected by emigration. Over a million Lebanese have left the country since the civil war began in 1975. Approximately 15,000 citizens—mostly educated young people—depart Lebanon every month. According to Labaki, the majority of those who emigrated between 1975 and 1990 were Christians (75 percent in 1975, 65 percent in 1981, and 50 percent in 1989–90). Emigration has had devastating effects on Lebanon's economic capacity and has resulted in the loss of skilled managers, capital, and labor. Between 1974 and 1990, per capita income in Lebanon was reduced by more than two-thirds, or about half what it was before the civil war.[6] Emigration affected the Muslim community as well: since 1980, there has been a significant increase in the emigration of Muslim Lebanese to other Arab countries, the United States, and Australia.[7]

The emigration of young Christians is of major concern to the Maronites and to Christian leaders throughout the Middle East. Speaking at an ecumenical conference of Christian leaders in November 2000, Patriarch Sfeir asked, "How can we stop this drain in which our sons leave for countries beyond the Middle East?"[8] The patriarch's solution to the crisis—an improved economy and improved political stability—has so far proved unattainable.

Key to Lebanon's political and economic health is the return of the émigrés with their ability to invest in Lebanon. Lebanon currently labors under a $25 billion debt burden, one of the highest in the world. Unemployment is at 25 percent, a situation complicated by the presence of an estimated one million Syrian "guest workers" who labor for below the minimum wage. Massive reconstruction projects undertaken by the government after the civil war require a constant infusion of outside cash. Bank deposits of nonresidents currently account for only 12.9 percent of the total bank deposits in Lebanon, a figure that must increase substantially if Lebanon is to climb out of its economic crisis.[9]

In order to attract investment, the government must convince the expatriate community and other potential investors that Lebanon is a safe and congenial society. Christian expatriates, in particular, must be given special and explicit reassurances by the Lebanese government. Prime Minister Rafik al-Hariri took a step in this direction in March 1998, when he met with Patriarch Sfeir and the Maronite bishops for a frank dialogue on Christian concerns. The patriarch handed Hariri a twelve-page memorandum titled "The Truth about the Crisis." In effect a Maronite position paper (although claiming to speak for all Lebanese), the memorandum cited the government's fiscal and economic shortcomings, the deficiencies of the Lebanese judiciary, and Lebanon's rampant political corruption and social ills. It made pointed reference to Maronite concerns about Maronite political marginalization and the unequal relationship between Lebanon and Syria, calling for strong governmental reforms.[10]

The Maronite community's disaffection stems from the terrible economic and political losses it suffered during the Lebanese civil war—although ironically, some of these losses were caused by the bloody internecine battles between opposing Christian factions. After the adaptation of the Ta'if Agreement in 1989 (which officially ended the civil war and gave greater power to the Muslim community), Maronite parties were either outlawed or weakened, Maronite participation in political life decreased, and Christian emigration accelerated. Maronite political leadership is now divided into nationalist groups (some of whom are in exile or in prison) whose commitment to Christian domination of Lebanon and alliance with Israel led the country into civil war, politicians who curry favor with Syria, and moderates who seek Lebanon's independence and sovereignty but within the context of appropriate relations with Syria.

The meeting with Hariri and "The Truth about the Crisis" solidified Patriarch Sfeir's role as a populist political leader. In assuming this role the patriarch walks a fine line. He risks being perceived as a parochial leader and defender of the Maronite community rather than as a prophetic voice who articulates the future of the entire country. Given the fragmentation of the Maronite community, however, the patriarch's voice is crucial. He has become its de facto political spokesman and source of hope for Muslims and Christians alike.[11]

The patriarch's prominence has as much to do with geography as with political circumstances. He is the only leader of a major Christian community who resides in Lebanon, and, as such, he can speak independently and without government restraint. Although his authority and outspokenness have generally been applauded, some would like to see his role confined to convincing the Maronites to return to full political and social participation in Lebanese affairs with a view to reforming the system, not to directing governmental reform personally. An editorial in a Beirut newspaper exhorted the patriarch to concentrate on "convinc[ing] his co-religionists that if they truly want to participate in national life on a scale that befits their importance to the country's long-term being, they must produce a viable alternative to the existing system."[12]

Lebanon's Relations with Syria

Patriarch Sfeir and other Christians have repeatedly called for the withdrawal of Syrian troops from Lebanon, criticizing the government's position that these 35,000–40,000 soldiers are necessary to preserve Lebanon's security. To the patriarch and his followers, the troops are a painful reminder of Syria's dominant role in Lebanon's political, social, and economic life. After Israel ended its twenty-two-year occupation of south Lebanon in May 2000, Christians argued that there was no longer any justification for a Syrian military counterpresence and increased demands for Syrian withdrawal. The death soon afterward of long-time Syrian leader Hafiz al-Asad and the ascension to power of his son Bashar, who was initially perceived as being more moderate than his father, fueled hope for a Syrian withdrawal. In September 2000, the Council of Maronite Bishops characterized a Syrian withdrawal as necessary to "cementing the best possible relations of brotherhood" between Syria and Lebanon.

Members of the Lebanese Parliament took up the call, with Walid

Jumblat, Nassib Lahoud, and other parliamentarians urging the government to "embark seriously on adjusting" Lebanese-Syrian relations.[13] Politicians, including Nabih Berri, speaker of the Parliament, traveled to Bkerki, the patriarchical seat, for meetings with Patriarch Sfeir. After his conversation with the patriarch, Berri gave the opposition hope by reiterating that "the redeployment of Syrian troops in the country would be completed 'in the near future' in compliance with the Ta'if Agreement and according to a timetable agreed upon by Beirut and Damascus."[14]

Although Berri's words were little more than a restatement of provisions set out in the Ta'if Agreement, Prime Minister Hariri felt compelled to counter them. In an interview with Vatican radio and television in April 2001, Hariri made it clear that Lebanon's national interest required keeping Syrian troops in Lebanon. Reminding his audience that Ta'if did not call for immediate Syrian withdrawal, Hariri added a cautionary note to the patriarch: "No one other than the Beirut government is entitled to make any decision on this."[15]

Patriarch Sfeir agreed with Hariri that the church should not be involved in negotiations with a foreign government. The patriarch reserved the right, however, to remind Lebanese that both Lebanon and Syria are sovereign governments and to continue to call for the normalization of Lebanon's ties with Syria. At the same time, he was careful to stress that "this call stems from feelings of friendship, which we would like to preserve between the two countries." In the patriarch's view, "normalization" would include formal diplomatic ties with Syria, which were not established when the two countries gained independence, and assurances that Lebanon, like other "sovereign and independent countries," was "free to make its own decisions"—including the withdrawal of Syrian troops from its soil. Only after normalization, the patriarch insisted, would claims such as "Lebanon does not exist in history or geography," "Lebanon's borders were fabricated by the French mandate," "the Syrian and Lebanese people are one people in two countries," and "the presence of Syrian troops is part of national security and guarantees balance in the country" be put to rest.[16]

When he pointedly refused to accompany Pope John Paul II on his historic visit to Syria in May 2001, the Patriarch Sfeir underscored his role as the most prominent critic of Lebanese government policies. In an interview in *La Croix* magazine explaining his decision not to go to Damascus, the patriarch said, "I can already hear their comments. 'Look, the patriarch came. There are no problems.' But I insist there is a problem: the Syrian occupation."[17]

By August 2001, the Syrian presence in Lebanon had become a political flash point. The accelerating conflict between Israel and the Palestinians once again threatened Lebanese security. Israeli jets regularly violated Lebanese airspace. Border areas such as the Shab'a Farms, characterized as Syrian rather than Lebanese territory by Israel, and the Alawite Muslim village of Ghajar became the sites of numerous confrontations between Israel and Hizballah. The Lebanese government reacted to these tensions by taking an even firmer pro-Syrian position regarding the deployment of Syrian troops in Lebanon. It ordered the arrest of some 200 supporters of the banned Lebanese Forces and the Free Patriotic Movement after a crowd at a reception for the patriarch, who had just returned from his visit to south Lebanon, rang with shouts of "Syria out!" (Although the patriarch sternly rebuked the crowd, warning that confrontational rhetoric was not the way to solve political issues, that was not enough to prevent the government from taking strong retaliatory action.)[18] The situation was further inflamed when plainclothes police who made the arrests assaulted a number of dissidents.

The public prosecutor in the case justified the arrests by asserting that the accused were serving the interests of Israel. "The state will show no leniency," he stated, "toward anyone who threatens national security or seeks to undermine Lebanon's relations with a sisterly state (Syria)."[19] On the opposing side, the arrests were condemned by the Christian parties as a ploy to isolate Christians further by unfairly characterizing them as Israeli lackeys.[20] The patriarch dismissed the arrests as deplorable and the charges as not credible, a view seconded by the Beirut's Orthodox Christian bishop Elias Aoude. In the Muslim community, however, most notably among the Shi'a leaders, suspicions remained that Israel was behind the calls for Syrian withdrawal and that the arrested were traitors. The merest suggestion of collaboration with Israel was sufficient to revive Muslim suspicions of Christian "betrayal." Shi'a clerics condemned the undermining of national unity and warned that they would oppose all "suspicious calls" for the "full recovery of sovereignty" that targeted Lebanon's relationships with Arab countries, especially Syria.[21]

The arrests and subsequent religious polarization represented a serious setback for Lebanese moderates of all faiths who were struggling to achieve national reconciliation. Loss of hope for reconciliation threatened Lebanon's broader agenda of political stability and economic recovery, and it damaged efforts to stem the tide of emigration of educated young Lebanese and lure prosperous émigrés back to assist in the economic recovery. Hopes for the peaceful resolution of Lebanon's border conflicts with Israel also faded. With two Christian journalists standing accused of being directly sponsored by Israel in their campaign to "pacify" the border and charged with treason—a capital offense—it was difficult to envision Hizballah joining the newly founded Druze-Maronites alliance in any effort to pacify Lebanon's border with Israel.

Lebanon and the Middle East Peace Process

When Israel ended its twenty-two-year occupation of south Lebanon on 24 May 2000, Hizballah assumed an orderly control of the region. Despite the creation of several thousand new refugees when the families of members of the South Lebanon Army (SLA) fled into Israel because they feared retribution by Hizballah, there was a remarkable absence of violence and retaliation. In the words of Hizballah's secretary-general, Sayyed Hassan Nasrallah, the end of the occupation represented "a true victory for all the Lebanese."[22]

In the initial euphoria that followed the Israeli withdrawal and certification by the United Nations that the withdrawal was in accord with UN Resolution 425, most observers assumed that the Lebanese army would move quickly into south Lebanon to secure the Israeli-Lebanese border. This hope was dashed when Lebanon refused to accept the UN certification, contending that the Israelis continued to occupy the Shab'a Farms, considered by Israel to be Syrian territory captured during the 1967 Arab-Israeli war.

Lebanon's claim to the Shab'a Farms surprised many observers. In the words of Staffan de Mistura, the UN secretary-general's personal representative to south Lebanon, the area was an "unusual, previously unheard of flashpoint."[23] The United Nations regarded Lebanon's claim as dubious: Following the 1973 Arab-Israeli war, Syria had sent maps to the United Nations that showed the Shab'a Farms as lying inside Syrian territory. The UN Disengagement Observers Force had monitored the area as part of the cease-fire lines on the Golan Heights, while UNiFiL, established in 1978 to oversee an Israeli withdrawal from Lebanese territory, had never operated there.[24] Although Syria's foreign minister, Farouk al-Sharaa, sent a letter to UN Secretary-General Kofi Annan in May 2000, supporting Lebanon's claim to at least part of the Shab'a Farms, the UN Security Council decreed that Israel did not have to withdraw from the area in order to satisfy UN Resolution 425.

Hizballah launched a campaign to liberate Shab'a Farms in October 2000. In the first ten months of the campaign, Hizballah conducted seven operations against Israel, killing three Israeli solders, wounding thirteen, and capturing three. In response, Israeli planes destroyed two Syrian army radar stations in Lebanon and launched attacks in which fifteen civilians were wounded and one Hizballah fighter killed. These acts of violence, in tandem with heightened conflict on the West Bank and in Israel, threatened once again to embroil Lebanon in the Israeli-Palestinian conflict. Because Israel holds Syria responsible for Lebanese security and has already retaliated against Syrian military installations in Lebanon, the odds for a military confrontation between Israel and Syria have increased—both in Lebanon and in Syria. It is also likely that Israel will wreak fresh destruction on Lebanon's newly rebuilt infrastructure.

Palestinian refugee camps in south Lebanon may once again become centers of active resistance against Israel, further jeopardizing Lebanon's fragile security. Although there is no evidence that Hizballah is directly involved in the Palestinian intifada, it has been accused by Israeli sources of underwriting the rebellion. Hizballah's television station, al-Manar, continually airs programs about the plight of the Palestinians and advocates the liberation of Jerusalem, complete with images of the Dome of the Rock and resistance fighters going into battle. In its greeting to Pope John Paul II during his visit to Lebanon in May 1997, Hizballah reminded the pope that in the case of the Palestinians, "a whole nation has been deposed from their land under the pretext of establishing a safe homeland for another people."[25]

Sources within Hizballah have more than hinted that the organization is ready to join in the Palestinian struggle. In an address to a group of Palestinians in Jabal Amel on 13 August 2001, Sayyed Hassan Nasrallah warned that "with the development of events inside Palestine, we are getting closer to the challenge. . . . We have to be prepared . . . so we can take up our legitimate *jihad* [holy war] and responsibility beside our people in Palestine in order for them to continue in this battle which will be decisive for the fate of the entire region."[26] Ze'ev Schiff, military correspondent for the Israeli daily *Ha'aretz*, views such activities as evidence of Hizballah's sponsorship of the Palestinians, warning that "Hizballah is expected to continue its direct involvement in the Palestinian confrontation . . . and may even act within the Green Line. This gives current events a dangerous regional twist, since Iran stands behind Hizballah. Israel will have to face some difficult decisions."[27]

At the same time, moderates in Lebanon and the Arab world were baffled that the United States was not doing more to stem the violence between Israel and the Palestinians. Most Arab political observers believed that only the United States had the power to end the conflict. They were puzzled and alarmed by the Bush administration's passivity as the United States—in the phrase of Secretary of State Colin Powell—continued to "assist but not insist," that is, not impose a solution.

The national security advisor to President Hosni Mubarak of Egypt, Osama el-Baz, expressed the feelings of most Arab states when in August 2001 he predicted that the Bush administration risked damaging its influence in the Middle East, even more than its prestige, if it failed to take a more active role in the Israeli-Palestinian conflict. American inaction, el-Baz warned, might bring Islamic extremists to power in moderate Arab countries. "In all the Gulf countries you should take a look at what is being said about the United States in the mosques." He continued, "[American inaction will encourage the] growth of fundamentalist trends in the region. If this happens, it will seriously hurt United States interests."[28]

The stunning terrorists attacks on New York and Washington on 11 September 2001 refocused American attention on the Middle East. In response to the attacks, Secretary Powell quickly set about creating an anti-terrorism coalition that sought to include the United Nations, NATO, the European Union, the Organization of American States, and the Organization of the Islamic Conference. The weak link in this plan was the Organization of the Islamic Conference, whose "Arab street" might perceive the coalition to be directed against Muslims rather than against terrorism, a judgment influenced by the widespread belief that the United States was not an objective broker in the Israeli-Palestinian conflict.

In Lebanon, there was worry that a U.S.-led war on terrorism waged against Muslims could lead to a conflict between Muslims and Christians. Religious leaders tried to head off potential conflict by stressing religious unity. Sayyed Mohammad Hussein Fadlallah, a leading Shi'a cleric, reassured Lebanese Christians that they need not fear a backlash against them in retaliation for an imminent war on Islamic extremists. "I tell every Christian among our citizens and every Christian in the Middle East region that we are one people. We are the product of one womb. We have lived together for 14 centuries as Muslims, Christians, and Jews."[29] However, while strongly deploring the attacks of 11 September, Fadlallah also issued a *fatwa* (ruling) stating that "it is not permissible for any Islamic state, ruler or political organization to extend any assistance to the United States in its war against a Muslim country or group."[30] On the Christian side, Patriarch Sfeir appealed to the United States to solve the political, security, territorial, and economic problems that gave rise to terrorism.

Addressing an issue he normally avoids, the patriarch stated, "At the forefront of these problems is the Palestinian cause, and specifically, Jerusalem."[31]

Secretary Powell and American policymakers anticipated the linking of the war on terrorism with the Israeli-Palestinian conflict and attempted to break the connection. In a press briefing on 13 September, Powell stated that he had been in contact with "Prime Minister Sharon and Chairman Arafat and with Foreign Minister Shimon Peres of Israel trying to move forward the process of a cease-fire in the region, trying to begin those meetings that we have been talking about, which would lead to implementation of the Mitchell Plan. I am still hopeful that something can be done in the next several days to have that first meeting, and we will be in close touch with the leaders as the next days unfold."[32]

On 2 October 2001, in another attempt to reassure the Palestinians and the Muslim world of his objectivity, President George Bush stated that he has always supported the vision of a Palestinian state, "so long as the right of Israel to exist is respected."[33] On 19 November, in a major policy address at the University of Louisville, Secretary Powell asserted that just as the United States had liberated Kuwait from Iraqi occupation and paved the way for the Madrid Conference, which began the Israeli-Palestinian peace negotiations that led to the 1993 Oslo Accords, it would now "capture the spirit of Madrid and create a renewed sense of hope and common purpose for the peoples in the Middle East."[34] He envisioned a Middle East where "two states—Israel and Palestine—live side by side within secure and recognized borders." To accomplish this goal, Powell said, Palestinians must stop terrorism and violence against Israelis so that innocent people can "live their lives free from terror as well as war," and "Israel must be willing to end its occupation, consistent with the principles embodied in Security Resolutions 242 and 338, and accept a viable Palestinian State in which Palestinians can determine their own future on their own land and live in dignity and security."[35] Powell attempted to resume the Middle East peace process by sending retired Marine Corp General Anthony Zinni to negotiate a cease-fire between the Israelis and Palestinians. General Zinni's two trips to the region (late November 2001 and early January 2002) were severely hampered by the continuing violence between the two parties.

At the same time, Hizballah was being identified as a target in the new war on terrorism. On 22 October 2001, Hizballah—pledging that the war on terrorism would not stop its resistance to continuing Israeli occupation of the Shab'a Farms—launched a wide-scale attack on Israeli forces there.

The raid provoked Israeli retaliation, but no casualties were sustained on either side. After the attack, a U.S. Embassy adviser reportedly told Lebanese officials that the operation "did not help achieve stability, was uncalled for, and was particularly grave under the present international conditions."[36] On 2 November the U.S. State Department announced that it was adding Hizballah (along with the Popular Front for the Liberation of Palestine, Hamas, the Palestinian Islamic Jihad, and the Popular Front for the Liberation of Palestine–General Command) to the list of Al-Qaeda terrorist organizations. Israel complained that Hizballah and Hamas were not on the original list of twenty-two organizations and sixty-six "terrorist" groups, issued on 24 September. Hizballah's secretary-general Sayyed Hassan Nasrallah then accused the United States of reacting to the wishes of Israel.[37]

Although Hizballah had already been identified by the U.S. State Department as a terrorist organization because of its role during the Lebanese civil war in the U.S. Embassy and Marine barracks bombings and the kidnapping of U.S. citizens, its inclusion in the Al-Qaeda list represented a significant change. It meant that the United States could not only freeze any assets Hizballah had in American banks but could exclude from the United States all foreign banks that did not do the same.

The government of Lebanon thus found itself in a difficult position. If it complied with the demand to freeze Hizballah's assets, it risked alienating a powerful military and political constituency and causing political instability. Throughout the Arab world, Hizballah, which was instrumental in the Israeli withdrawal from Lebanon, is renowned as the first Arab force to achieve a victory over the Israeli military. Since the Lebanese civil war, Hizballah had also attained respectability as a national political movement. Freezing its assets, Hizballah secretary-general Nasrallah warned, "would lead the country to a civil war."[38] If Lebanon refused to comply, however, it risked political and economic retaliation from the United States and the antiterrorism alliance.

Prime Minister Hariri decided that the lesser of the two risks was international retaliation and so rejected the U.S. demand to freeze Hizballah's assets.[39] Hariri held out hope that he could convince the United States and the coalition against terrorism that Hizballah was a Lebanese resistance movement, not a terrorist organization, a position that was shared by most Lebanese politicians, Christian and Muslim alike.[40]

As this epilogue is being written, the definition of Hizballah continues to cause conflict between the United States and Lebanon. In meeting with Lebanon's president Emile Lahoud and Foreign Minister Mahmoud

Hammoud on 15 December 2001, Assistant Secretary of State for Near East Affairs William Burns acknowledged that "Hizballah has a number of different dimensions, as a political party, as a social welfare organization, but the United States continues to be concerned about terrorist activities that go well beyond . . . the borders of this country."[41] Secretary Powell reiterated this position in an interview on 9 January 2002, stating that "all parties in the region will be well advised to control organizations such as Hizballah and all the others who have not yet renounced terror and violence against civilians as a means to a political objective."[42] The fact that Hizballah's secretary-general Nasrallah challenged Muslim clerics who have decried the suicide bombings in Israel as sacrilege, and called for more such attacks, reinforces the perception that it is terrorist organization. "These suicide attacks are the weapon that God gave to this nation, and no one can take it away," Nasrallah declared. "Do not listen to those who say these types of attacks go against Muslim *Sharia* [law]."[43]

The new war on terrorism has placed Lebanon in the crosshairs of international conflict. As it has for the past twenty-five years, Lebanon will continue to suffer the consequences of a failed peace among Israel, the Palestinians, and Syria.

Conclusion

Although "Lebanonization" has faded from the political lexicon, Lebanon still faces challenges in the twenty-first century that cannot be met with its material and spiritual resources alone. As the authors in this volume have demonstrated, global and regional politics and internal conflicts continue to shape the Lebanon's political structures and political discourse. In order to fulfill the dreams of a future revival, Lebanon needs the assistance of all those who support the rule of law, human rights, and a just peace in the Middle East.

Notes

1. Boutros Labaki, "The Christian Communities and Economic and Social Situation in Lebanon," in *Christian Communities in the Arab Middle East: The Challenge of the Future,* ed. Andrea Pacini (Oxford: Clarendon Press, 1998), 223–46.

2. Carole H. Dagher, *Bring Down the Walls: Lebanon's Postwar Challenge* (New York: St. Martin's Press, 2000), 88.

3. Ibid., 86.

4. Labaki, 255.

5. Dagher, 149.

6. Labaki, 242–46.

7. Ibid., 228–30.

8. Abdo Matta, "Sfeir Sounds Alarm for Region's Christians," *Daily Star* (Beirut), 21 November 2000.

9. Dagher, 149.

10. Ibid.

11. See Labaki, 232, on the appeals made by Shi'a merchants and Sunni politicians to the patriarch for a redress of their grievances against the government.

12. "Sfeir's Opportunity," *Daily Star* (Beirut), 13 August 2001.

13. See Mona Ziade, "Bkerki Has Ruffled Lots of Feathers," *Daily Star* (Beirut), 23 September 2000; Abdo Matta, "Sfeir Scoffs at Syrian Claims of Having Averted 'Genocide,'" *Daily Star* (Beirut), 2 October 2000; and Abdo Matta, "MP Lahoud Calls for 'Serious Discussion' of Ties with Syria," *Daily Star* (Beirut) 12 November 2000.

14. Abdo Matta, "Calls for Action to Follow Berri's Move at Bkerki," *Daily Star* (Beirut), 30 November 2000.

15. Nafez Kawas, "Premier Spells Out Stance on Syria to Vatican," *Daily Star* (Beirut), 24 April 2001.

16. Abdo Matta, "Patriarch Urges Diplomatic Ties with Damascus," *Daily Star* (Beirut), 14 November 2000.

17. Quoted in "Where's Sfeir?" *Middle East International*, 18 May 2001, 13.

18. Mona Ziade, "State Cracks Down on Aounists, LF in Security Sweep," *Daily Star* (Beirut), 8 August 2001.

19. Ibid.

20. "Christians 'Are Not Israeli Allies': Politicians Say Stereotype Is Becoming Lame as Criticism of Crackdown Continues," *Daily Star* (Beirut), 17 August 2001.

21. "Sfeir Dismisses Accusations of Plot to Partition Country," *Daily Star* (Beirut), 13 August 2001.

22. Ranwa Yehia, "Nasrallah Reaches Out to Christians," *Daily Star* (Beirut), 27 May 2000.

23. Nicholas Blanford, "Post-Liberation South Still a 'Sad Story,' De Mistura Says Beirut Has Neglected Its Duties to the Region," *Daily Star* (Beirut), 20 August 2001.

24. Ibid.

25. "Greetings to the Honorable Supreme Pontiff Pope John Paul the Second" (http://almashiq.hiof.no/lebanon/30 . . . 324.2/hizballah/hizballah-baba.html).

26. "Hizballah Close to 'Joining Battle,'" *Daily Star* (Beirut), 13 August 2001.

27. Cited in Michael Jensen, "Implicating Hizballah," *Middle East International*, 23 February 2001.

28. Jane Perlez, "U.S. 'Inaction' Weakens Arab Moderates, Egypt Aide Warns," *New York Times*, 16 August 2001.

29. Mona Ziade, "Christians Told: 'You are Safe,'" *Daily Star* (Beirut), 22 September 2001.

30. Maurice Kaldawy, "Fadlallah Issues Coalition Fatwa," *Daily Star* (Beirut), 19 September 2001.

31. Mona Ziade, "Religious Leaders Close Ranks in Face of New War: Sfeir, Fadlallah Say 'Christians and Muslims Are One People,'" *Daily Star* (Beirut), 21 September 2001.

32. U.S. Department of State (International Information Programs) "On-The-Record Briefing (1300 hrs) Secretary Colin L. Powell Remarks to the Press Washington, DC 13 September 2001" (http://www.state.gov/secretary/rm/2001/index.cfm?docid=4910). The Mitchell Report of May 2001 (based on UN Resolutions 242 and 338, "Land for Peace") called on Israel and the Palestinian Authority to act swiftly and decisively to halt the violence, rebuild confidence, and resume negotiations "in the spirit of the Sharm el-Sheikh agreements and understandings of 1999 and 2000." See U.S. Department of State (International Information Programs), "Sharm El-Sheikh Fact-Finding Committee, 30 April 2001" (http://usinfo.state.gov/regional/nea/mitchell.htm).

33. U.S. Department of State (International Information Programs) "Bush Confirms U.S. Support for Palestinian State as Part of Settlement, 2 October 2001" (http://usinfo.state.gov/regional/nea/summit/1002bush.htm).

34. U.S. Department of State (International Information Programs), "Secretary Colin L. Powell, 'United States Position on Terrorists and Peace in the Middle East,' Remarks at the McConnell Center for Political Leadership, University of Louisville, Kentucky, 19 November 2001" (http://www.state.gov/secretary/rm/2001/index.cfm?docid=6219). This vision of U.S. policy was also restated by Assistant Secretary of State for the Near East William Burns on 12 December; he stated that "the realization of the vision of a Palestinian state existing alongside Israel in peace and security will be difficult but possible to achieve." U.S. Department of State (International Information Programs), "Vision of Palestinian State at Peace with Israel Is Possible, 12 December 2001" (http://usinfo.state.gov/regional/nea/summit/1212brns.htm).

35. Powell, "Remarks."

36. Elie Hourani, "Lahoud Denies U.S. Envoy Issued Warning," *Daily Star* (Beirut), 25 October 2001.

37. Nicholas Blanford, "Hizballah Unshaken by U.S. Order to Freeze Its Funds," *Daily Star* (Beirut), 5 November 2001.

38. Cilina Nasser, "Nassrallah: Accepting U.S. Demands Could Lead to Civil War," *Daily Star* (Beirut), 12 November 2001.

39. Nafez Kawas and Khalil Fleihan, "Hariri Presses Diplomatic Offensive," *Daily Star* (Beirut), 12 November 2001.

40. Elie Hourani, "Politicians Refuse to Back U.S. Stance on Hizballah," *Daily Star* (Beirut), 7 November 2001.

41. Khalil Fleihan, "Burns Thanks Beirut for Help in War on Terror," *Daily Star* (Beirut), 15 December 2001.

42. U.S. Department of State (International Information Programs), "Interview on Middle East Broadcasting Centre by Hisham Melham, Secretary Colin L. Powell, Washington, D.C., 9 January 2002" (http://www.state.gov/secretary/rm/2002/index.cfm?docid=7148).

43. Nicholas Blanford and Cilina Nasser, "Nasrallah Encourages More Suicide Attacks," *Daily Star* (Beirut), 15 December 2001.

Appendix

Mathematical Model Explaining the Obstacles to an AEMU

The following mathematical model has three components. First, it assesses the initial position of Lebanon relative to the target variables of a potential AEMU. Second, it puts the correct weight on these variables. Third, it measures the effect of each unit change in Lebanon's or the AEMU's macroeconomic policy instruments on the target variables. Models developed by Frankel (1988) and Humpage (1990) provide the base for the model used in chapter 11. (See p. 205, notes to chapter 11.)

Let there be a function of two target variables for Lebanon specified in (1) and a similar one for an Arab country K in (2).

(1) $XL = 1/2\ w_y Y^2 + 1/2\ w_u U^2$

(2) $XK = 1/2\ w'_{y'} Y'^2 + 1/2\ w'_{u'} U'^2$

where X represents a quadratic loss to be minimized, L stands for Lebanon and K for country K, Y is Lebanese output expressed relative to its optimum, U is the current account expressed as a percentage of GDP and relative to its optimum, w_y is the relative welfare weight placed on output and w_u is the relative welfare weight placed on the current account, and a (') denoting the analogous variable for country K. Y and U represent two target variables, although the specification could include more.

The following equations use only one policy instrument (even though the model allows for many): g for Lebanon (and g' for K), standing for government expenditure as a percentage of GDP and approximating the criterion for fiscal policy convergence or the budget-deficit-to-GDP ratio. The marginal welfare effects of changes in these policy variables are shown by:

(3) $dXL/dg = w_y(Y)Y_g + w_u(U)U_g$

(4) $dXL/dg' = w_y(Y)Y_{g'} + w_u(U)U_{g'}$

(5) $dXK/dg = w'_{y'}(Y')Y'_g + w'_{u'}(U')U'_g$

(6) $dXK/dg' = w'_{y'}(Y')Y'_{g'} + w'_{u'}(U')U'_{g'}$

The policy multiplier effect of government expenditure on output is given by Y_g and of government expenditure on the current account balance by U_g, etc. The model could be solved by setting the derivatives equal to zero with the target variables Y and U first expressed as linear functions of the policy variables g and g', etc.

If Lebanon and country K take the policies of each other as given, which is currently the case in a noncoordination situation (Nash noncooperative equilibrium), one needs only equations (3) and (6). Equations (4) and (5) do not apply, as each country ignores the effects that its policies have on the other country. Cross-country effects enter only in the coordinated solution, which is the standard reason why the noncoordinated equilibrium is suboptimal.

If policies were to be coordinated, the above system of equations would illustrate the uncertainties or the main obstacles preventing a successful international policy coordination deal: uncertainty regarding the initial position of the target variables Y, Y', U, U'; the welfare weights w_y, $w'_{y'}$, w_u, $w'_{u'}$; and the government expenditure policy multipliers Y_g, $Y_{g'}$, U_g, $U_{g'}$, etc.

The results of Frankel (1988) and Humpage (1990) show that uncertainties are so large that the signs of the crosseffects in equations (4) and (5) cannot be determined with confidence. This implies that, for example, Lebanon cannot be sure whether it should ask country K to expand or contract its government spending (variable g') to increase Lebanon's own welfare. These uncertainties represent serious obstacles to policy coordination.

Theoretical literature specifies that all countries need to start discussion on where to move their targets. In the case of an AEMU, additional deliberations would have to be conducted regarding the structural economic differences of member nations. Lebanon would need to study the costs and benefits of each move. Lebanon would also need to determine the initial position of its and other Arab countries' target variables, the appropriate weights of the targets, and the policy multipliers in order to prevent coordination from reducing benefits. If different countries were to place different weights on different variables, the benefits of a potential union could be jeopardized.

Contributors

Michael F. Davie is a professor of geography and a researcher at the Center for Urbanization in the Arab World, University of Tours, France.

Kail C. Ellis is the founder and former director of the Center for Arab and Islamic Studies at Villanova University, where he is an associate professor of political science and dean of the College of Liberal Arts and Sciences.

Nabeel F. Haidar is a professor of chemistry and vice-president for academic affairs at the Lebanese American University, Beirut.

Fouad Hamdan was Lebanon campaigner and media coordinator for the Greenpeace Mediterranean office in 1995–99. He is currently communications director of Greenpeace Germany, based in Hamburg.

Mona Chemali Khalaf is the director of the Institute for Women's Studies in the Arab World, the Lebanese American University, Beirut.

Hafeez Malik is a professor of political science at Villanova University and editor of the *Journal of South Asian and Middle Eastern Studies*.

Julie Peteet is chair and associate professor of anthropology at the University of Louisville.

Mohammad Sammak is secretary-general of the Islamic-Christian Committee for National Dialogue, Beirut, Lebanon.

Paul Nabil Sayah is the Maronite archbishop of Haifa and the Holy Land and associate general secretary of the Middle East Council of Churches.

Kirsten E. Schulze is a lecturer in international history at the London School of Economics.

Wassim N. Shahin is professor and dean of the School of Business, Lebanese American University, Byblos, Lebanon.

Index

Note: Page numbers in italics indicate tables.

www.ingramcontent.com/pod-product-compliance
Lightning Source LLC
Chambersburg PA
CBHW020856270326
41928CB00006B/739